In Honour of War Heroes

COLIN ST CLAIR OAKES AND THE
DESIGN OF KRANJI WAR MEMORIAL

Athanasios Tsakonas

© 2020 Athanasios Tsakonas

Published in 2020 by Marshall Cavendish Editions
An imprint of Marshall Cavendish International

A member of the
Times Publishing Group

Other Marshall Cavendish Offices:
Marshall Cavendish Corporation, 800 Westchester Ave, Suite N-641, Rye Brook, NY 10573, USA • Marshall Cavendish International (Thailand) Co Ltd, 253 Asoke, 16th Floor, Sukhumvit 21 Road, Klongtoey Nua, Wattana, Bangkok 10110, Thailand • Marshall Cavendish (Malaysia) Sdn Bhd, Times Subang, Lot 46, Subang Hi-Tech Industrial Park, Batu Tiga, 40000 Shah Alam, Selangor Darul Ehsan, Malaysia

Marshall Cavendish is a registered trademark of Times Publishing Limited

National Library Board, Singapore Cataloguing in Publication Data
Name(s): Tsakonas, Athanasios.
Title: In Honour of War Heroes : Colin St Clair Oakes and the Design of Kranji War Memorial / Athanasios Tsakonas.
Description: Singapore : Marshall Cavendish Editions, [2020] | Includes bibliographic references.
Identifier(s): OCN 1175571771 | ISBN 978-981-4893-36-7 (paperback)
Subject(s): LCSH: Oakes, Colin St. Clair. | Kranji War Memorial (Singapore) | War memorials—Singapore—Design and construction. | War cemeteries—Singapore—Design and construction.
Classification: DDC 725.94095957—dc23

Printed in Singapore

Contents

Foreword   5

Preface   7

CHAPTER 1   Introduction   14

CHAPTER 2   Writings   32

CHAPTER 3   The Architects   45

CHAPTER 4   Architecture   71

CHAPTER 5   Colin St Clair Oakes   92

CHAPTER 6   Singapore   122

CHAPTER 7   Kranji   148

CHAPTER 8   Building a War Cemetery   182

CHAPTER 9   Post-War   220

Notes   252

Bibliography   280

Index   285

Foreword

Mrs Victoria Wallace, DL
Director General
Commonwealth War Graves Commission

During my time as Director General of the Commonwealth War Graves Commission (CWGC), an organisation dedicated to the commemoration of the 1.7 million men and women of the British, Imperial and Commonwealth forces who died in the two world wars, I have visited many of the cemeteries and memorials around the world where their bodies lie buried or where their names are engraved. I have always been struck by the uniformity of purpose and design that is displayed at these places of remembrance and pilgrimage – regardless of where you are in the world, you immediately know when you are standing in a CWGC cemetery. And yet, if this is not too much of a contradiction, each and every cemetery and memorial is also unique and intrinsically different from any other. Each has its own character and sense of place which differentiates it.

A change in the horticultural treatment and types of plants in the headstone borders; a subtle shift in the alignment and layout of the graves; the differences in the positioning and placement of various features and structures, such as the Stone of Remembrance and the

Cross of Sacrifice; and the location of the cemetery or memorial in its surrounding landscape, all ensure that no two cemeteries or memorials are the same.

None of this is down to chance. It is the work of various architects, designers, horticulturists, planners and builders who have worked collaboratively over the years to create these special places.

I was delighted to be asked to write the foreword for this study on one of these architects, Colin St Clair Oakes. While much has been written about the original architects who were engaged by the Imperial War Graves Commission (as it was then) after the end of the First World War to bring the vision of the Commission to life, very little has been written about the second wave of architects who picked up the mantle from their illustrious predecessors, and embarked on a new phase of design and construction after the Second World War.

The template for the cemeteries and memorials had already been established, but rather than restricting this new generation of architects, it in some ways liberated them to develop those ideas further from a sound and solid base. Freed from the need to 'start from scratch', they could take the ideas of their predecessors and expand and develop them. Nowhere is this more evident than in Oakes's design for the Singapore Memorial, which sits within the surrounding Kranji War Cemetery. Its clear, simple, sweeping lines, its nod to modernism, could not be more different from Lutyens's mathematically complex series of intersecting arches which form the Thiepval Memorial, or Blomfield's Menin Gate in Ieper, adorned as it is with various embellishments and decorations, two of the most celebrated memorials created by the Commission after the First World War.

It is particularly timely to look at the creation of the Singapore Memorial and Kranji War Cemetery now, in this 75th anniversary year of the end of the Second World War, and I hope you will enjoy this fascinating insight into this magnificent site and its no longer overlooked architect.

Preface

On the Australian Government's Office of Australian War Graves (OAWG) website, their definition of those physical sites designed to commemorate the fallen is as follows:

> A war memorial is a commemorative object intended to remind us of the people who served in and died as a result of war. War memorials may take many forms, but common to all of them is the intention that they remind us of those we have lost to war.[1]

The OAWG then proceeds to highlight the various forms such memorials could take, from the simple mounted plaque through to 'grand museums and monuments'. These memorials are subsequently categorised by *where they are*, *by whom they are dedicated*, and *to whom they are dedicated*. Interestingly, at this juncture, only the categorisation *where* is expounded: 'Battle exploit or battlefield memorials are sited near where those they commemorate fell in given battles. Prisoner of War (POW) memorials may be at the site of the former POW camps. War memorials can sometimes be found where units were or are based.'[2] In the case of Australia, this is a salient point as most if not all the significant sites of commemoration are found outside the country, in fields both close and afar, underlining the nation's imperial origins and history of overseas engagements.

After listing the principal war memorials for each State and Territory, OAWG then lists numerous overseas memorials under their remit. Among the Second World War memorials situated in Southeast Asia, three are in Malaysia, namely Parit Sulong Memorial in Johore, Sandakan Memorial Park, Sabah, and the Surrender Point Memorial on Labuan Island; Indonesia hosts the Nurses Memorial (Vyner Brooke Memorial), on Bangka Island; in Thailand, the Hellfire Pass Memorial Museum & Walking Trail and the Siam-Burma Railway; and ten sites in Papua New Guinea, including Kokoda, Milne Bay, Rabaul.

Interestingly, not a single war memorial is identified for Singapore, a significant site of memory that otherwise should be dedicated to the almost 15,000 troops of the Australian Imperial Forces who were captured by the Japanese upon the fall of Britain's 'impregnable fortress' and rendered prisoners of war. This omission of arguably one of Australia's great military catastrophes speaks volumes about the uneasy relationship the country continues to exhibit with this significant wartime memory, almost 80 years after the event. Australia's inability to suitably address the commemoration of an ultimately failed defensive campaign to prevent the Japanese onslaught through Malaya ending in the fall of Singapore, commensurate only to the tragic events on the Gallipoli Peninsula during the First World War, leaves an unfinished chapter in its military history.[3]

Changi Prison, on the other hand, site of incarceration for most of the Australian servicemen and staging post for the thousands transported to the notorious Siam-Burma Railway, many of whom would not return, has over the years been the subject of numerous scholarly articles, books, television and film productions, and museum exhibitions. Intermittent government-to-government discussions with the Singapore authorities on preserving parts of the former gaol site as some form of memorial, have yielded little result, the occasional artefact transfer aside. The reticence of both nations in finding common ground and conclusively accepting and acknowledging this episode with its own dedication, renders the symbolism of hosting annual commemorative events at Singapore's Kranji War Cemetery and Memorial, under the authority and management of the Commonwealth War Graves Commission, all the more uncomfortable by them *not* being at Changi.

Singapore's reluctance to amplify through commemoration this doomed British 'imperial' cause stemmed in part from its need to embrace the economic and social-cultural realities of its new-found post-independence position. This was compounded by the role its former occupier Japan would go on to play in the development of its industries and the sensitivities such regional relationships offered. The official opening of Kranji and unveiling of its memorial in 1957 did not greatly figure in the collective imagination, neither resonating with the growing population, the majority of whom trace their roots from further afield, nor representing the suffering the civilian population endured during those almost four years of occupation. For Singaporeans, a dedicated memorial to their dead would only be erected in 1967, a decade later. Kranji thus became perceived as an anomaly from the past, a foreign enterprise sitting uncomfortably within the nation's modern history.

This book does not set out to debate the merits or otherwise for selecting Kranji in lieu of Changi in the establishment of the Commission's primary war cemetery in Singapore. Its aim is to chronicle how the many participants in this endeavour all came together with a single goal to achieve a dignified resting place for their fellow comrades. For in the immediate aftermath of the conclusion to the bloodiest conflict to affect all of Asia, the urgent need was to account for the thousands of prisoners of war who survived, identify where the many thousands of their fellow prisoners had been sent to, and collate the records of those known to have died or designated missing. At this time, the welfare of the living took precedence over those who died, and it was the armed forces of Britain and Australia that offered this immediate assessment and relief through their war graves registration units. Amid all this, the foresight of the Commission in dispatching officers whose very task was to make assessments of and recommendations towards permanent burial grounds was salient at the very least.

Instead, the choice of Kranji over the immediate symbolism that Changi offered the commemoration process posed this author an interesting question – how throughout the preceding 74 years since the end of the war, and 62 years since the unveiling of the Singapore Memorial to the Missing, the understanding of the founding of this site and the design of its memorial have escaped a more thorough scrutiny. Indeed, the sheer lack of material on the cemetery's designer, the British architect Colin St Clair Oakes, who as Principal Architect to the Commission was the only Principal Architect of the Second World War, informs us of how society rapidly put behind it the war and its effects, preferring to bask in the post-war optimism rather than reflect on the tragic recent past. Oakes himself is in fact complicit in this, one of millions who served during the Second World War and then went back to their lives upon being demobilised, preferring to compartmentalise the past lest it overwhelm them.

It is this collective amnesia of Kranji's design process and its architect – including by those very institutions that partook in the trauma of that period, such as the Imperial War Graves Commission, the architectural fraternity and its schools, and historians in the United Kingdom, Singapore and Australia – that warrants further interrogation. I have sought to uncover through historical investigation how a structure so elegant in its simplicity yet timeless in its projection could have escaped critical scrutiny – an architectural monument on a small hill offering shelter to over 24,000 names of Allied servicemen who came to tropical Southeast Asia from near and far, and gave their lives for a cause, their bodies never to be recovered. Their names are inscribed in perpetuity on the white Portland stone slabs that line the walls.

Beginning this search for answers on the Kranji War Cemetery and Memorial and how it came to be founded along the northern edge of Singapore island began with a single name, that of its architect. Little was known about this man who otherwise appeared as a footnote to the monument and any official description of it. It was an online encounter with a PhD dissertation submitted in 1968 by a University of Cambridge student, and the effort by the alumni office at Clare College, that introduced me to Oakes's eldest son, Michael. My deep gratitude in gaining an opening into the life and work of Oakes, and the assistance with making his papers and background accessible, is extended to all his four children, Sally Thomas, Valerie Secretan, Bill Oakes and Michael, along with their families.

The primary research material that formed the basis of this work was sourced from the extensive archives of the Commonwealth War Graves Commission at Maidenhead. I am sincerely indebted to the archival team of Andrew Fetherston, Michael Greet and Ian Small, who tirelessly assisted me with locating the relevant papers, clarifying the workings of the Commission through the ages and providing the photographs and drawings that comprise a significant portion of this book. Similarly, the following British institutions proved invaluable in piecing together the research, in particular the Imperial War Museum, British Library, Royal Institute of British Architects, The National Archives, the British Film Institute (BFI) National Archive, Ministry of Defence, Royal Academy, Croydon Council and the Victoria & Albert Museum, in particular the RIBA Drawings and Archives Collection. Mention must also be accorded to Edward Bottoms from the Architectural Association, Peter Fisher of London Metropolitan University, David Wiggins of the Museum of Military Medicine, Dr Jane Harrold of Britannia Royal Naval College, Dartmouth, and Judith Wright, Senior Archivist at Boots UK, who along with Sophie Clapp kindly directed me to Oakes's extensive post-war reconstruction work for Boots whilst their Chief Architect.

My gratitude is also extended to Stephen Wyatt, whose play 'Memorials to the Missing', introduces Chapter 3 on the Architects. This dramatic work serves to reinforce the inspiration I drew from the late architectural historian Gavin Stamp and his 2006 study of Sir Edwin Lutyens's Somme Memorial. This significant structure's context within the broader history of commemorating the war dead in *The*

Memorial to the Missing of the Somme served as my intellectual template for how a detailed study on a memorial and its architect could be achieved. It is the one book that has not left my side these past few years whilst working on Oakes and Kranji.

Thank you also Alessandra Giovenco, Archivist at the British School at Rome, who kindly made available Oakes's records during his time in Italy; Ron Taylor of the Far East Prisoner of War (FEPOW) online community and its members; and Yoke Lin Wong for producing the informative maps.

In Singapore, I would like to acknowledge the National Library Board and the team at *BiblioAsia*, the library's journal, that provided me the platform to contribute an earlier essay on Oakes and Kranji. Mention is also warranted to Sarafian bin Salleh and Jerome Lim, who assisted in locating some of the military burial grounds; the kind staff at St George's Church; Fiona Lim for her research assistance; and Joseph Chia (谢福崧) and Teo Seng Yeong (张成雄) from the Singapore Hui Ann Association.

Closer to home, I am indebted to the generous assistance given by the research staff at the Australian War Memorial who helped me navigate its vast archival resources. Similarly, my thanks extend to the National Library of Australia, National Archives of Australia, Australian Army History Unit, Office of Australian War Graves, Department of Veterans' Affairs, the Australian Ex-Prisoners of War Memorial, Military History & Heritage Victoria and Virtual War Memorial Australia. Across in New Zealand, thanks to Peter Ireland, Richard Wolfe, William Hamill of the University of Auckland and Caroline McBride of the EH McCormick Research Library at the Auckland Art Gallery.

Being able to contact direct descendants of many of the book's participants, and receive their generous support throughout this journey, has been a personal highlight, and I cannot thank the following enough: Bill Brown, Janet Sebald, Mike and Matthew Brindley, Carol Greening, Alisdair Ferrie, Vicky Nash, Peter William, Glenda Godfrey, Ho Yap Hoi (何益辉), Yeo Bin Seng (姚平生), and Ho Ki Han Alvin (何纪涵).

Finally, particular mention must be extended to Chee Soo Lian, whose editing and writing advice over the last two years of this project guided it to a recognisable format before being submitted to the publishers; Writers Victoria for providing an early comprehensive structural edit and recommending the expanded chapter format; Melvin Neo and Justin Lau from Marshall Cavendish for helping realise a manuscript into a book; Professor Anoma D. Pieris for her patience over this journey and providing a scholarly sounding board to researching and writing history; and the many other friends and colleagues throughout the UK, Australia and Southeast Asia who though not individually listed here offered their greatly appreciated advice and friendly direction across the journey.

Athanasios Tsakonas
Melbourne
15 August 2020

Unveiling ceremony of Kranji War Memorial, 2 March 1957

CHAPTER 1

Introduction

On a bright and early Saturday morning on 2 March 1957, the shallow mist that often formed in the surrounding rubber plantations of Kranji during the night had gradually lifted, filling the sky with the white towering cumulonimbus clouds so typical of the tropics. The month of March in Singapore marks the official end of the north-easterly monsoon and the beginning of the warm, dry season. Ceremonies and events would often be hosted in the early hours, before the rising temperatures and high humidity made it uncomfortable for all who resided in the island state, especially those visiting from temperate latitudes.

Slowly pulling into an open car park at the base of the small hill, a motorcade with the British Union flag fluttering off the bonnet was met by representatives of the armed forces and Singapore government officials. The Governor and Commander-in-Chief of Singapore, Sir Robert Black[1], had arrived to preside over the official unveiling ceremony of the newly constructed Singapore Memorial at the Kranji War Cemetery. Amidst a silence that had fallen among those gathered, many of whom had arrived at dawn, Black was received by Air Chief Marshal Sir Arthur Longmore, Vice-Chairman of the Imperial War Graves Commission. Although not in breach of protocol, it was unusual for royal support to be absent during the event; this was not the

case in the opening ceremonies of numerous other major war cemeteries throughout the world. The Duke of Gloucester, also President of
the Imperial War Graves Commission, was noticeably absent because
of the ongoing political instability throughout Malaya and Singapore.
So was John Hare, 1st Viscount Blakenham, the recently appointed
Secretary of State for War and Chairman of the Commission. Seeking
a face-saving and honourable alternative, the Commission turned to
Black, who had served as an intelligence officer during the war before
being captured and interned in Singapore's Changi prisoner-of-war
camp. With the endorsement of the Colonial Office, and acquiescence
of Singapore's government – which was represented that day by the
Chief Minister Lim Yew Hock – it thus fell upon the Governor to act
as the representative of the British monarch, as guest of honour for the
occasion.[2]

Adorned in the traditional Court Uniform of the Colonial Service,
with its white drill, gilt buttons and white sun hat plumed with ostrich
feathers, Black projected the unmistakeable image of the Empire and
all it represented. Yet, this image was incongruous with the reality of
the times. The post-war period in Singapore, which briefly saw violence, disorder, malnutrition and high unemployment, had made way
for an economic recovery through the growing demand for rubber and
tin. The early 1950s also saw rising discontent among the local populace. The British government's failure to defend the island – their
'impregnable fortress'[3] – had shattered the Empire's credibility with the
local population and inspired the latter's political awakening. Rising
anti-colonial sentiment and nationalism saw deadly riots break out,
in particular the Hock Lee incident in 1955, ostensibly on account of
failed negotiations between the Hock Lee Amalgamated Bus Company
and its workers. Less than a year later, similar agitation and unrest
would erupt at the Chinese High School, both incidents underscoring
the modernisation trajectory of Singapore's local population. Having
arrived two years earlier in 1955 and astutely reading the local mood for
independence, Black would quietly advise the government in London
on the desirability of independence, and proceed to set in motion the

Sir Robert Black, Governor of Singapore, arriving for the unveiling ceremony

steps to achieving self-rule for the island. Within a few days of the unveiling of the Memorial, the first of three constitutional talks on self-government – commonly referred to as the Merdeka Talks – would be convened in London. This would culminate in the United Kingdom agreeing to grant the island complete internal self-rule, paving the way for the establishment of the State of Singapore the following year, in August 1958. The unveiling of the Singapore Memorial would thus become one of the last major official events Black presided over before departing Singapore later that year to take up the governorship of Hong Kong.

Beyond the stone-clad shelters that framed the formal entrance to the cemetery, a guard of honour had been assembled with soldiers lining the gently inclined grassed walkway up to the Memorial. It comprised contingents from the Royal Navy, the Commonwealth Armies and Air Forces, the Police, and the Singapore and Malayan Army and Air Forces. The band of the 2nd Battalion, The Royal Welch Fusiliers, played during its mounting and dispersal. And in strict tradition, it was the wreath-bearers who first marched through, followed by the procession of the Reverend Canon Victor J. Pike, Chaplain to the Queen and

17

Chaplain General to the Forces. Governor Black followed closely after, receiving the Royal Salute, then inspecting the Guards of Honour.[4]

Alongside the assembled dignitaries and representatives of the various Commonwealth governments, almost 3,000 invited guests had gathered among the neat rows of uniform white headstones and carefully tended orchids. They were there to bear witness to the conclusion of a process commenced over a decade earlier in the immediate aftermath of the war. Among them were over 500 next-of-kin, whose loved ones were interred within the cemetery or had their names inscribed on the memorial. They had come mostly from Singapore, Malaya and nearby countries in Southeast Asia. Ten relatives from the United Kingdom, eleven from Australia and New Zealand and one from Canada had made the arduous trip from homelands thousands of miles away.[5] Compared to the situation in Europe, where the majority of war graves were found in close proximity, either within the UK or just across the English Channel, the long distance and high fares to Singapore were a deterrent. But with the assistance of the British Legion and the War Graves Commission, a charter plane was arranged, and for the sum of £200, the relatives in the United Kingdom contingent were able to make the journey. Similar arrangements were put in place with government assistance for the Australian contingent, comprising mothers, fathers, wives and former prisoners of war.[6]

Overlooking the Straits of Johore to the north, the Singapore Memorial formed the backdrop to the war cemetery and the assembled guests. A gracious wing-like structure supported by 12 pillars, their Portland stone inserts were inscribed with the names of over 24,000 servicemen who had no known graves. Fronting each pillar, a sentinel from each of the represented services stood at attention, head bowed. At the centre, beneath the central pylon rising to the sky, was a curved stone panel draped with the Union Jack and carrying the inscription dedicated to the unveiling of the Memorial. It was here that the Governor took his position and delivered his address to the assembled guests and the thousands listening back home on the wireless. In a concise oration invoking Abraham Lincoln's poignant Gettysburg Address,

Black reminded those gathered that 'it was for them to dedicate themselves to the task ahead so that the dead shall not have died in vain'.[7] And in commemorating those soldiers and airmen whose names the memorial would maintain in perpetuity, Governor Black unveiled the Singapore Memorial.

Covering the ceremony was the British Broadcasting Corporation (BBC) World Service, through their new Far East correspondent Anthony Lawrence. Lawrence, in his distinct clipped tone, provided a vivid running description of the day's events. Reported in both radio and television news programmes later that evening[8] to living rooms thousands of miles away in the United Kingdom, Australia, New Zealand, South Africa and Canada as well as those closer to home in Singapore and Malaya, the BBC's coverage gave the sense that due recognition was finally being accorded to the many who had sacrificed their lives in Southeast Asia. The ceremony was also filmed, with screenings held soon after back home. This was one of the first major events covered by Lawrence, who would go on to become one of the most highly regarded and influential BBC foreign correspondents, covering the Cultural Revolution in China, the independence of Malaya and Singapore, and the Vietnam War.[9]

A lone bugler from King Edward VII's Own Gurkha Rifles then stepped forward to sound the 'Last Post', and the lament 'Lochaber No More' was played by Pipers of the King's Own Scottish Borderers. The Reverend Canon Pike dedicated the Memorial, and Reveille was called. Sir Reginald Blomfield's Cross of Sacrifice, its Christian symbolism a mere few metres away on account of an additional row of graves which were not in the earlier plan, was an appropriate prop for the prayers that followed. The Reverend I.E. Newell, representing the Far East Air Force, led those gathered in 'Let Us Pray' and the Reverend Cannon Pike read from 2 Thessalonians of the New Testament and pronounced 'The Blessing'. To address the multicultural, multi-faith origins of the many fallen Commonwealth servicemen who fought on behalf of the British Empire, the Nadzir Ugana Haji Ibrahim bin Yusoff, the Bhawan of the 1st Battalion, 2nd Gurkha Rifles, Pundit Bhoj Raj Sharma and

Pipers of the King's Own Scottish Borderers performing
at the unveiling of Kranji War Memorial

the high priest Venerable Sek Hong Choon offered Islamic, Hindu and
Buddhist prayers, respectively. The Senior Roman Catholic Chaplain of
the Far East Land Forces, the Reverend P. Tobin, accompanied by the
Reverend P.F. Bailey, concluded the ceremony's liturgy with a reading
of a prayer of lament, Psalm 130.[10]

Following the laying of wreaths at the base of the Cross of Sacrifice, the Governor took the general salute, and the national anthem
'God Save the Queen' rang out across the site. A flypast of six de Hav-
illand 'Vampire' jet fighters from the Far East Air Force punctured
the sky in a salute, their white, interwoven atmospheric trails lingering overhead. Governor Black and his entourage then fanned out to
inspect the Memorial and read out the acknowledgements of all those
involved in the creation of the War Cemetery. The spirit and gener-
osity of the occasion was best reflected in a photograph appearing in

the local Chinese newspaper *Nanyang Siang Pau* the following day. Attired in a white linen suit, a smiling Ho Bock Kee, the builder of the Memorial, was seen receiving the Governor's handshake, a gesture of appreciation for the completion of the Memorial. The ceremony, steeped in the formalism of an established protocol dating from the beginnings of the Imperial War Graves Commission in 1917, would be officially over by mid-morning.[11]

The unveiling ceremony at Kranji was not unique. Over the past decade, numerous similar ceremonies had been held across Europe, North Africa, the United States, Canada and the Middle East, coinciding with the completion of war cemeteries, monuments and memorials. In Asia itself, there were 21 major war cemeteries, in an administrative district that stretched from Karachi in the west to Hong Kong in the east, from Assam in the north to Singapore and Ceylon on the equator. By March 1957, given the difficulties encountered with the distances, access to materials and skilled labour, 12 of the war cemeteries had been completed, six were under construction and three remained to commence.[12] In fact, the first such unveiling ceremony in Asia had taken almost a decade after the conclusion of the war. It was only in January 1955, having endured internal conflicts, independence struggles and a myriad of other delays, that the Sai Wan Memorial within the Sai Wan War Cemetery in Hong Kong was unveiled, its classical form serving as a backdrop to the terraced graves overlooking the South China Sea. Similar ceremonies in Delhi and Karachi followed soon after in the latter half of 1957, the Rangoon Memorial in Taukkyan War Cemetery in 1958, and Chittagong War Cemetery in 1962. These rituals, centred on a memorial or war cemetery, often represented a fitting and overdue acknowledgement of the thousands of servicemen and women who died in the war; their remains were either never found or never positively identified. They also provided relatives and friends of the deceased with a physical monument to visit and commemorate their loved ones. The scholar Jay Winter offers that 'war memorials marked the spot where communities were reunited, where the dead were symbolically brought home, and where the separations

of war, both temporary and eternal, were expressed, ritualized, and in time accepted'.[13]

Yet amidst the pomp and ceremony of that day, the architect of Kranji War Cemetery and Singapore Memorial, Colin St Clair Oakes, was not in attendance. After the war against Japan ended, at the behest of the War Graves Commission, Oakes had immediately set off to Asia to advise on the location and layout of the many war cemeteries being established hurriedly by the Army. In the decade after, his professional practice was largely dependent on these sites, to which he would return to evaluate their suitability and what preliminary preparation the war graves units had undertaken. This also involved developing the conceptual schemes through to their realisation. However, for all these years of emotional investment in the Commission's foray into Asia, Oakes did not attend any official unveiling or opening ceremony of the many war cemeteries and memorials he had designed throughout India, Bangladesh, Hong Kong and the countries in Southeast Asia. In a varied career that saw him study in Rome, work in Bengal and fight in Burma before taking up an appointment as Principal Architect for the Imperial War Graves Commission, Oakes was by 1957 content to remain at home in rural England with his wife and four children, work in his garden and contribute to the rebuilding of a Britain still emerging from the devastation of the war years.

This book examines the Imperial War Graves Commission's work in Asia following the conclusion of the 1939–45 war, through the design narrative of the Kranji War Cemetery and Memorial. It argues that Kranji is a distinctive product of the wartime opportunity afforded a relatively unknown young architect. As the fifth and final Principal Architect appointed by the Commission, Oakes's undertaking of the design responsibility for the majority of the war cemeteries and memorials throughout South and Southeast Asia came about because of his military service background along with the experience of having lived and worked in Asia.[14] It proved an astute choice, as Oakes introduced a modernist sensibility to these sites of commemoration and pilgrimage, in the process defining his future career. Similarly, Kranji is framed within the wider context of these sites of difficult memories. Whilst spanning vast geographical distances between nations of disparate cultures and societies, the war cemeteries' shared architectural heritage produces a common history with its own narrative: the advance of the Japanese campaign and its subsequent military confrontation and retreat.

With its creative origins emanating from the design principles founded by the Commission for the Great War in 1917, the design of Kranji was a collaborative process involving many participants. These included the British and Australian War Graves Units dispatched immediately after the surrender who were responsible for the collection and concentration of the deceased, the Imperial War Graves Commission and its officers and advisors, through to the local builder appointed to transform a once-temporary burial site into the permanent site of commemoration as it is known today. Kranji's design was

Killed during the final battles on the Western Front, the bodies of Australian troops, each with its simple wooden cross, are gathered for burial at a cemetery being constructed at Guillemont Farm, 3 October 1918.

24

also informed through its architect's education process and life experiences. And the island's location along the equator was an important consideration. Kranji would take well over a decade to fulfil its architect's vision.

Above all, Kranji symbolises the contemporary amnesia that befell similar sites throughout the region. An essentially British or 'imperial' project created in a colonial outpost with its populace seeking independence, Kranji has a contested history. From the Commission's perspective, this 'sacred site' represented the fallen soldiers and airmen of the Commonwealth forces during the war against the Japanese. Drawn predominantly from the ranks of the British, Australian, Dutch and Indian dominions along with members of the local Malay regiments, the bodies interred and names inscribed reflect a foreign enterprise far from their places of origin.[15] Though it may partly be attributed to its vast distance from the better-known and more well-patronised war cemeteries and memorials in western Europe, Kranji also speaks of its uncomfortable position within a society and culture vastly different from its predecessor. This discomfort denies the memorial the opportunity for multiple visitations and the accompanying vigils and commemoration that might occur elsewhere in Europe, further isolating the site.[16]

On the other hand, local Chinese combatants and civilians, unless associated with the imperial forces such as Dalforce or the Straits Settlements Volunteer Force, did not meet the Commission's criteria on qualifying personnel and were precluded from burial within Kranji War Cemetery.[17] Instead, the local community in a country with a majority ethnic Chinese population established their own sacred spaces of remembrance after independence from Malaysia in 1965. The most significant is the Memorial to the Civilian Victims of the Japanese Occupation.[18] Located in the civic quarter of the city, with its distinctive four identical pillars rising to the sky, the memorial annually hosts the most significant local commemoration – the surrender of Singapore to the Japanese on 15 February 1942. Along with VJ Day on 15 August, local appropriation of this memorial relegates Kranji to Remembrance

Day organised by the British, Anzac Day by Australia and New Zealand, and the occasional foreign-led pilgrimage and service.[19]

In examining the available writings on the Kranji War Cemetery and the commemoration and memorialisation of its war dead, Chapter 2 enables an understanding of how this site has been perceived through the various historical and cultural filters of the authors and their audience. Making use of scholarly writings in the disciplines of social geography, military history, political science and architectural history, each author's perspective on how the war cemetery and its memorial are viewed and appropriated by various stakeholders is revealed. We also explore that sense of fluid ownership that often serves multiple agendas.

Chapter 3 places the appointment of Oakes as the Commission's final Principal Architect for the Second World War sites within the broader timeframe and selection process that took place as the conflict was coming to its end. This enables an appreciation of the other architects and their contribution to the war cemetery and memorial effort. Similarly, the choice of Oakes itself poses questions as to the viable alternatives that were at the Commission's disposal. It argues that whereas Oakes was an unknown choice, the three architects who were overlooked – Arthur Hutton, James Ferrie and John Brindley – were all known to the Commission through their work on memorials, and had personal connections to Singapore. The sense of ownership and stakeholder interest in the Singapore site is best exemplified by the Australian architect and soldier Brindley, who not only designed a war memorial for Singapore, but was interned at Changi. Was this an opportunity missed to also commemorate the prisoners of war who survived?

The original tour by Major Oakes and Colonel Harry Obbard of the numerous battlefields, prisoner-of-war and labour camps, and burial sites throughout South and Southeast Asia frames Chapter 4. This was carried out on behalf of the Imperial War Graves Commission during the chaotic period following the war's end in late 1945–1946. As the appointed Advisory Architect and the Commission's Inspector for India and Burma respectively, these two men, recently demobilised from active service and seconded to the Commission, would produce the initial outline of those sites suited to becoming permanent war cemeteries and provide preliminary design layouts for the Army's War Graves Units to work to. Chapter 4 then introduces an understanding of the architectural principles that the Imperial War Graves Commission embraced after the war of 1914–18.[20] Through the vision of the Commission's founder and Vice-Chairman, Sir Fabian Ware, and the direction of its Artistic Advisor, Lieutenant-Colonel Sir Frederic Kenyon, the design of war cemeteries and memorials became a lasting legacy. It introduces the original Principal Architects and then considers the changing environment that greeted the Commission with the Second World War. The expansion of the Commission's role in Asia brought new challenges in working in such an unfamiliar environment. It introduced the need for a Principal Architect for the Asian theatre, leading to the tentative appointment of Colin St Clair Oakes.

A biographical account of Oakes forms the basis of Chapter 5. Unlike the Commission's other Principal Architects, who through their status and positions in British society at the time were recognised and written about, Oakes was an obscure figure. The son of an architect who served in the Great War, his trajectory through a local polytechnic would impress upon him the possibilities of modern architecture. A stint in Finland followed by selection to the British School at Rome marked a turning point for Oakes, with the friends and contacts he developed over two years in Italy guiding him throughout his life. This preceded his departure for Bengal as a government architect just before the outbreak of war and his subsequent enrolment and active service in Burma. It was because of this period in Asia that his credentials attracted the attention of the Commission.

The selection of Kranji in Singapore as the site for the permanent war cemetery and memorial to the missing airmen and soldiers throughout the Southeast Asia campaign is examined and developed throughout Chapters 6 and 7. According to the primary sources from the Commission's archives and Oakes's family records, it is apparent

27

that the preferred location was in fact not Kranji but a hilltop site to the centre of the island. Similar sentiments were voiced by representatives of the local Chinese community in a parallel quest to establish their own site of remembrance for civilian victims of the Japanese Occupation. The Australian authorities on the other hand were advancing the case for Changi, the site of incarceration for thousands of servicemen, to stage a national war memorial, going so far as to call for a design proposal. Through the tour of Asia that formed his assessment to the Commission's preference against considered advice, the design of Kranji offers an insight into Oakes's reading of the contemporary landscape after the war. It also marks an attempt to redress the conception of the war cemetery as an imperial project implanted into another society. The deliberations on the architect's background and his involvement in the Asian theatre of the war offer this study a new way of looking at Singapore's only war cemetery: as part of a wider body of similar sites of commemoration designed by Oakes throughout South and Southeast Asia.

Whereas the previous chapter made the case for Kranji's selection (if not the preferred site, then a suitable compromise given the unsettled period), Chapter 7 addresses the origins of what would become the Commission's major memorial to the missing airmen of the war in Asia. In accordance with the Commission's long-standing policy of promoting sites with significant war-time memories, the location offers different readings to the various stakeholders in the venture. For the British, the Japanese landing at Kranji shattered their perceptions of Singapore as an impregnable fortress, with the threat envisaged and planned for coming from the sea to the south. For the locals, Kranji was merely the last move in the Japanese push southwards through the Malay Peninsula, culminating in the surrender of the island seven days later. To the Australians, whose forces fought bravely along the Kranji coastline, inflicting considerable losses upon the invader, the location reflected the chaos of the battle and their inglorious retreat. Kranji will always be remembered as the easy opening afforded the Japanese Army to the island.

Sorting and reburial of remains at Kranji War Cemetery, 1946

Reflecting upon local contributions to Kranji, Chapter 8 explores the development of the permanent cemetery and its memorial through its local builder, Ho Bock Kee. As a migrant from China, with his skills and entrepreneurship Ho played a significant role in the building of post-war Singapore – a contribution often ignored in the recorded anthologies of Singapore's built history. Through oral interviews with Ho's second son and the Singapore Hui Ann Association, a picture emerges of an industry deeply ensconced in the construction of Singapore's war-associated built heritage. This allows us to better comprehend and appreciate the development of Oakes's design ideas and their realisation in the local context. This involves not only critiquing Oakes's built design, but also the landscape design, a considerable investment in the war graves enterprise. In this case, Mandy Morris's study of the quintessential war cemetery 'that is for ever England' frames our understanding of how Kranji evolved from the Commission's post-First World War ideas of war cemetery landscape. Through the efforts of Oakes, Obbard and the Singapore Botanic Gardens, the site became rooted in its tropical domain. Similarly, the need for the urgent founding of the Singapore State Cemetery, adjacent to the war cemetery, posed significant challenges to its previous hegemonic role in Kranji, representing a clear site for war memory and commemoration.

The final chapter opens with the human dimension of the official unveiling of the Singapore Memorial in 1957. Against the backdrop of political instability in Malaya and Singapore,[21] the ceremony marked an important shift in the relationship between the island state marching towards independence and its colonial rulers remembering their fallen. It had been ten years since Oakes first visited Singapore and began considering a likely site and its design. Oakes had by this stage relinquished his appointment with the Commission and taken up a new position as Chief Architect for the Boots Pure Drug Company. This would represent a full circle in his career – from designing sacred spaces for those who perished in the war, he would now turn to the rebuilding of London and numerous other cities and towns throughout Britain, cities scarred by the bombing damage wrought during the Blitz.

My interest in this war cemetery and memorial stems from an early appreciation of its solemnity within a contemporary landscape of rapid economic, industrial and social progress occurring in the country. A visit in early 1992 piqued my architectural interest in the why and how of its situation. At that time, the northern perimeter of the island contained a scattering of industrial estates, public utilities and farmlands, amongst which this solitary wing-like structure found itself placed. A subsequent search produced a solitary name of an architect without any further context. It raised a pertinent question of how one of the Principal Architects of the Imperial War Graves Commission had remained little-known and had subsequently not been accorded due recognition for his body of work. Where the other Principal Architects of the Commission like Reginald Blomfield, Edwin Lutyens, Herbert Baker and Louis de Soissons were invariably given due mention whenever they received promotions or honours, how did such an active participant in this post-war endeavour elude further examination and public awareness?[22]

Two decades later, after irregular yet periodic visits to the war cemetery, I decided to pursue further research into Colin St Clair Oakes. This enabled a better understanding of the extensive and still little-known body of work he left behind in Asia. These are the works that the majority of visitors to these sites would inevitably recognise for their significance to the Japanese campaign. However, they are unaware of the architectural connection between these sites. My research coincided with an increasing local awareness of the period of occupation under the Japanese. A similar rise in interest within Australia of the Anzac legacy and the quest for a national identity saw sites of difficult memories such as Changi, the Kokoda Track and the Siam-Burma Railway stimulate a growing appreciation and understanding of the period and its consequences. This resulted in ever-increasing pilgrimages and attendances at significant national events of commemoration, often led by military historians.

I hope that this study, through primarily focusing on the architecture and the process that led to its creation, will stimulate a greater awareness and appreciation of the background of an important architect and the historically significant memorial, offering another way of reading this site.

CHAPTER 2

Writings

It was barely six months after the defeat of Nazi Germany and a little over two since the surrender of the Japanese Imperial Forces. In the cold and overcast early morning of 14 November 1945, two former senior officers of the British Army and a third from the Imperial War Graves Commission quietly gathered at Hurn Airport, a few miles out from the southern English coastal city of Bournemouth. A Royal Air Force Base activated at the start of the war to serve transport and fight operations, the airport had been transferred to civilian control and had begun operating as Britain's only international airport. Two officers departed on an ex-military BOAC Dakota, whilst the third made his way to the nearby harbour of Poole, and departed by BOAC Empire flying boat.[1] A low-key affair, all three were setting off for an extended, and what was to become a challenging tour of the Indian subcontinent, Burma and the Far East. Hastily assembled by the Commission, and with only their personal kits, their orders were to visit the locations of some of the heaviest battles of the war against the Japanese and assess the numerous burial sites where Allied servicemen had been laid to rest. They were to then recommend the suitability of these sites in becoming permanent war cemeteries.[2]

Accompanying Major Andrew MacFarlane, the Commission's Deputy Director of Works, was Colonel Harry Naismith Obbard, seconded from the army as the Inspector for India and Burma, and Major Colin St Clair Oakes, an architect recently demobilised from active service. MacFarlane and Obbard were old hands in the ways of the British military, both considerably older than Oakes and veterans of the First World War. MacFarlane had been a Major with the Cameron Highlanders and was awarded the Military Cross for his actions on the Western Front. Upon his return to civilian life and joining the Commission as Chief Clerk of Works, he was actively involved in the construction of war cemeteries and memorials throughout France and Belgium, notably the Thiepval Memorial.[3] His role on this tour, beyond being the senior Commission liaison officer, was to survey the existing conditions of burial grounds and advise on their construction requirements.

Obbard, on the other hand, had been a career army officer, serving on the staff at the General Head Quarters (GHQ), New Delhi, before being loaned to the Commission for this tour. Commissioned into the Royal Engineers in 1916 and joining King George V's Own Bengal Sappers and Miners, Obbard saw active service in France and north-west Persia during the First World War. and was subsequently seconded to the Indian Army with service in Egypt and Burma during the Second World War. In addition to being tasked along with Oakes to assess and report back on the suitability of the various burial grounds to becoming permanent sites, Obbard had a second responsibility. It was to prepare a preliminary assessment towards an operational framework and policy for the Commission's establishing of an agency in the region. The new agency would be tasked with undertaking the planning, building and maintenance of the many war cemeteries that the Far East required. This would eventually cover an area stretching from the far western Indian subcontinent to the far east coast of the Pacific, including French Indochina, Hong Kong, and southwards to the Australasian coastline. Obbard would soon after returning retire from the Army and, along with a promotion to Brigadier, be appointed the Commission's Chief Administrative Officer for this new agency based in Penang, Malaya.[4]

The original itinerary was to visit all military cemeteries and burial grounds in Assam, Eastern Bengal and Burma so as to enable the advisory architect to make proposals for their general layout and architectural treatment. This would enable the war graves units on the ground, who were actively recovering remains and consolidating them, to better organise their operations and burial locations to avoid further exhumations and reburials in the future. As the scale of the conflict became better understood, the tour was subsequently extended to also include Ceylon, headquarters for Admiral Lord Louis Mountbatten, Supreme Allied Commander South East Asia (SACSEA) and South East Asia Command (SEAC). At the invitation of the Allied Land Forces South East Asia (ALFSEA), they also visited southern Burma and Thailand, advising the Army's Directorate of Graves Registration & Enquiries (DGR&E) on the number, location and layout of the military cemeteries from that dark theatre of the war.[5]

Covering over 26,000 miles by air, rail, road and water, the trip took them through north-east India and Bengal, visiting cities and remote towns such as Bhanipur (Bhowanipore), Sylhet, Jauhati, Jorhat, Kohima, Imphal, Silchar and Calcutta, before entering present-day Bangladesh into Chittagong, Maynamati and Dacca (Dhaka). They then entered the vast mountains and jungles of Burma through Rangoon, Toungoo, Magwe, Pegu and Mandalay, visiting the notorious Siam-Burma Railway and the concentration burial grounds located at either end – in Kanchanaburi, Chungkai and Thanbyuzayat. From Rangoon the party continued on to Singapore, before embarking on the return leg back to Delhi through Burma, Bengal, Ceylon and India. It was late February before MacFarlane and Oakes returned to London.[6]

There was also the difficulty of travelling in countries that were ravaged by the war and newly liberated, with little rest every day. The party had to contend with rudimentary accommodation, most often the type that had seen active service, such as straw bashas, tents and war-damaged buildings with meagre furniture, if any. Oakes was restricted to writing his notes and preparing sketches under hurricane lamps well into the night, all with the knowledge that the next day

TIBET

R. Brahmaputra

HIMALAYAS

CHINA

Chungking

R. Mekong

Sadiya
Dibrugarh · Panitola
Digboi
R. Brahmaputra
Jorhat
Ledo
Airlift to China (Hump Route)
Dimapur
ASSAM
Kohima
Sylhet
Silchar
Naga Hills
MANIPUR
Tamu
Imphal
R. Chindwin
Sumprabum

R. Yangtze

Kweiyang

Yunnanyi

Myitkyina
Mogaung
Paoshan

Kunming
Burma Road

YUNNAN

BENGAL

R. Ganges

Dacca
Agartala
Comilla
Tiddim
Kalewa

Indaw
Bhamo
Loiwing

Calcutta

Chin Hills

Kachin Hills
Lashio

R. Salween

Chittagong

Cox's Bazar
Maungdaw
R. Mayu
R. Kaladan

Akyab
Yenangyaung

Meiktila
Myingyan
Mandalay

SHAN
Loilem
Kengtung

STATES

Dien Bien Phu

Hanoi

Haiphong

ARAKAN

Magwe
Loikaw

BURMA

KAREN
HILLS

Kyaukpyu

Taungup
Prome
Zigon

Henzada
Pegu

R. Sittang
Toungoo
Chiengmai

Vientiane

R. Salween

R. Mekong

Vinh

FRENCH INDO-CHINA

BAY OF BENGAL

Gwa
Taukkyan

Bassein
Rangoon

Moulmein
Gulf of Martaban
Raheng

SIAM

Hue

Thanbyuzayat

Ye
Niki
Three Pagodas Pass

Chungkai
Kanchanaburi
Non Pladok
Bangkok

Siam-Burma Railway

Tavoy

ANDAMAN
ISLANDS

Mergui

Prachuab

Phnom Penh

Saigon

GULF OF SIAM

Victoria Point

Kra Isthmus

Surat

Ca Mau

NICOBAR
ISLANDS

Nakhorn

Phuket Island

Singora

Sebang Island

Alor Star
Sungei Patani

Kota Bahru

Taiping

MALAYA

Kuantan

Kuala Lumpur

SUMATRA

Strait of Malacca

Port Dickson

Malacca

Mersing

Kluang

Johore Bahru
Kranji
Singapore

++++ Railway
- - - International Border
▨ Elevation above 1500 feet
Kranji War Cemeteries

Miles
0   100   200

0   100   200   300
Kilometres

N

would bring more travelling, more burial sites and more civilian populations trying to salvage what remained of their lives after four years of war and hardship. Yet amongst all the personal discomfort the tour entailed, the conceptual ideas for the present-day Commonwealth war cemeteries in India, Myanmar, Bangladesh, Thailand and Singapore were sown, in readiness for their design development and approval before permanent works could finally commence. Upon their return, Obbard's final report on the tour recommended a total of 25 permanent war cemeteries be established in their administrative area of Asia: ten in India, six in Burma, four in Ceylon, and two in Singapore, as well as three specifically for the Siam-Burma Railway – two at the Siam end of the line, and one at the Burma end.[7]

Writing on Kranji

Jean-Louis Cohen, in his 2012 book, *Architecture in Uniform: Designing and Building for the Second World War*, presents a unique perspective on the role of architects and architecture during the Second World War. Citing such examples as English architect Hugh Casson's designs of camouflage and William Holford's hostels for women in munitions factories, Cohen's central premise is that the opportunities the war provided to design participants on all sides of the conflict were fundamental to the process of modernisation. This revelation reinforces the validity of modernism in architecture and its subsequent growth and export across the globe during the post-war years.[8]

Yet in this extensive study centred around ten themes, Cohen interestingly does not dwell far beyond North American and European sources, offering very little by way of Asian examples to his argument. Neither does the study interrogate the architecture for the dead, nor those architects serving the Imperial War Graves Commission. Only in his concluding chapter, in a section entitled 'Architecture of Memory and Oblivion', is the topic of commemoration raised. This is through the design of monuments for battlefields and the victims of war or violence, rather than memorials for fallen soldiers. It is also in this section that Japanese efforts at commemoration are first introduced, through competition entries for memorials and monuments, notably Kenzo Tange's winning pyramid design for the foot of Mount Fuji as part of the Daiôta or Greater East Asian Co-Prosperity Sphere, the Empire of Japan's imperialist policy for those countries under its occupation. The book's noticeable omission of war cemeteries and the architects who designed them may suggest they were not considered participants in this modernist agenda.[9]

Scholarly writings[10] on the Imperial War Graves Commission and its work tend to fall within three distinct yet often overlapping areas of study. Firstly, there are the many historical studies of the institution itself and its founding as the consequence of the First World War. They include Sidney Hurst's *The Silent Cities* (1929), Fabian Ware's *The Immortal Heritage* (1937), Philip Longworth's *The Unending Vigil* (1967) and David Crane's *Empires of the Dead* (2013). To a lesser extent, Julie Summers's *Remembered: A History of the Commonwealth War Graves Commission* (2007) and an abridged follow-up, *British and Commonwealth War Cemeteries* (2010), also fall into this category. Secondly, there are those studies where the emphasis is on the war cemeteries and memorials. The history of the Commission is an important aspect but it serves as an accompaniment to the Commonwealth war cemeteries themselves. In this case, the written works attempt to make sense of the numerous sites across the world, by either focusing on those of the First World War, those that include the Second World War, or works that investigate a particular group or subset of war cemeteries. Edwin Gibson and Kingsley Ward's *Courage Remembered* (1989) and Bart Ziino's *A Distant Grief* (2007) are examples. The final method in studying the history of the Commission is either through studying the many design practitioners that contributed to the development of the war cemeteries and memorials, or by focusing on a solitary work that embodies a unique aesthetic characteristic. Accounts on individual servicemen within the Commission's cemeteries also fall into this category. Jeroen Geurst's *Cemeteries of the Great War by Sir Edwin Lutyens* (2010) and Kristine Miller's *Almost Home* (2013), which looks at the war cemetery landscape designs by Gertrude Jekyll, are notable examples

37

of this final method. Gavin Stamp's *The Memorial to the Missing of the Somme* (2006), which examines the Thiepval Arch and its design by Lutyens, offers an understanding of the Commission through this single monument built to commemorate the war dead.

In the case of Kranji War Cemetery, the English-language literature produced since its establishment and consecration in 1947 has been limited, which is in stark contrast to the available material on Changi. As Singapore's most significant prisoner-of-war and internment site, Changi assumes an indelible position within both popular imagination and the intellectual memorialisation and commemoration discourse on the Pacific War. While Kranji is somewhat peripheral to popular war memory, Changi has come to represent harsh prisoner-of-war experiences in broader British and Australian war-time narratives. The writings that do exist tend to place Kranji within various scholarly frameworks, primarily the broader discourse of the Imperial War Graves Commission's history and its work around the world. The exception is Arthur Lane's *Kranji War Cemetery* (1995), which, aside from providing a detailed account of the battles across Malaya until the fall of Singapore, incorporates a roll of honour of all casualties interred within Kranji War Cemetery and inscribed on the memorials. Lane was a former prisoner of war of the Japanese and his work serves as the official burial register, located in the Register Box within the cemetery's east Entrance Shelter.

First published in 1967, Philip Longworth's *The Unending Vigil: A History of the Commonwealth War Graves Commission* is the most notable example of locating Kranji within the broader Commission discourse.[11] Commissioned by the war graves agency itself, the book is arguably the definitive reference on the founding and the workings of the Commission, broaching as it claims, the 'political, constitutional, administrative, financial, social, aesthetic and technical'[12] aspects. And yet Longworth makes patently clear in his prefatory note that the bulk of the text is devoted to the Commission's earlier years, due in part to the belief that interest lies in the Commission's founding and its formation of policies. In this otherwise engrossing 250-page account, only a few pages are devoted to the work in Asia. Kranji is accorded only a single sentence, whilst the portrayal of the continent verges on the pejorative – 'the most difficult region, however, was the Far East'; 'the cemeteries in the Far East suffered the worst delays of all'; 'incorruptible clerks of works were always hard to find'.[13] These statements are compounded by the knowledge that the majority of the 'Asian' war graves sites are not in the 'Far East' but situated in the geographic arc between the Indian subcontinent through to Singapore at the southern tip of the Malay Peninsula. The Far East in fact incorporates some of the better organised, constructed and maintained sites, notably Sai Wan War Cemetery and Stanley War Cemetery in Hong Kong.

The representation of Asia and Kranji is marginally better developed in other primary resources on the Commission. Major Edwin Gibson and G. Kingsley Ward's *Courage Remembered* chronicles a more detailed survey of the key war cemeteries and memorials across the world, providing facts and figures on each, invaluable to those intending to visit. It brings a better understanding of the war graves work in Asia to a wider readership through its descriptions of selected sites in India, Burma, Malaya, Indonesia and New Guinea. In writing about the Singapore Memorial, not only are the casualty numbers and their countries of origin listed, but its unveiling is recorded and Colin St Clair Oakes is credited with its design: 'It consists of a building of a dozen piers carrying a flat roof, with a tall central tower surmounted by a star, the whole at first glance not unlike the tail unit of a giant aeroplane.'[14] And yet Gibson and Ward's most important contribution might be in identifying the renewed interest shown in the war cemeteries and memorial sites since the mid to late 1980s, in particular by veterans and their relatives.

Julie Summers's *Remembered: A History of the Commonwealth War Graves Commission,* along with a photographic exhibition of the Commission's cemeteries and memorials around the world, was released in 2007 to coincide with the 90th anniversary of the Commonwealth War Graves Commission (CWGC).[15] Her follow-up book, *British and Commonwealth War Cemeteries,* published a few years later in 2010, is presented as an accessible companion for travellers visiting the war graves sites. Though according only three pages to the Commission's work in Asia, it is one of the first published accounts that gives Oakes due recognition for designing the war cemeteries in the 'Far East' and for the pre-eminent use of the pedestal headstone with bronze plaque inscription. The Singapore Memorial at Kranji is mentioned as holding the names of not only those servicemen who died in the battle for Singapore, but importantly also those who died during the three and a half years of captivity under the Japanese.[16] In a series of colour photographs and accompanying captions, Summers also highlights Oakes's other sites such as Chungkai ('started by prisoners of war'), Kohima ('this beautiful terraced cemetery') and Sai Wan ('the magnificent view of the harbour').[17]

As with Longworth, the understanding of Kranji in these works is viewed nominally through a Eurocentric lens, and as an effect of the institution and its ideals. Kranji is reduced to becoming one of the few cemeteries created from the 'distant' war against Japan, yet somehow fitting within the wider war graves endeavour. This complements the numerous battlefield guides, brochures and journal articles prepared by the Commission and its agents, offering a rudimentary outline of the cemetery's history and its place within the wider Asian theatre of the conflict. The architect if at all mentioned is in a cursory note.

Outside the 'imperial' view, the most comprehensive tome written on Kranji emanates from a local. Singaporean Romen Bose's *Kranji: The Commonwealth War Cemetery and the Politics of the Dead* (2006) offers the first detailed insight into the establishment of the Kranji War Cemetery, and importantly, one that is told from the perspective of the country it is situated in. Bose comprehensively details all of Kranji's individual memorials and explores the politics of the cemetery's approval and funding, along with an account of the official unveiling of the Memorial. Incorporated a few years later as a chapter within Bose's 2012 comprehensive *Singapore at War: Secrets from the Fall, Liberation & Aftermath of WWII*,[18] it also introduces the development of the Singapore State Cemetery, located adjacent to the war cemetery, for the interment of the nation's post-independence leaders. Bose's work marked an important shift in the local perception of Kranji, contributing positively to the flourishing local writing on how the war of 1939–1945 was remembered.

From the late 1980s onwards, both the Singapore government and local heritage groups began to show a renewed and somewhat nostalgic interest in battlefield histories of the Japanese invasion and occupation of the island state. Books, journal essays and newspaper articles along with exhibitions, tours and public events sought to analyse the Second World War and its effects on the local population and the built environment, as distinct from prisoner-of-war histories. State narratives increasingly appropriated the memory of the British abandonment and subsequent Japanese occupation to emphasise self-reliance and the concept of total defence.[19] The scholarship of social and military historians and geographers focused on making sense of Singapore's many public monuments, memorials, war-era military structures and museums that were dedicated to remembering the war, highlighting how the public's collective memory of these places was shaped. An emerging discourse on Singapore's post-colonial history raised important questions of national identity. Academics Brenda Yeoh and Hamzah Muzaini described the prevailing literature as tending to 'analyze these spaces of memory as loci of "personal mourning" or as symbolic manifestations of imperial identities'.[20] It coincided with an expanding scholarly focus on 'memoryscapes' – the study of unofficial and official forms of memorialisation. This is illustrated in the research of local and expatriate scholars such as Yeoh and Muzaini, Lily Kong, Kevin Blackburn, Karl Hack, Kevin Tan, Jon Cooper, P. Lim Pui Huen and Diana Wong.[21]

Within this new trope, local cemeteries, monuments and places of 'difficult memories' or 'deathscapes'[22], including Kranji War Cemetery, are analysed from a subaltern perspective. It places emphasis on their social and political understanding from a local population outside the usual hegemonic power structures. Architecture is re-imagined through their interaction with the public. Where once such sites offered only an imperial version of the event, this new context indicates how their meanings are being embraced as part of a national historiography for state and non-state agencies alike. It also underlines how memories are spatially and culturally appropriated by foreigners and locals. In doing so, each participant reflects their own objectives.

Under the scholarship of human geography and social sciences, Yeoh and Muzaini's *Contested Memoryscapes* incorporates a dedicated chapter on Kranji, '"Rescaling" War Memories at the Kranji War Cemetery and Memorial'. The authors argue that 'despite the plural nationalities of the war dead honoured within them, Commonwealth memorials continue to be manifestly perceived as reflections of "Britishness"'.[23] This applies equally to their landscape and topographical settings. Citing Lily Kong's study on 'deathscapes' in geography, 'Cemeteries and Columbaria, Memorials and Mausoleums', they suggest that the design of the landscapes was intended to create the impression of the dead lying within a garden representative of their respective 'homelands' within the British Empire.[24] Similarly, referencing Mandy Morris's essay 'Gardens "For Ever England"', they argue that the landscape of Kranji was designed as 'part of a geographical imagining of the British Empire, and the making of a tangible imprint of British presence'.[25] It creates an awareness in the modern audience that Kranji is an entirely foreign subject, devoid of any local connections or impressions. Furthermore, any act of appropriation of the Kranji War Cemetery for local narratives is seen as a positive and long-overdue outcome, appeasing post-colonial sensitivities.[26]

This local appropriation of an otherwise foreign edifice is not the exclusive domain of Singaporeans. Australians, through the number of their war dead in Singapore, have constructed their own narratives. In a similar vein to Yeoh and Muzaini, making use of personal stories and experiences, Bruce Scates's *Anzac Journeys* charts the pilgrimages of Australians to Kranji and other such 'traumascapes of war'.[27] He offers an Australian perspective on how such sites, invariably located overseas and replete with the history of fighting for the 'motherland', affect visitors. These include veterans returning to former battlefields, prisoners returning to sites of punishment, and widows, children and parents grieving for loved ones. Through the testimonies of their memories of the war, the culture of loss, bereavement and commemoration, Scates examines the sense of place embodied in each pilgrimage through what he terms the 'shadow of memory'.[28] Kranji, along with Chungkai and Kanchanaburi in Thailand and Thanbyuzayat in Burma, serves as the setting for captivity narratives.

Yet with all writings in which the Kranji War Cemetery and Memorial occupy an integral part, the common threads linking the various disciplines are the servicemen interred and inscribed within. The architecture of the site, while framing the location as a war cemetery, is nevertheless often portrayed as ancillary to their main narratives. Whether an imperial edifice to Britishness, contested memoryscape for national identity or a site of pilgrimage for battlefield tourism, Kranji is above all a physical reminder of a difficult period in time. A case in point is John McCallum and Lee Robinson's 1982 Australian war film, *The Highest Honour*.[29] In the closing scenes, an epilogue appears to inform its viewers that 'ten Rimau prisoners, executed on July 7th, 1945, one month before the war ended, are today buried in the Kranji War Cemetery in Singapore'. Based on Yuzuru Shinozaki's book of the true account of Operation Jaywick and Operation Rimau by Z Special Unit during the war, the scene then pans to Lutyens's stone and its inscription, fading out as an act of remembrance to the true-life servicemen upon whom the film is based. Although providing a minor cameo, Kranji bookends the events of a group of ten Australian commandos, who, while undertaking a raid in Singapore harbour, were captured and subsequently interrogated in Outram Road Jail. They would be tried for perfidy and espionage in a Japanese military court and executed by beheading at Pasir Panjang on 7 July 1945, approximately one month before the war ended. Their remains were then dumped in three unmarked graves, which upon recovery after the war ended were re-interred at Kranji. The bodies of two other team members were discovered on Merepas Island in 1993 and were also recovered and transferred to Singapore for burial in August 1994.[30] This film, an Australian-Japanese co-production, offers Kranji War Cemetery as the crucial link between an atrocious war-time event and the people who suffered the ultimate penalty on account of it.

Where authors do tackle the architecture of Kranji, it is either through physical description, as in the form of the Singapore Memorial and what it could represent, or through the greater design discourse on the war graves project. In this case, Kranji has been invariably viewed either in its modern context or as part of the overall 'Britishness' of all the war cemeteries. Philip Longworth would be one of the earliest writers to make the connection to the shift from traditional to contemporary architecture through the projects in Asia. 'Only the architects in the Far East showed much modernism. The Singapore Memorial at Kranji is roofed by a graceful continuous slab from which springs a tall pylon – like the tail-plane of an aircraft.'[31] Yet Longworth fell short of crediting Oakes with this modernism and acknowledging his work. Instead he identifies that it 'was probably [Edward] Maufe, the new artistic overlord, who most truly represented the Commission's post-war aesthetic in his work as Principal Architect for the United Kingdom'.[32] The research would prove otherwise.

CHAPTER 3

The Architects

In Stephen Wyatt's widely acclaimed 2007 BBC radio play, *Memorials to the Missing*, the British playwright imagines a speech delivered by Sir Fabian Ware at the unveiling of Sir Edwin Lutyens's Thiepval Memorial. Crossing back and forth to his work with the Red Cross at the commencement of the Great War in 1914, it chronicles the struggles he encountered thereafter in having the casualties buried where they fell and providing them with uniform headstones without distinctions of class, rank or faith. Meanwhile, somewhere near the front lines in northern France, the architects Lutyens and Herbert Baker, along with Charles Aitken, Director of the Tate Gallery, engage in a boisterous debate on their personal predilections for the design of the war cemeteries and how a memorial to the thousands of missing servicemen could be envisaged.[1]

Interspersed with actual recordings of present-day visitors to the war cemeteries, Wyatt presents a 'chorus' of three soldiers of the war, all of whom had perished in the fighting, and who are introduced through their accents as One (north country), Two (upper class) and Three (cockney). Testifying on their tragic fate and the attempts to identify their remains, the three 'missing' expound the merits of Ware's principles for the war dead. But they also reflect on the futility of monuments and memorials, constantly reminding the audience that behind the elegant designs and materials lie the many human tragedies that war creates. Wyatt's closing reflections are poignantly voiced by missing soldier Three:

> I remain a name on a wall in a monument. Nobody's ever visited me. The only person I really cared for was married to someone else and I'm sure she soon forgot me. I'm just a memory. Except a few weeks ago a sergeant in today's army brought his squaddies along. And they looked and they stared and they felt uncomfortable faced with where their own lives might end. But at least they understood something about duty and service. One of them even read my name out loud. I wonder which war he was off to fight in.[2]

Directed by Martin Jenkins and first broadcast on 8 November 2007 for BBC Radio 4's 'Afternoon Play',[3] the award-winning drama brought to a new generation the story of the Commonwealth War Graves Commission (CWGC). By setting the story around the founding and unveiling of Thiepval Memorial, Wyatt sheds light on the architectural element so interwoven with the established protocols associated with bereavement and commemoration of the war dead. The title itself is taken from a chapter in British writer and architectural historian Gavin Stamp's 2006 book, *The Memorial to the Missing of the Somme*. Described as the 'principal, tangible expression of the defining event in Britain's experience and memory of the Great War',[4] Lutyens's triumphal arched memorial is inscribed with the names of almost 73,000 men whose bodies were never identified after the Battle of the Somme. Stamp's detailed study of the design and building of the memorial, along with a tour of Lutyens's Arras Memorial in Faubourg d'Amiens British Cemetery, would become the inspiration for Wyatt's momentous work.[5]

Imperial War Graves Commission

There was no formal war graves organisation upon the outbreak of the Great War on 28 July 1914. Instead, the first few months saw the difficult task of recovering, identifying and burying the battlefield dead fall to the Joint War Committee of the British Red Cross Society and the Order of St John of Jerusalem. This was alongside their regular duties in transporting wounded soldiers from the front lines to hospitals in the rear. Neither was the concern and treatment of the dead a foremost priority. The history of Britain's war-time burials in earlier conflicts saw the remains of officers mostly returned home to their families to make arrangements, whereas those of common soldiers were dumped in mass graves. The first memorial honouring the war dead, from the Battle of Waterloo, was only unveiled in 1889, after an order of Queen Victoria was issued. The Crimean War (1853–1856) saw a military cemetery established 20 years after its conclusion, for the thousands who died of their injuries and disease. And by the time of the 1914–1918 industrial-scale death and destruction on the Western Front, the sentiment of the fighting man towards his post-mortem fate could not have been lower.[6] The English poet Edmund Blunden, himself a veteran of that war through action in Ypres, the Somme and the Battle of Passchendaele, would recount that in the 'rapid ruin and chaos and oblivion of the front line with its enormous process of annihilation, perhaps not many soldiers retained the confidence that the dead – themselves, it might be, to-morrow or the next instant – would at length obtain some lasting and distinct memorial'.[7]

In September 1914, a 45-year-old former school teacher, Fabian Ware, having been rejected from serving in the British Army on account of his age, arrived in north-east France and was given command of a mobile Red Cross 'flying unit'. Consisting of a disparate group of private vehicles and volunteer drivers, Ware set about imposing a level of discipline on this ambulance unit and organising its operations with the primary role of searching out and caring for the French wounded, on account of being initially attached to the French I Cavalry Corps, and later, to the French X Corps. Throughout this early period of the war, they also took care to record the location of burials and what identification there was, of the British dead, encountered along the way. Gradually, this expanded to sending out search parties further afield, often during lulls in the fighting, to record the ever-increasing numbers of isolated and scattered British burial sites. At their own request, the Red Cross Society had also provided Ware's unit with the means to mark and register these graves in whatever location they might be found. But it was Ware's realisation that whilst many English graves did not have their positions recorded or registered, neither was there an entity responsible for their maintenance. That October marked

Sir Fabian Arthur Goulstone Ware

the beginning of the unit's expansion beyond merely identifying the graves, to also providing them a semblance of dignity with a proper timber cross and painted inscription.[8]

Ware was not alone in this endeavour. Richard Norton, the noted American archaeologist and director of the American School of Classical Studies at Rome, similarly volunteered his services to the Allied campaign. Soon after the war commenced, Norton placed his scholastic pursuits aside and set about establishing the American Volunteer Motor Ambulance Corps in London during the fall of 1914.[9] Beginning with two cars and four drivers, by October that same year he had 10 ambulances in the field. By 1917 the service had attracted almost 600 volunteer drivers, many of whom were recent graduates of American colleges, and 300 ambulances, before it was taken over by the American Army with the United States' entry into the war. What distinguished Ware's efforts was in fact a consequence of the war – which the British public believed would be 'over by Christmas' of 1914 – having settled into a stalemate of trench warfare and mass casualties, often fighting over mere metres between opposing front lines. The sheer scale of the dead and wounded saw Ware's Red Cross Mobile Unit and its personnel taken over and enlarged by the British Army in October 1915. In 1916, the Army established the Directorate of Graves Registration and Enquiries (DGR&E), a department under the command of Ware, with the sole responsibility for preserving records of burials and providing the means for graves to be marked and identified.

And yet as the war continued and expanded beyond France and Belgium to other theatres further afield such as the Gallipoli peninsula, British soldiers were dying and being laid to rest alongside thousands of men from the Dominions who had heeded the call to serve and defend the Empire. These men from Canada, Australia, New Zealand, South Africa and Newfoundland, from India and from all the British Colonies, who had travelled thousands of miles to give their lives in these foreign fields, would have the effect of seeing the powers of the Director extended, as Director-General, to all theatres of the war. Ware and the DGR&E were now responsible to the Adjunct-General to the Forces at the War Office, Sir Nevil Macready. Macready, a career army officer, had recommended to the War Office the transfer of control of Ware's Graves Registration Committee from the Red Cross to the British Army, and would play an instrumental role in assisting Ware draft the proposal for an 'Imperial Commission for the Care of Soldiers Graves'.[10]

Dominion representatives had also been appointed to a National Committee for the Care of Soldiers' Graves, of which the Prince of Wales was President. And with the need to attend to the demands of the deceased's relatives for the care of their loved ones' graves after the war, it was apparent that the great numbers of non-professional soldiers that had formed the New Armies would force the United Kingdom to consider this new endeavour with the full co-operation of its Dominions. A new entity would need to be formed, one in which the interests of its member states had equal standing as those from London, and was responsible to all the partner governments of the Empire. In March 1917, King George V submitted to the British Prime

Minister David Lloyd George a Memorandum incorporating the proposals set out by Ware and the DGR&E, for the formation of a permanent Imperial organisation tasked with the care and maintenance of the graves of all those servicemen who had fallen in the war. It would also be empowered to acquire land for the establishment of cemeteries and to erect permanent memorials within these sites. Placed on the agenda for the Imperial Conference scheduled later that year, a resolution recommending the adoption of this new organisation was moved on 13 April, and on 21 May 1917 the Royal Charter was granted, establishing the Imperial War Graves Commission.

Over the next two decades, the sheer size and complexity of the Commission's endeavour would become clearer and better appreciated. What began with a few selected 'experimental' war cemeteries[11] along the former front lines in France and Belgium would by 1939 expand to a total of 15,846 burial grounds that contained war graves. This was within 107 countries across six continents.[12] The war of 1914–1918 had seen an astonishing loss of life among its combatants, with the total number of Commonwealth war dead amounting to 1,104,890. Of these, 587,117 casualties were identified and buried in known graves, while 517,773 were recorded as 'Missing'. Of this latter figure, however, 180,861 had been found but not identified and were buried as 'Unknown'. These men would be commemorated on Memorials to the Missing, with the Commission designing and erecting 86 separate memorials within 30 countries.[13]

This task, the scale of which also required a greatly expanded organisational structure and the kind of management discipline normally associated with a multi-national corporation or an empire, could still not be deemed completed. Although the discovery of British and Commonwealth bodies by local inhabitants on former battlefields was diminishing with the passing years after the war ended, the Commission's accounting and reporting period 1938–1939 still saw 377 British dead recovered in France and a further 155 in Belgium.[14] And in an ominous portent of what was to come, the threat of war became more insistent in the latter half of 1938, and the Commission recognised they might again be called upon to tend to the dead. In the introduction to their 20th Annual Report for 1938–1939, they offered a well-informed plea to the war-mongers to avoid a repeat of the disastrous recent past:

> [T]he Commission, representing, in a way that no other body can, the dead of the last war, have always been conscious of possessing a unique influence which they could and should exercise in international affairs. By fostering, and indeed by leading the peoples of other nations to cultivate, the remembrance in common of the dead of that war, the Commission were persuaded that they might make a practical, as well as a sentimental and emotional, contribution to the maintenance of peace.[15]

Designing for the War of 1939–1945

Acutely aware of the need to establish further war cemeteries upon the conclusion of the Second World War, the Commission commenced contingency plans from the onset of the hostilities. With the previous war, limited as it had been to defined geographic regions such as north-east France and Belgium, the Italian Alps, the Balkans and the Gallipoli peninsula, access to the grave sites was often possible through the shifting of the front lines. In the case of the present 'total war', the sheer geographic scale and scope of the conflict across all of Europe to the western edges of Russia, North Africa, the Middle East, and the Asia-Pacific, along with the advance in mechanised and air warfare, made reaching the battlefield sites an untenable proposition. It was not until January 1943 that the Commission was able to foresee in the near future a region sufficiently liberated in which to commence its work.

At a special meeting of the Commission held at their London headquarters on 26 March 1943, a few weeks shy of the complete Allied liberation of North Africa and Egypt, a proposal was forwarded by the War Office[16] for the Army Graves Service to hand over selected cemeteries within areas of the Middle East that had been recently liberated. With precedent established from the previous war in which the first cemetery contract was awarded a mere eight days after Armistice, the Commission approved the first resolution in the commencement of its work for the Second World War: the taking over from the DGR&E of those cemeteries in areas no longer the scene of active operations.[17]

Five resolutions were proposed and approved that Friday morning, the first of which activated the Commission's involvement. The fourth resolution paved the way for the Director of Works, Lieutenant-Colonel Frank Higginson, to prepare preliminary estimates for the cost of constructing those initial war cemeteries, and the methodology by which they could be undertaken. The fifth resolution, as in the case of the fourth, required an allocated budget from the Finance Committee. It was approval for the creation of a North African administrative area with dedicated staffing and facilities to enable the Commission to undertake their construction and maintenance works throughout the region. Like the Commission's previous operations, the UK Treasury was to provide initial funding with the participating countries and Commonwealth Dominions[18] contributing their allocated share in proportion to the number of graves each required. An Imperial War Graves Endowment Fund, which had been established and contributed to by the participating countries in 1925 to provide for the permanent maintenance of the cemeteries from the First World War, would be called upon to provide principal funding for the second. Annual contributions from the participating countries thereafter would ensure the Commission was able to maintain its work.[19]

It is the second and third resolutions that most interest this study. These two statements, moved by Sir Robert Gordon-Finlayson for the Commission and seconded by E. MacLeod representing the High Commissioner for Canada, were key in establishing the architectural direction the war cemeteries and memorials would take. Based on the unanimous approval of the Commission's past work in developing war cemeteries, it was decided that the 'same general architectural and horticultural treatment be accorded wherever possible to the cemeteries resulting from the present war as was accorded to those resulting from the last war'.[20] Importantly, this was qualified by directing that any substantial departures or variations in detail from these architectural and horticultural norms be referred to the Commission.

The Principal Architects

In line with the principles first laid out in Sir Frederic Kenyon's 1918 report, *War Graves: How the Cemeteries Abroad will be Designed,* and again based on precedent, the third resolution called for the appointment of a Principal Architect for the designing of cemeteries in those liberated areas of North Africa the Commission could take over.[21] It also called upon the Commission to request that their Architectural Advisor put forward a recommendation for a candidate. The intention was to appoint a suitably credentialled senior architect for each theatre of war, under whom younger architects who had served in the forces would work. Where Lutyens, Blomfield, Baker, Sir Robert Lorimer, Charles Holden and others, as 'men of a standing beyond criticism', had served the Commission in the past, it would again fall upon Kenyon to suggest the Principal Architects, commencing with Hubert Worthington for North Africa.[22]

Sir Frederic George Kenyon

Worthington (1886–1963) was a graduate from Manchester University's school of architecture and had spent the two years between qualifying and the outbreak of the First World War working as an assistant to Lutyens, in whom he had found inspiration. The war saw Worthington serving as a Captain with the 16th Battalion Manchester Regiment, where he was severely wounded during the offensive on the Somme, by accounts surviving overnight in a shell hole before being rescued. His subsequent return to practice would coincide with a spell in academia as Professor of Architecture at the Royal College of Art and lecturing at Oxford University and Hull during the 1930s. In keeping with another of Kenyon's directives that the Principal Architect visit the sites selected for cemeteries and ensure no work be undertaken that would prejudice their design and ultimate maintenance once construction had commenced, within a few months of his appointment on 26 July 1943, Worthington had departed for an arduous seven-week tour from the Suez Canal through to Algeria.[23]

By January the following year, the Commission turned its attention to the war cemeteries and memorials that would be required closer to home. Developments at Brookwood in Surrey, at 37 acres the largest Commonwealth war cemetery in the UK, and at the Royal Air Force regional cemeteries scattered across the country, had led the Commission to seek its second Principal Architect. The timing, however, coincided with the death of the person most intimately associated with the architectural expression that defined the Commission – Lutyens.[24] Almost a year since the passing of Blomfield, the men who had provided the Commonwealth war cemetery with its ubiquitous 'Stone of Remembrance' and 'Cross of Sacrifice', respectively, had made way for a new generation of designers to take the Commission forward. And on 19 January 1944, on the advice of Kenyon, the architect Edward Brantwood Maufe (1882–1974) was put forward and appointed Principal Architect for the UK.[25]

Like many of his contemporaries, Maufe was an early admirer of the 'Lutyens style', and his pre-war buildings exhibited early links with the Arts and Crafts movement.[26] Cultivating an early interest in architecture, Maufe, after an apprenticeship under the London architect William Pite, would go on to graduate from Oxford whilst also studying design at the Architectural Association (AA). The advent of the First World War saw his fledgling career interrupted, whereupon after a short stint with the Royal Naval Volunteer Reserve, he enlisted in the army. Serving with the Royal Garrison Artillery on the Salonika Front in northern Greece, this experience altered his design sensibility, shifting it to an austerity likened to Swedish modernism – his war memorial design as an expansion of the Lutyens memorial at Tower Hill is a salient example. Within a few years of his appointment, Maufe would become the Commission's honorary Chief Architect, taking responsibility for coordinating the work of the four other Principal Architects. He would succeed Kenyon as the Commission's Artistic Advisor.[27]

By the middle of 1944, the war in Europe had taken a distinct turn in favour of the Allies. The D-Day landings on the Normandy beaches in northern France on 6 June culminated with the liberation of Paris 11 weeks later on 25 August. By September, most of France had been freed from German occupation. Meanwhile, the Italian campaign which had commenced the previous year with the 10 July Allied invasion of Sicily, had made slow progress, albeit with enormous casualties, pushing their way northwards and taking possession of Rome on 4 June 1944. Whilst Fascist Italy collapsed following the toppling of its leader Benito Mussolini in July 1943, stiff resistance put up by a determined German defence ensured the country would not be fully liberated until almost two years later, on 2 May 1945. It was in this context of the war's progress that the Commission began turning their attention to the war cemeteries that would be required for both countries.

The Commission had begun considering its role in continental Europe from as early as June 1944, when they dispatched the architect Louis de Soissons on an exploratory tour to Italy to report on the extent of the construction works required. With the assistance of their Area Superintendent in Italy, Count Guido Nobile Memmo,[28] the assessment found that the cemeteries from the past war were in good condition and that those regions retaken by the Allies were suitably stable to commence urgent planning for the new sites. To this end, the Commission's 262nd meeting, on 18 October 1944, saw Kenyon outline the merits of the two Principal Architects upon whom the design of war cemeteries for Italy and France would be entrusted, de Soissons and Philip Hepworth, respectively.

Canadian by birth, and arguably the most enigmatic of the Commission's architects, Louis Emmanuel Jean Guy de Savoie-Carignan de Soissons (1890–1962) descended from French nobility; his father Charles was the 37th Count of Soissons. Widely acknowledged as a classical architect and town planner, his long association with Ebenezer Howard on the garden city of Welwyn developed in him a deep humanism.[29] This would be reflected in the considered detailing of the 46 war cemeteries he designed for Italy and Greece after the Second World War. After a childhood move to London, de Soissons went on to study at the Royal Academy School and the École des Beaux-Arts in Paris, culminating in 1913 with a three-year scholarship at the British School at Rome. While the interruption by the First World War saw de Soissons enlisting and serving in Italy with distinction,[30] it was the following conflict that would affect him profoundly. His eldest son, Philip, whilst serving with the Royal Navy, was killed in action on 23 May 1941. His name is commemorated on the Portsmouth Naval Memorial, of which the extension for the Second World War was designed by Maufe, de Soissons's colleague.

As with de Soissons, and indeed Worthington before him, Philip Dalton Hepworth (1890–1963) had similarly been awarded a scholarship to the British School at Rome (BSR). After initial studies at the AA in London and the École des Beaux-Arts in Paris, his admission to the BSR in 1914 was, however, short-lived. With the outbreak of war, he returned and joined the Royal Engineers. Commissioned as a Lieutenant, Hepworth saw active service in France. Returning to architecture after the war, his influence by the Beaux-Arts manifested in the municipal projects he undertook. The start of the Second World War saw Hepworth apply to re-enlist, but his age restricted him to serving in the Home Guard, where he was soon appointed to the Royal Academy of Arts' Planning Committee, chaired by Lutyens, for the rebuilding of London following the damage caused during the Blitz. He went on to design war cemeteries for France, Belgium, the Netherlands and Germany.[31]

The Australian War Graves Service

Whilst the design and development of war cemeteries was well under way in Europe and North Africa, the Commission was grappling with the magnitude of the task at hand in the far reaches of the Indian sub-continent, Southeast Asia and the Far East. The end of war in Europe had witnessed the emergence of a new global power structure, with an ascendant USA pitted against its former ally, the Soviet Union. It marked the beginning of the Cold War era, dividing the continent into western and eastern blocs. Meanwhile, the unconditional surrender of Imperial Japan four months later on 2 September 1945 did not signal the end of all hostilities in Asia. The decline of European colonial empires coinciding with the Japanese defeat had the unintended conse-quence of resurrecting long-standing independence struggles. Amidst festering anti-colonialism and political upheavals in India, Burma, Malaya and Indonesia, the desire of those colonies to seek self-de-termination prolonged the attaining of a lasting peace in the region. And unlike the geographic convenience in accessing Europe from its headquarters in the UK, the preparation, planning and logistics the Commission needed for an extended visit to Asia was considerably challenging. It was apparent that this new role would require people of special abilities, along with careful liaison with the Colonial Office, South East Asia Command (SEAC) and the Australian Army War Graves Service.

From Australia's perspective, the war in Asia had arrived at its doorstep. Whereas the British, Dutch and French 'empires' were impacted through the surrender of their colonies on the other side of the world, the ongoing war raging in New Guinea, Borneo and the south Pacific was an existential one for Australia. The Japanese bomb-ing of Darwin along the northern coastline of the country and subma-rines entering Sydney Harbour served to clearly reinforce that belief. The failure of the Singapore strategy and loss of almost a quarter of its overseas soldiers – with more than 15,000 captured – stunned the country. If the lesson harshly learnt from the disastrous 1915 Dar-danelles campaign was to never again place Australian troops under

British command, the fall of Singapore proved the last straw in its military dependence on the motherland. It marked a significant shift in foreign policy. A security alliance with the USA was now of utmost priority. Australian Prime Minister John Curtin announced in his 1942 new year's address to the nation that 'Australia looks to America, free of any pangs as to our traditional links or kinship with the UK... as its keystone, which will give our country some confidence of being able to hold out until the tide of battle swings against the enemy'.[32] Under command of General Douglas MacArthur, Supreme Commander of Allied Forces in the Southwest Pacific Area, thousands of American troops were soon dispatched to Australia to shore up local confidence. Fighting alongside the Australian troops, they would begin the island-by-island liberation push northwards to Japan.

Recovery of Commonwealth casualties throughout this campaign fell primarily to the Australian Army's War Graves Service, through its Graves Registration and Enquiries (GR&E) Units and War Graves Units.[33] This was to be expected given the active involvement of the Australian Army throughout the conflict in this region and the proximity to Australian forward bases and the mainland to replenish and resupply those units with materials and personnel. What units of the British Army War Graves Service were provided, the British Army's ongoing involvement with the India-Burma theatre of the war saw their resources concentrated there, along with the Siam-Burma Railway after liberation.[34]

Although not intended as a comprehensive description, a rudimentary understanding of the war graves service is important for this study. In this instance, Jack Leemon's memoir, *War Graves Digger: Service with an Australian Graves Registration Unit,* provides a rare insight to the operations of such units, the author having served in one and later becoming an Officer-in-Command.[35] Focusing on the British War Graves Services, Seumas Spark's PhD thesis, *The Treatment of the British Military War Dead of the Second World War,* offers a scholarly account of their operations, the template upon which the equivalent Australian services were initially raised.[36] There is also the Australian

Army's set of guiding protocols and practices for their graves units during the Second World War, spelt out in their FSPB manual, *Identification of Bodies, Burials, Graves Registration, Disposal of Effects, Burial of Enemy Dead,* issued in early 1942.[37] Citing from Leemon's first-hand account, which is consistent across all three references, the functioning of the war graves service is best summarised as follows: Initial responsibility for the burial of a fallen soldier lies with his unit. A 'Burial Return', along with a description or map marking the grave, is then completed, upon which the War Graves Unit is assigned the duty of 'Location, Identification and Re-Location'. The degree of difficulty in locating the sites then often depends on the quality of the description or map, the altering of physical terrain either by natural growth or unnatural disturbance such as further fighting in the area. It is also compounded considerably through time lapsed from initial burial until recovery. Positive identification tends to be more challenging, often requiring some level of forensic or investigative work on the part of the unit. It begins with the exhumation of the grave and collection of items of identity, if any, whilst the remains are bagged and identifying tags attached. This may include the reports provided by the deceased's unit, personal items left on the body, physical traits or if required, dental records.[38]

It is the final stage of relocating the remains that most concerns this study. A series of Memorandums and instructions issued by the Directorate Graves Registration throughout May 1943 to all Staff Officers Graves Registration and GR&E Units clarified the burial protocols in place. In the first instance, each set of remains is buried in a designated new 'Temporary War Cemetery' or an allocated area within an existing civilian cemetery,[39] laid out in an alpha-numeric grid of rows and sections. Christian and Jewish personnel are buried together, with a separate plot provided for all non-Christians, such as Chinese, Muslims, Hindus, etc. Each individual grave is then marked by either a standard white wooden cross for those identified as Christian, a Shield of David for those identified as Jewish, and suitable markers for other beliefs. Often, a simple grave marker was provided for all.[40]

Burial grounds created by prisoners of war, on the other hand, either inside or within proximity of their internment camps, often saw the graves arranged in sections by nationality. This was the case in Changi and Kranji, with their diverse groups of internees, and where the scarcity or availability of materials informed their markers. The cross or grave marker would be then inscribed with name, rank, unit, regiment number, and 'known' date of death. Any doubts to the identification ensure the preceding 'Believed to be...' before the further details. Upon the erection of the cross at the head of a grave, a photograph is recorded, a print of which is sent to the next-of-kin.[41] Where the remains are unidentifiable or cremated, they are collated in a common grave and the details of those missing are inscribed alongside others, on a common marker. In all instances, the primary intention was to provide a dignified burial ground for fallen servicemen until informed decisions were made as to the permanent site of commemoration and remembrance.

Command of the Australian War Graves Service (AWGS) fell upon its Director, Lieutenant-Colonel Athol Brown. Headquartered in Melbourne, the AWGS's role in the direction of the Commission's work in Asia was significant. With primary responsibility for all Australian theatres of the war, in particular New Guinea, New Britain, Solomon Islands, Singapore, Malaya and Borneo, its proximity to northern Australia through bases in Darwin and Brisbane made them an invaluable asset to the Commission's operations. They were similarly beneficial to the United States Army Forces in Australia (USAFIA), through an arrangement reached whereby any burials of American servicemen undertaken or discovered were advised to the nearest American Headquarters.[42] Their knowledge of the region also ensured pragmatic design decisions in the face of the tropical environment, far from the easy access routes of the past. With New Guinea and Borneo prone to frequent earthquakes, torrential thunderstorms and cyclonic activity on account of their location along the rim of the Pacific Ocean basin, the challenges in establishing and maintaining permanent war cemeteries in Australia's immediate neighbourhood were many.

The strong social, cultural and military ties between the UK and its former Dominion in the antipodes ensured an interoperability between AWGS and its British Army counterpart. Overlapping of their war graves services was common given the shared military roles both countries played, in particular in Malaya, Singapore and the Siam-Burma Railway. This was not lost on the Commission amidst the dilemma it encountered in having to contend with maintaining British war graves and those of its Dominions in an unprecedented vast area on the other side of the world. As it were, the Commission had reached out and commenced preliminary discussions with the Australian government from 1944 on the viability of establishing a formal presence through an affiliated agency, similar in structure to those operating in Canada and South Africa. The Vice-Chairman, Ware, had in fact requested the Australian government allow Brown, en route to Egypt on military duty, to extend his journey onwards to London and attend the Commission's monthly meeting of January 1945.[43] Aside from the intended discussions on the likely workings and geographical sphere of interest of an Australian agency, it offered the Commission's senior hierarchy an opportunity to assess Brown himself.

Discussions held between Ware, Brown and Stanley Bruce, Australia's High Commissioner to the UK[44], prior to the formal meeting had their intended outcome in that a provisional agreement was reached in relation to the establishment of an Agency of the Commission in Australia. It was only a matter then of moving a resolution to that effect, though not before the Commission and Brown vowed to resolve three pertinent issues affecting both parties. The first concerned the maintenance of war graves within Australia on account of the government's decision to administer and finance all the First World War graves directly. As the Commission had correctly anticipated, the lack of a dedicated Endowment Fund providing a regular source of income had the foreseeable consequence of declining maintenance standards. Brown proposed that it be put to the Australian government to make an additional contribution to the Commission's own Endowment Fund to satisfy this quandary. Furthermore, an altogether separate Endowment Fund, administered this time by Australia, was the solution for the second issue – the variance between Australia and the Commission on the entitlement of war graves. Australia regarded those servicemen who died after the official termination of the First World War (31 August – 1 September 1921) as entitled to full war grave recognition. Contrarily, the UK had decided for its own forces that only those graves of servicemen who died before that date would be marked and maintained by the Commission.

The third item revolved around the sensitive issue of the Agency's area of interest. Geographically larger in size than the Canadian Agency (which along with its hinterland also maintained war graves in the USA and Alaska), it inevitably encompassed territories and islands that fell under the purview of the Colonial Office. It also had to contend with countries such as New Zealand, which maintained their own graves at home and in territory within her military control. Fiji, although a British colony, had seen thousands of its locals volunteer for the Fiji Infantry Regiment, attached to New Zealand and Australian army units during the war. Hong Kong on the other hand, also a colony of the British Empire, was excluded on the objections of the Canadian Agency, who had a direct interest through the maintenance of a sizeable number of Canadian graves there. As it stood, the resolution was moved for the Agency to undertake the Commission's work in the 'Commonwealth of Australia, and certain parts of the Pacific to be clearly defined later'.

The Agency's sphere of interest would only be finalised in September 1946, with Java, Sumatra and Hong Kong excluded, whilst Borneo was included. Significantly, after considerable deliberations from all the Dominions, the war graves in Japan would henceforth fall under the responsibility of the Anzac Agency. This coincided with events five months earlier when the Australian government's Minister of the Interior ratified the original resolution through an Instrument of Appointment of the Anzac Agency. On that same day, 17 April 1946, the nomination of Brown as Secretary-General to head the new Anzac Agency was also approved.

Born in Sydney in 1905, Athol Earle Brown had at the young age of 14 enlisted in the Royal Australian Navy, serving two years as a midshipman at the tail end of the First World War. His post-war career as Company Manager and part-time member of the Active Citizen Military Forces proved beneficial to the army when he re-enlisted in 1940, joining the 2/8th Field Regiment (Artillery). Assigned to the Australian 9th Division, Brown embarked that November on the troop ship *Strathmore* for the North African campaign. He would return home wounded in August 1941, unfit for further front-line active service. However, the outbreak of war against Japan a few months later saw him reassigned to the hast-ily assembled Graves Services and by March 1942, he was appointed Assistant Adjutant-General, Graves Registration. His managerial acumen and organisational skills would be aptly suited to the unfold-ing events in Asia over the next four years. And yet one of his greatest challenges emanated closer to home.

Athol Earle Brown

On the night of 5 August 1944, while the Graves Services were making initial preparations to rapidly expand their tasks in Asia on the back of the retreating Japanese forces, 1,104 Japanese prisoners of war attempted to escape their internment camp outside the small country town of Cowra in New South Wales. In the ensuing escape attempt and manhunt, 234 Japanese soldiers died, along with four Australian servicemen. The Graves Services were dispatched to Cowra the following day to coordinate recovery and burial services, and the ensuing military cemetery would be the first established by the service in the war against Japan.[45] Brown's efficient and compassionate han-dling of the deceased from both sides was a precursor to his ensuring Australia's fallen servicemen and civilians were dutifully attended to five months later. By the following year, 1946, Brown was appointed Secretary-General of the Imperial War Graves Commission.

Brown's post-war tenure heading up the Anzac Agency began with his setting in motion an ambitious design and works programme. Hundreds of upgraded and new war cemeteries and memorials were designed and completed throughout Australia, Southeast Asia and the South Pacific.[46] Many of these had their origins in the Australian War Graves Group. Aside from the major war cemeteries in all of Australia's state capitals, there were also sites dedicated for Australia's wartime enemies. The Cowra Japanese War Cemetery was eventually developed and consecrated in 1964. It consolidated those prisoners of war who perished in the 1944 breakout, with aircrew shot down over northern Australia and Japanese civilian internees who died in Australia.[47] The Anzac Agency also undertook the establishment of the Tatura German Military Cemetery in central Victoria. Opened in 1958, this first foreign war cemetery in Australia was for the reburial of 250 German internees, prisoners of war and civilian internees who died whilst detained in Australia during both world wars. Then there was the only Commonwealth war cemetery to be established in mainland Japan, arguably the Agency's most significant challenge and accomplishment. Located in Yokohama, the cemetery contains the graves of Commonwealth servicemen, the great majority of whom died in Japan as prisoners of war. It comprises four main areas, accommodating the UK; Australia; Canada and New Zealand; and the Indian Forces 1939–45.

The Imperial War Graves Commission, meanwhile, aware of the progress being made by the Australian War Graves Group, had commenced their own preparatory work in the region. Brigadier J.K. McNair, Director of Graves Registration and Enquiries, War Office,[48] was approached with a view to examining the Commission's existing organisation structure for India and Burma. He was to make recommendations for its adaptation to better undertake the Commission's work resulting from the Second World War. As it stood, the undertaking in India was substantial. There were some seven new war cemeteries in India and seven in Burma to contend with. Casualties had occurred and were continuing to occur throughout the entire country. There was also the issue of incorporating the work from Malaya and Ceylon. And the Government of Burma was not as yet functioning. Likewise, Kenyon, in his capacity as Artistic Advisor, was asked to put forward a name for appointment as Principal Architect to India and Burma. It was noted that this appointment had to be made with more care. McNair, coming from an army background, suggested the architect should be of the right calibre and know India well. And so it was in August of 1945, two years after the first Principal Architect was appointed, that the Commission carried a resolution on commencing with considered deliberations for an architect for Asia.

An Architect for Asia

In considering its scope of work in Asia, the Commission had always wanted a senior architect to visit the British war cemeteries of the ongoing war in India, Burma and South East Asia Command (SEAC). The architect's brief was to settle all existing and proposed cemetery boundaries, submit designs for the 'beautification' of those cemeteries initially formed by the GR&E units, prepare proposals for the development of new war cemeteries, and inspect and make recommendations regarding sites for new cemeteries. This scope had been approved at the Commission's 272nd meeting alongside the approval of a temporary inspectorate in India which would oversee the execution of the work.

Inherent difficulties in gaining access to the hundreds of scattered sites had made delays inevitable and an urgency set in. This came along with limited transportation options, being so soon after the ending of hostilities. What transport was available was prioritised for the repatriation of thousands of servicemen and prisoners of war. The Commission had also been considering picking the architect from among those already associated with the Commission, ostensibly to save time but more importantly to ensure a predictable outcome. But interestingly, it was aware of at least two architects, Arthur Hutton and James Ferrie, who had the requisite experience in war cemeteries and memorials and had served in the armed forces. They were also well entrenched in

Asia, with invaluable local knowledge of the conditions and resources available. Furthermore, an Australian option had presented itself with the conclusion of the war: a young architect who as a prisoner of war in Singapore had upon liberation designed a war memorial for Changi on behalf of the Australian government.

Trained in the Glasgow School of Architecture, Arthur James Scott Hutton (1891–1982) had served with distinction in the Royal Engineers during the First World War. Upon demobilisation he joined the Imperial War Graves Commission in northern Europe, working as an Assistant Architect under Baker, Blomfield and Lutyens. By the time he left the Commission in 1926 for a Public Works Department position in Kenya, Hutton had assisted in and designed 67 war cemeteries, most notably the Mazargues Indian Cemetery and Memorial in Marseilles, France.[49] An Assistant Government Architect role brought him to Singapore in 1935, where he remained until the last days before the surrender. In a daring escape with 68 other Public Works Department officers from a sinking vessel, they swam to safety on a nearby island. He eventually resurfaced in Ceylon, whereupon he was called back to the UK to train for the return to Malaya with the attacking forces and help set up the civilian administration. The war's end saw him return to Asia in 1946 and become Chief Government Architect for the Malayan Union in Kuala Lumpur.[50]

Fellow Scotsman James Westwater Ferrie had only just qualified as an architect in Glasgow before signing up and serving in the Burma campaign. Involved in the decisive battle of Kohima in Nagaland, north-east India, he could lay claim to having designed one of the first war memorials of the recent war in Asia. In his mid-twenties, and a Lieutenant in the Royal Engineers, 2nd Division, Ferrie was asked to design a memorial in tribute to the men of his division who had fallen in fighting the Japanese. After negotiations with the local Naga tribesmen, Ferrie selected a 20-foot-high, 19-ton boulder resting in the area of Garrison Hill that had seen some of the fiercest fighting. Two hundred tribesmen brought the stone down from the hill and placed it in a standing position, in line with their long-held cultural traditions.[51] In what would become one of the great evocative epitaphs of remembrance, the regiment's Padre, the Reverend Francis Maclauchlan, would select from an approved list prepared by the War Graves Commission, the text by John Maxwell Edmonds of Simonides's verses on the Battle of Thermopylae:

> When you go home,
> tell them of us and say,
> for your tomorrow,
> we gave our today.[52]

Set within a semi-circular grey dressed stone wall, Ferrie's memorial to the 2nd Division was unveiled by Commander of the 14th Army, Lieutenant-General William Slim, in November 1944. It would be one of many erected upon Garrison Hill by other regiments involved in

James Ferrie's early sketch and watercolour rendering of the proposed memorial to the 2nd Division at Kohima War Cemetery, 1944. The horror and carnage of the battle of Kohima is captured in the shattered landscape and tree stump that represents the fatal wounding of Ferrie's commanding officer, Major Jimmy Langdon.

the battle, but with its inscription a key attribute, Ferrie's memorial was chosen by the Imperial War Graves Commission to be retained and integrated into the final design layout of the Kohima War Cemetery. Ferrie moved to Singapore after the war in 1948 and joined the office of Palmer and Turner Architects, one of the island's oldest design practices. Branching out on his own four years later, he became one of Singapore's and the region's most prominent architects.

A single black-and-white photograph, retrieved from the Australian War Memorial's archives, is all that exists to remind us that another consideration for Principal Architect to Asia was available to the Commission. Whereas both Hutton and Ferrie were British subjects, the image portrays the young architect John Brindley, an Australian. The photograph presents an alternative vision of what has now become one of the Commission's most important sites commemorating the war against Japan – the Singapore Memorial at Kranji. Captured by an official photographer of the Australian Army's Military History Section, a kneeling Brindley is seen alongside the watercolour renderings of his prize-winning war memorial design for the Changi Prisoner of War Cemetery.[53] Taken on 15 September 1945, ten days after the liberation of Changi, the design competition was open to all Australian prisoners of war and included a £100 prize, not an unsubstantial sum of money at the time. The healthy physical condition of Brindley does, though, pose questions as to whether the process was a morale-boosting exercise for the public back home – or, more probably, an impassioned statement by the Australian Government, through their War Graves service, identifying Changi as the symbol of their darkest hour.

Emanating from rural New South Wales, Brindley (1913–1999) had worked as an architect before the onset of war saw him joining the Citizen Military Force, then enlisting in Sydney with the 2/19th Battalion, 8th Division. His dispatch to Singapore soon after the Japanese bombing of Darwin saw his unit involved in some of the heaviest battles in Malaya, fighting a rearguard action down the peninsula. At the infamous battle at Parit Sulong Bridge, where many of his comrades were machine-gunned trying to cross the river or bayoneted

Lieutenant John M. Brindley, an Australian 8th Division ex-POW of the Japanese, with his prize-winning design for a war memorial for the Changi Prisoner of War Cemetery, 15 September 1945

when surrendering, Brindley managed to survive, only to become a prisoner of war with the fall of Singapore. His internment at Changi saw him assigned to a work detail repairing war-damaged buildings and infrastructure throughout the island. It also offered him an opportunity to sketch and watercolour numerous scenes of occupied Singapore. Following three and a half months on the Siam-Burma Railway, he returned to assume teaching duties at the 'University of Changi' established by the prisoners of war, and designed many of the chapels that sprang up in the camp. Upon his return home, Brindley went back into private practice, undertaking many public and civic institutions across regional and rural Australia. This included one completed war memorial. As part of his design for the Royal Australian Engineers Chapel in Moorebank, NSW, Brindley incorporated a small memorial commemorating the fallen 'Sappers' from all conflicts. It consists of a Christian cross made with timber from a sleeper of the Siam-Burma Railway sitting atop a stone pedestal from Changi Prison.[54]

Appointment of Oakes

Although all three architects were well-credentialled and met the criteria of having served in the forces, they were overlooked. The answer to the Commission's dilemma would come through what proved to be

one of the last acts of its now ageing Artistic Advisor Kenyon, shortly
before his retirement. By early autumn 1945, Kenyon had made enquiries of the Royal Institute of British Architects (RIBA) to put forward
suitable candidates for the Commission's consideration. A number
of architects were soon presented, none of whom impressed Kenyon
enough to recommend. It was only on 2 October 1945 that Cyril D.
Spragg, Secretary of RIBA, replied with a further candidate, a Major
Colin St Clair Oakes, who had recently disembarked in the UK and
been discharged from active duties. Indeed, Spragg would commend
this selection, highlighting his practical experience in India, service
record in Burma and career as student, notably as a Rome Scholar in
Architecture at the British School at Rome.[55]

Piqued by Oakes's experiences in Asia, yet cautious of his 'relatively' young age of 36, Kenyon interviewed him but did not mention
an actual appointment as Principal Architect.[56] The Commission after
all was conservative, and its architects of that generation were from a
Beaux-Arts–Classical background and had all served in the previous
war. But Kenyon needed someone who understood India and Burma,
had served in the war, and could respect the Commission's principles.
Above all, the candidate needed to travel urgently to the sites in Asia,
evaluate the existing burial conditions and establish a programme for
their development.

Kenyon, satisfied he had found the right person, wrote with his
suggestion to both Brigadier F. Higginson (Director of Works) and
H.C. Chettle (Director of Records and Deputy Controller of the Commission). Both concurred and Oakes was appointed as an Advisory
Architect to undertake the immediate tour to Asia. It would take
another two years for the appointment as Principal Architect to be
made. On 1 March 1947, the scope of designing the war cemeteries
for the vast and difficult Far East was given to Colin St Clair Oakes, 'a
man of the new generation who had served in the Second War'.[57]

CHAPTER 4

Architecture

It is the policy of the Commission to create cemeteries for and memorials of the war dead of the Commonwealth at or as near as possible to the places where they died. In consequence the cemeteries, though following a general pattern of design, have individual characteristics derived from rocks and soil, the climate and vegetation of each locality as well as from the contours of the site. Each cemetery becomes a natural part of its surrounding scenery and no two are identical.[1]

Writing in the September 1953 issue of the *Journal of the Royal Institute of British Architects*, under the title 'The Imperial War Graves Commission: Architectural Work following the 1939–45 War', the unknown author frames the war cemetery within the broader architectural discourse of the period. The article identifies that war cemetery architecture must be subservient to both its site location and the design template developed by the Commission after the Great War. Furthermore, it implies that the architect's creative scope is limited to designing within the margins of what is essentially a military graveyard. Although some scope for individuality in gateways and ancillary buildings may be afforded, the architect's work is 'principally a matter of skilful landscaping and layout in embodying these elements'.[2]

The war of 1939–45 provided vastly different challenges from the previous. The scope of this conflict spanned the globe, and with the entrance of Japan in 1942, brought the Commission to the eastern-most edge of Asia and the south Pacific. These are regions in which climate, topography, vegetation and soils differ markedly from what the Commission was conversant with through its work within the European continent and North Africa. This included the perception that labour standards in construction and gardening might not be up to the expectations the Commission had become accustomed to.

At the same time, with the significant expansion of air warfare, the subsequent casualties, both found and missing, had increased tremendously.[3] The Commission first began deliberations over commemorating the Royal Air Force (RAF) airmen who went missing in action in early 1945, though concerns had been raised a few years earlier. Since October 1942, officers and men of the RAF who had died in the small British enclave of Gibraltar, on the southern tip of the Iberian Peninsula, had been buried at sea with no headstone or marker in the local cemetery to identify them. As for the missing airmen and crew, whose numbers far exceeded those buried, there was growing concern as to how to commemorate them.[4] And while active planning would not commence for another few years, this set the context not only to design for new environments, but provide a new series of memorials and commemorative spaces for the Commonwealth air forces.[5] It afforded the Commission a unique opportunity to design for the modern era.

Within these new structures of commemoration, gathering spaces for annual pilgrimages and public remembrance ceremonies alike, the architect was given greater freedom of creative expression:

> The memorials to the missing – to those who have no known graves – are on a different plane. In these, the architect has full scope for original, truly monumental design. The sole essential element is the provision of space for the inscription of names. Beyond that, questions of symbolism, form and

materials are for the architect to consider unfettered. Thus, the design of these memorials is largely a personal expression and they arouse far greater variation in approval than do the cemeteries.[6]

Expanded over two subsequent issues, the journal article featured selected works from the five Principal Architects appointed for the war cemeteries and memorials the Second World War generated – Edward Maufe, Hubert Worthington, Louis de Soissons, Philip Hepworth and Colin St Clair Oakes. Mention was also made of Gordon Leith, who as an Advisory Architect to the Commission undertook work in his native South Africa.[7]

It was in the October issue that Oakes's work in Asia first came to the attention of the wider architectural fraternity and general public. It was also a portent of the many troubles his various projects encountered. The sheer distance and physical difficulty in accessing the various sites, along with the prevailing political disturbances in these post-war societies, meant a great deal of the work had been delayed. And in the case of those few war cemeteries partly completed, obtaining access for good photographs proved challenging to the Commission. Of the eight war cemeteries Oakes had commenced designing since 1946, only two by that stage had been suitably developed and were close enough to completion to be published – Kranji War Cemetery in Singapore and Sai Wan Bay War Cemetery in Hong Kong. Absent were the projects from India (undergoing independence from the British and separation from Pakistan), Burma and Malaya (both enduring insurgencies and insurrections) and Thailand (under authoritarian rule).

The Architecture of the Imperial War Graves Commission

In introducing Fabian Ware's *The Immortal Heritage*, a retrospective account of the workings of the Imperial War Graves Commission, the English poet and author Edmund Blunden observed that those who visit the war cemeteries in many parts of the world 'must be impressed and even astonished at the degree of beauty achieved by the creators and guardians of these resting places ... drawn to these cemeteries by their harmonious grace and dignity of architecture, of tree, shrub, grass, and blossom'.[8] Written in 1937, 20 years after he founded the Commission, Ware's account identified architecture as one of the primary legacies gained after the systematic concentration of war graves within hundreds of permanent burial sites. It suggests an acknowledgement that the war cemetery through its architectural treatment had earned an aesthetic gravitas usually accorded to temples and civic institutions.

The architecture of the Imperial War Graves Commission had its inception alongside the founding of the organisation. Indeed, the Commission's very policy of dignified burial is entwined with the aesthetics that manifestly represent that dignity. Three years into the Great War, the Prince of Wales addressed a minute to the Imperial War Conference, enclosing a memorandum by Ware, then Director-General of Graves Registration and Enquiries. Submitted to the representatives of the Government of Empire, who had assembled in London for the conference, the memorandum and its terms were approved by a resolution of the conference, and on that spring day, 13 April 1917, the body known as the Imperial War Graves Commission was brought into being.[9] At the same conference, the Commission presented and obtained approval for three guiding principles for the control of its work in building the war cemeteries: The memorials should be permanent; the headstones should be uniform; and there should be no distinction made on account of military or civil rank.[10] They would prove a starting point for formulating a detailed set of design guidelines by which every war cemetery of the Empire would be planned, constructed and maintained in perpetuity.

Being prominent architects of that period, Edwin Lutyens and Herbert Baker, along with Charles Aitken, Director of the Tate Gallery and the author Sir James Barrie, were invited by Ware in early 1917 to tour the British battlefield cemeteries near the front lines in north-east France.[11] It was intended they subsequently report back to DGR&E with advice on a series of suitably broad ideas for the post-war design of these burial sites. Aside from reaching an agreement that each grave be individually marked and that a uniform headstone be used for all burials, the collaborative process became problematic and ground to an impasse. With each architect offering divergent opinions on a suitable draft design – Lutyens propelling towards abstract monumental design and the centrality of a secular War Stone, Baker placing more importance on sentiment and the literal symbolism of a Christian cross as the most important monument – their artistic differences threatened to derail the momentum of the Commission's work.

The Commission soon found themselves in a quandary. Between opening the process through a public competition for a multitude of designs, or undergoing an internal process whereby one or two of the more prominent architects were selected to decide upon the general design principles, tentative efforts at both choices proved to be unsuccessful. Lutyens, Baker and Aitken had not been able to collectively agree on any clear design direction. Aitken had sided with Baker and similarly recommended a cross, while Lutyens was firmly adamant a secular altar would neither alienate any religion nor those for whom no religion was the preference. The resulting process became estranged and counter-productive, leaving Ware with few options. In one of the most astute decisions made, the Commission approached Sir Frederic Kenyon, Director of the British Museum and a lieutenant-colonel in the army who had served in France, to act as their Architectural Advisor.[12]

Oxford-educated and with a background in palaeography, Kenyon (1863–1952) was a renowned Greek and biblical scholar, and brought with him a scholastic rigour and military temperament to the task at hand. These two attributes would be called upon as his initial task entailed focusing and reconciling the numerous disparate design opinions that had found vocal expression, particularly in the artistic circles. Consequently, his primary duty was to decide between the various proposals submitted to him as to the architectural treatment and laying out of the war cemeteries. And at the Commission's meeting of 20 November 1917, it was resolved that Kenyon be formally appointed, along with the categorical reminder that the most important principle guiding his endeavour would be the 'equality of treatment'.[13]

Kenyon's Architectural Principles

Duly appointed with a mandate to investigate and report back, Kenyon soon departed for the battlefield sites of France and Belgium in the winter of 1917–18, and saw for himself the rudimentary and extenuating conditions upon which burials had been undertaken. Many had been formed in connection with the hospitals and casualty clearing stations, often arranged with some level of forethought and deliberation. But for the majority of those whose remains could be retrieved, they were either collectively buried in small, hastily prepared cemeteries or in the thousands of single and isolated graves scattered along the length of the front lines. The immense number of casualties and the scale of the task in providing a dignified resting place was daunting. Whereas many of the graves were located behind the fighting and some basic care had been taken, along with a simple cross or timber marker and a few pencilled notes to identify the fallen, others had suffered irreparable damage through the ebb and flow of the shifting battle lines. But it was the sense of a collective identity in the military cemeteries, as laid out by the French and British armies through their respective Graves Registration Units, that was to have the most lasting impact on Kenyon.

> The communal cemeteries are a jumbled mass of individual monuments of all sorts and sizes and of all variety of quality ... and the result is neither dignified nor inspiring. Side by side with these, the military cemeteries, whether French or English, with their orderly rows of crosses... have both dignity and inspiration. It is this impression which it is sought to perpetuate in the treatment now proposed for permanent adoption.[14]

Kenyon's final report, *War Graves: How the Cemeteries Abroad will be Designed,* was issued to the Commission a little over two months later, at its meeting on 24 January 1918.[15] In its preparation, Kenyon sought out at home and abroad the various representatives of the principal interests involved, namely the Army, relatives of the fallen, religious denominations and the various artists, in the hope of seeking consensus. He also made a point of seeking out the positions of India and the many Dominions who contributed men to the war. Yet it was the artistic classes – whose strengths he understood all too well, together with their limitations – that would impress upon him most strongly. Considering all the advice rendered to him by the 'eminent' architects and others, Kenyon was able to navigate the varying opinions and elucidate an architectural programme, setting forth clear design principles. This architectural template would be used on most if not all of the war cemeteries, including those of subsequent wars. It would forever define the Imperial War Graves Commission.

The Commission's most significant principle, 'equality of treatment', determined that individual monuments be forsaken in lieu of a common memorial, with no distinction between military ranks of soldiers and officers. Neither was there to be any distinction between each man's social standing in civilian life. This collective uniformity of the graves marked by headstones, amongst carefully manicured green lawns, would symbolise the 'military idea, giving the appearance as of a battalion on parade, and suggesting the spirit of discipline and order which is the soul of an army'.[16] This 'order' would furthermore serve to define the cemetery as one of the war and be clearly evident to those passing by or visiting.

The headstones themselves, nominally 2 feet 6 inches in height, 1 foot 3 inches wide, and 3 inches thick, would be made of limestone, quarried from the Isle of Portland, and embedded in a concrete base. A curved top would ensure water runoff towards the sides, preventing staining on the face. Inscribed on their face would be the regimental pattern of the deceased's unit, their religious symbol and a few details such as name, regiment and date of death. Furthermore, Kenyon recommended that a short inscription along the base of the headstone, of not more than three lines, be added if requested and provided by the deceased's next-of-kin. These were subject to censorship and intended to be in the form of a text or prayer – 'it is clearly undesirable to allow free scope for the effusions of the mortuary mason, the sentimental versifier, or the crank'.[17]

In outlining how the cemeteries would be designed, Kenyon also made the distinct point that horticultural design was as important a feature of the site as the architecture. 'The main architectural features of each cemetery will be given by the trees or shrubs planted in it, with regard to which the designer and the horticultural expert must work hand in hand.'[18] A pragmatist, Kenyon took great care not to show preference for either Lutyens's idea of the monument in the garden or Baker's 'English garden'. Instead, he inserted a caveat in his report placing the landscape design on an even footing with the architecture, well aware that otherwise, the architectural treatment could overwhelm it. He further clarified that the horticultural experts alone could advise on what trees and flowers were suitable to the local conditions. His intention was that the war cemetery should not be a place of gloom, but through an expanse of grass and bright flowers, it should reflect an environment of brightness and life. A year later, the Assistant-Director of the Royal Botanic Gardens Kew and Botanical Advisor to the Imperial War Graves Commission, Captain Arthur W. Hill, delivered a lecture outlining the framework for the war cemetery horticultural scheme. Published in the *Journal of the Royal Horticultural Society,* the lecture-cum-article entitled 'Our Soldiers' Graves' reinforced Kenyon's notions of landscape as an elemental ideology.[19]

The epitome of an understated English elite gentleman, Kenyon was well acquainted with and appreciative of the system of patronage in the arts. In his opinion, it was desirable that the artistic merit of the whole cemetery should be entrusted to those architects in whom the public had confidence, and who had 'earned' the right to be regarded as representative of British architecture.

> I do not believe that in matters of art the best work is produced by a committee. I would rather go back to the mediaeval tradition of a master architect or painter, surrounded by a school of disciples, who under his guidance, and with

greater or less degrees of subordination, did their work and learnt to be masters in their turn.[20]

Kenyon therefore recommended that a selected few Principal Architects be appointed for the various cemeteries, largely grouped on geographical grounds, with a number of younger architects working under their direction. And that those young architects must have served in the war. While following the general design principles, an important consideration was that they be 'free to work in accordance with the dictates of their genius'.[21]

Over the next few months, Lutyens, Baker and Reginald Blomfield were formally invited to serve as Principal Architects for the Commission.[22] With the realisation of the sheer scale of the work and its spread across the former battlefield sites of Europe, North Africa and the Middle East, further senior appointments were an obvious necessity. The initial three Principal Architects were soon joined by Robert Lorimer, Charles Holden, Sir John James Burnet and Edward Prioleau Warren. Lorimer, a prominent Scottish Arts and Crafts architect, would be the Principal Architect responsible for Italy, Macedonia and Egypt, creating notable works including the Memorial to the Missing at Lake Dorian in Greece, the Scottish National War Memorial in Edinburgh and the three naval memorials at Portsmouth, Plymouth and Chatham. Holden would become Principal Architect for France and design the war cemeteries at Passchendaele and Polygon Wood. He would be better known for his London Underground designs created in the interwar period. Burnet, whose architectural firm would go on to become an influential force in British modern architecture, would be tasked with the war cemeteries in Palestine, Gallipoli and Suez, most notably the Lone Pine War Cemetery and Memorial. Warren, who was both architect and archaeologist, would undertake the War Cemetery in Basra, Mesopotamia (Iraq).

Stone of Remembrance and Cross of Sacrifice

What followed was the evolution of artistic ideas into firm architectural elements, the first of which involved the central monument. Kenyon intended that this monument be 'simple, durable, dignified and expressive of the higher feelings with which we regard our dead',[23] and most notably, it should be located in every war cemetery, bar the very smallest. Sketching on the back of an envelope whilst in France, Lutyens, a strong advocate for secular architecture, proposed a great memorial altar stone stripped of all adornment, allowing everyone of all faiths, and those without, to interpret its symbolism. Writing to Ware upon his return from France in his Memorandum of August 1917, Lutyens describes this abstract monumental form as 'one great fair stone of fine proportions, 12 feet in length, lying raised upon three steps, of which the first and third shall be twice the width of the second; and that each stone shall bear in indelible lettering, some fine thought or words of sacred dedication'.[24] Wherever possible, it was to be located on the eastern side of the cemetery, with the graves lying before it. Gavin Stamp identifies that Lutyens 'modelled and enlivened the Stone with entasis – the application of a slight convex curve to a surface or vertical element to correct the visual illusion of concavity'.[25] With the exception of the very smallest burial sites and those in locations which were difficult to access – for example, the Asiago plateau in the Italian Alps, northern Greece and some parts of Papua New Guinea – the Stone would become an intrinsic feature in all of the Commission's war cemeteries. Originally termed a War Stone, it was over time formally accepted as the Stone of Remembrance.

The inscription itself would emanate from another 'gentleman of highest artistic qualifications' – the British author, poet and Nobel laureate, Rudyard Kipling. Kipling, whose only son was killed on the Western Front in 1915, joined Ware's Imperial War Graves Commission. In his capacity as Literary Advisor, he suggested the memorial phrases 'Known unto God'[26] for the gravestones of unidentified servicemen, and 'Lest we forget', from his 1897 Christian poem 'Recessional', for use in war remembrance services.[27] Yet his most significant contribution was to Lutyens's Stone, where he called upon a quote from the Book of Ecclesiasticus, 'Their name liveth for evermore.' The full verse reads: 'Their bodies are buried in peace; but their name liveth for evermore.'[28] Lutyens, firmly believing in a secular architecture and the equality of remembrance, initially opposed the full line. It was only with the intervention of Kenyon, in his capacity to make a final decision, that the initial phrase was cut and the second part of the verse accepted, thus underlining the Stone's abstract symbolism.[29]

The Stone of Remembrance and its symbolism was also the subject of an impassioned speech before the House of Commons in May 1920. The Imperial War Graves Commission, a mere three years after its founding and struggling under severe funding constraints, found its very existence being called into question. A young Winston Churchill as Secretary of War, addressing a boisterous and sceptical House, rose

Lutyens's Stone of Remembrance in the forecourt at the entrance to Kranji War Cemetery, August 1957

to the defence of the institution and invoked the longevity of Lutyens's 'ten-ton great stone' as an endearing symbol of the British Empire:

> [E]ven if our language, our institutions, and our Empire all
> have faded from the memory of man, these great stones will
> still preserve the memory of a common purpose pursued by a
> great nation in the remote past, and will undoubtedly excite
> the wonder and the reverence of a future age.[30]

The Stone's eschewal of all religious and cultural symbolism was a cause for concern for Kenyon. With an eye to the greater public, and to placate Baker and Aitken, Kenyon envisioned the cemeteries augmented by the iconic character of a cross – to define the Christian Empire and serve as a symbol of the self-sacrifice made by those who lay within the grounds.[31] The Cross of Sacrifice, designed by Blomfield, was shaped as an elongated Latin cross with proportions somewhat reflecting the Celtic cross of northern Britain, so as to avoid comparison with the crucifixes seen in French cemeteries. Originally carved from white Portland Stone, as used for the headstones, granite or any other white limestone commonly found in France, Belgium and Italy was often substituted. Mounted on the front face, and sometimes also the rear face, is a mediaeval bronze sword with its blade pointing downwards to an octagonal stone base. The Cross of Sacrifice would come in four heights, scaled proportionally, allowing it to be applied to cemeteries of differing sizes.[32] And in keeping with the Commission's awareness of the cultural diversity of the Commonwealth, it would be modified in regions where religious sensitivities or physical conditions made its erection impractical. Across the mountains of northern Greece, its replacement consisted of a locally sourced stone cairn, conical in shape and with a small stone cross atop. In Turkey and in those cemeteries of solely Indian or Hindu soldiers, it was omitted altogether.

Kenyon, seeing the merits of both ideas in the appeasement of the secular and the religious, thus recommended that these two forms of monuments, the Stone and the Cross, be combined, within

View of Blomfield's Cross of Sacrifice from Kranji War Memorial towards the entrance of the cemetery. The Straits of Johore is in the background.

each cemetery. With most war cemeteries having a main axis and an entrance axis, the guiding principle was the Stone as the primary focus, and the Cross with its height serving as an orienting feature identifying the war cemetery from afar. Together, the two memorials would become the universal mark of the Commonwealth war cemetery, at home and abroad.

Selecting Young Architects

Whereas the Principal Architects were designers of repute and high standing in British society at the time, the criteria for selecting the young architects were to have a far more lasting impact. Kenyon strongly recommended that preference be given to those architects who had served in the armed forces, and indeed clarified his intentions by insisting that those architects who did not serve should not

83

be accepted for the work. For his conviction was that those 'who have themselves served, and whose comrades lie in these cemeteries, are best qualified to express the sentiment which we desire the cemeteries to convey'.[33] Indeed, for the war cemeteries and memorials of the First World War, some of the most significant were by the Commission's Assistant Architects and recently returned servicemen such as William Bryce Binnie (Nieuport Memorial), Harold Chalton Bradshaw (Ploegsteert Memorial to the Missing), William Harrison Cowlishaw (Pozieres Memorial), George Hartley Goldsmith (Villers-Bretonneux), Noel Ackroyd Rew (Bailleul Road), Leslie Daniels Barrett (Mosul) and John Reginald Truelove (Noyelles-sur-Mer Chinese Cemetery). Wilfred Clement von Berg, who served in both world wars, designed Bedford House in Ypres, Belgium. Verner O. Rees, one of Lutyens's assistants and designer of the Memorial to the Missing at Soissons, would go on to become President of the Architectural Association.

The idea of giving preference to young architects who had served in the war was a noble one. Their return home in 1918 saw a great many struggle in the war's aftermath with the stagnant economic conditions let alone the physical and psychological state they found themselves in. The work the Commission provided was well received and it allowed them, in their own small way, to offer respects to their fallen colleagues. In her essay, *Architects in the First World War*, Cathy Wilson suggests that of the 4,336 members of the Royal Institute of British Architects (RIBA) in 1918, over 1,300 or almost one-in-three served in the First World War, of which 230 would not return.[34] Indeed, the call for volunteers at the outbreak of the war saw many in the architectural profession signing up. The Architectural Association (AA) formed their own War Service Bureau to assist architects and architectural assistants in enlisting. The AA's own President joined the Royal Engineers, the regiment of choice for many in the design professions, the other popular regiment being the Artists Rifles or 28th Battalion London Regiment. RIBA formed the Architect's War Committee and arranged among other critical services to look after the work of young architects called up. The war effort also had the effect of restricting construction activity on the home front, compounding an already dire industry. But the most pertinent activity undertaken by the profession was the *RIBA Journal* maintaining a roll-of-honour throughout the four years of conflict. Through printing the names of all members who had enlisted, along with their rank and regiment, the roll recorded the names of those members, members' sons and RIBA staff killed in action, wounded or listed as missing in action.[35] It became a mental reminder for those architects who upon returning joined the Imperial War Graves Commission and designed the very memorials and headstones upon which the names of the fallen were subsequently inscribed.

In contrast to the abundance of young and available architects hungry for work and willing to become assistants to their 'eminent' peers after the First World War, there would be no such repeat upon the conclusion of the second. The cost of materials and labour had risen significantly since the last war, compounded with the mass demobilisation of servicemen and the scarcity of food and accommodation that awaited them back home. The pressure to rein in the ever-increasing cost of building and maintaining new and existing cemeteries would be the most pressing concern for the Commission.[36] Under tight fiscal control from the Treasury, the Commission could not afford to pay the prevailing market rates, and struggled accordingly to recruit qualified professional and technical staff. This shortage in attracting staff of the right calibre, along with occasional slips in quality control, saw an inevitable slowdown in the production of design ideas into actual works. The works in South Asia, Southeast Asia and the Far East would be particularly affected.[37]

Whereas the European theatre for the Imperial War Graves Commission would have four Principal Architects allocated, and the proximity to the United Kingdom was a key criterion in attracting adequate numbers of technical support, Asia would prove more challenging. It was a new frontier for the Commission, and aside from the direct responsibility they had in India through subsuming their old agency, they required further sub-branches to administer the new cemeteries and memorials. Subsequently, and under control from the Delhi offices, new offices were established for India, Burma and the region encompassing Malaya, Indochina, the Dutch East Indies and Hong Kong. Australia and New Zealand, through forming their own Anzac Agency with the agreement of the Commission, had already taken over responsibility for the war graves closer to home in Java, Sumatra, Papua New Guinea and the South East Pacific. And yet only a single Principal Architect, Colin St Clair Oakes in 1947, was formally appointed for the vast area encompassing Asia.

It was the Commission's own in-house Architects who stepped up and took on a greater role in the delivery of the vast majority of the war cemeteries and memorials in Asia. They saw out the tail end of the Commission's second grand development project that had commenced with the end of war in Europe in 1944. Where Oakes provided initial thoughts and conceptual ideas through his first inspection tour of the region from 1945 to 1946 and the follow-up in 1947, returned service-men and architects such as Henry John Brown, Ralph Hobday, Alan Stewart, George Vey, and Architectural Assistant Richard Duckham ably assisted in developing the designs and in many cases initiated their own concepts into realised sites. Otherwise obscure in the public domain and little known or acknowledged in the written history of the Commission, their staff cards and handwritten notes on the formal design assessment, budget and approval reports known as 'Form A' display an astute understanding of Kenyon's founding architectural principles, and a self-confidence in adapting their designs to the con-temporary conditions of the time and locations.

With his military service in the War Office followed by Major in the Royal Engineers, Brown was one of the Commission's earliest post-war appointments in 1944. A practising architect before enlisting, the army would instil in him considerable executive experience in the organisation of construction works, a key requisite for his role as the Commission's Senior Deputy Director of Works and Advisory Archi-tect. Responsible for the design of a great number of war cemeteries in India and newly created Pakistan, as well Burma and Ceylon, he would also later assume part of Oakes's extensive portfolio with the latter's impending departure from the Commission's service. Delhi, Karachi, Kirkee, Madras, Colombo, Kandy and Trincomalee were all highly accomplished examples of Brown's design direction, but his most significant legacy was to be in Burma. Taukkyan War Cemetery, the largest of three war cemeteries in Burma, was the consolidation site for those burials from Mandalay, Meiktila, Akyab and Sahmaw, which were proving difficult to access and maintain. Brown deftly adapted Oakes's original concept ideas and created one of the most elegant sites of commemoration, the Rangoon Memorial. Unveiled by General Sir Francis Festing, Commander-in-Chief of the Far East Land Forces, in July 1958, the Memorial accommodates the inscribed names of nearly 27,000 servicemen of the Commonwealth who died in Burma and had no known graves. It would also be Brown's concluding piece for the Commission. He departed soon after for a London architectural partnership with L.C. Moulin. They would conceive the LIC Building in Madras (Chennai), India, which upon completion in 1959 was the tallest building in the city and has remained an important modernist landmark ever since.[38]

Hobday joined the Commission's staff as Architect in North Africa in 1944, and under the direction of the Principal Architect Worthington he was involved in the preliminary designs of war cemeteries there. Appointed back to London, and under the supervision of Maufe, who was by then the Commission's Advisory Architect, Hobday would for the most part of his career design hundreds of small war grave layouts and memorials within war cemeteries in the United Kingdom. Acknowledged as a 'sound architect with a talent for simplicity in design and a fine artistic sense', his work on the Brookwood 1939–1945 Memorial in Surrey and Lyness Royal Naval Cemetery in Orkney cemented his design reputation.[39] Stamp acknowledges Hobday's considerate design of the monumental staircase within Lutyens's Memorial to the Missing of the Somme in Thiepval.[40] Yet, facing the manpower constraints for the Asian theatre, and appointed Senior Architect, Hobday would be drafted to oversee the approval of the many sites in that region, along with responsibility for the design of the Ambon War Cemetery in Indonesia.

Maynamati and Rawalpindi War Cemeteries in Pakistan, designed and completed in 1953 and 1958 respectively, were the creations of Stewart. They were preceded by the war cemetery section of the Bidadari Christian Cemetery in Singapore (1952), and followed by the Kuala Lumpur (Cheras Road) Civil Cemetery in Malaya (1954). Unlike Brown, Hobday and Vey, who were newly recruited direct from the armed forces upon their demobilisation in 1944, Stewart came to the Commission in 1951 after a spell in private practice. Becoming the District Works Officer for the Middle East followed by District Officer for the Commission's Southern Region a few years later, he would also have a hand in designing numerous war and military cemeteries in the Middle East and Greece, along with memorials for the Indian subcontinent. He was the last of the senior designers for the Commission, along with Duckham (Memorial at Addu Attoll, Maldives), with their departures in the late 1960s.[41]

It is telling, therefore, that without the guiding hand of the Principal Architects, the Assistant Architects and in-house Architects were able to execute the high standards expected of the Commission, even as the works programme was drawing to its conclusion. The design precedents first set by Lutyens and Blomfield and developed over the past 40 years were holding these final war cemetery schemes together, regardless of who was designing them. For although each war cemetery differed between their individual sites, from country to country, and each design feature required specific thought and detailing, the basic principles put forth by Kenyon in 1917 offered each architect a refined template that ensured a uniform identity and quality was achieved. If any war cemetery was emblematic of this architectural flux the Commission found itself encountering towards the tail end of the 1950s, it was Digboi War Cemetery in north-east Assam, India. Credited to Stewart, the sketch design was in fact prepared by a young architecture student, Norman Kates, who was on the Commission's staff at the time. A 'simple' rectangular and level site catering to the graves from a nearby cemetery, bereft of any vegetation, the design was endorsed by Vey and certified by Maufe in his role as Artistic Advisor. Digboi would be approved in early 1955 for construction.[42]

Post-Architecture

By the mid-1960s, the primary construction programme of the by now renamed Commonwealth War Graves Commission in establishing war cemeteries and memorials was nearing completion. This was aptly reflected in the number of formal meetings being conducted, the first of which had taken place nearly 50 years prior, on 20 September 1917, six months after the Commission had been constituted by Royal Charter. Since then, they had met once a month until the commencement of the Second World War, several times annually throughout the period of hostilities, and once a month in the post-war period until 1964, when most of the construction activities resulting from the Second World War came to an end.

The focus of the Commission would soon turn to principally one of maintenance, alongside other roles focused on remembrance. They would embark on a review and reorganisation of their vast administrative structure, by then spanning most of the globe, and see the closing of selected regional offices and adjustments to the size and territorial scope of their area offices. Along with millions of war graves within thousands of war cemeteries built since 1917, the Commission also continued to maintain nearly 40,000 non-Commonwealth war graves throughout the world, under arrangements with the foreign governments concerned. It was incumbent on the Commission to rein in expenditure and increase efficiency, along with centralising as much control as possible back to their headquarters in London. This period also coincided with two important milestones, the first of which was the 50th anniversary of the end of the First World War. In April that same year, Maufe, the Commission's Chief Architect and Artistic Director, who had taken over from Kenyon and overseen the architectural programme since 1949, retired. He was succeeded by an architect of the present generation in Lord William Holford as Artistic Advisor, the appointment reverting to its former title, marking a subtle shift in the priorities of the architectural direction thenceforth.

Holford would oversee the last remaining projects in commemorating the dead of the 1939–1945 war, including the erection of a Cross of Sacrifice in Rhodes War Cemetery in the Dodecanese island in November 1969. In December, Dar es Salaam War Cemetery in Tanzania was completed and inaugurated, consolidating the remains throughout the country of both First and Second World War Commonwealth casualties. The remaining stages of the Mosul War Cemetery in Iraq were completed soon after in 1970, bringing to an end major works for the Second World War.[43]

Although the war cemeteries established throughout the world had their security safeguarded by treaties, the Commission faced challenges that were more the consequence of post-war urban and social development. It was noted at the 51st Annual Meeting, 1969–70, that the 'growth of cities and towns, the construction of new motorways, and the general increase in populations have in recent years multiplied the problems which the Commission has faced in protecting them and their surroundings'.[44] The Commission had to call upon their ingenuity, technical and diplomatic skills to address these problems and enable affected cemeteries to remain in situ, unaltered. Landscaping and screening was often deployed to conceal unsightly new buildings nearby. At the Yokohama War Cemetery, careful negotiations with the local authorities would see the realignment of a projected new motorway, avoiding the destruction of numbers of large trees providing shelter over the burial plots. In consultation with the Zambian Government, numerous war graves scattered throughout the country were regrouped within a new Commonwealth War Cemetery, making it possible that their future long-term maintenance was assured.[45]

Over the next four decades and by now into the 21st century, the Commission settled into their role as custodians of the war dead of the Commonwealth. Where remains of deceased servicemen were found in former battlefields, well-established protocols were activated and new war graves were dug and headstones erected. Old and dilapidated headstones and other building elements were repaired or replaced. General improvements were made to the horticulture of sites and their public amenities in keeping with the times. In so doing, the acumen and skill of the Commission's tradespeople and staff were constantly on display. Annual commemoration events, remembrance ceremonies and educational tours contributed to the Commission remaining in the public imagination. An extensive archive was also activated, offering an opportunity for the public and scholars alike to locate the fallen and their final place of rest, and research both the history and workings of the Commission, as well as each war cemetery and memorial.

In 2008, though, the Commonwealth War Graves Commission would be once again called upon to resurrect the core expertise it was founded to undertake. Through the historical research of a retired Australian teacher, Lambis Englezos, and an analysis of aerial photographs, a mass grave was discovered on the edge of Pheasant Wood (Bois Faisan) in northern France, near the border with Belgium. Further investigation revealed the presence of human remains; 250 bodies were subsequently recovered during excavation works in 2009. Using modern DNA analysis, the men were identified as British and Australian soldiers who had died on 19 July 1916 during the Battle of Fromelles.[46]

It would be almost 50 years since the Commission last had the need to appoint an architect for a new war cemetery. And in the case of this new mass grave discovery, they were called upon not only to provide the management for the project but to construct a new war cemetery for the reburial of the recovered bodies. The Commission turned to the architect Barry Edwards, who upon receiving confirmation of a suitable site nearby on account of the original location being prone to flooding, drew up plans and design sketches for the new cemetery. The location, on the outskirts of Fromelles, almost 120 metres away from the mass grave, offered a higher elevation that allowed for the Cross of Sacrifice to stand out from the surrounding skyline. Edwards also considered the orientation of the grave plots, facing them southwards so as to avoid shadows on the face of the headstones. And in deference to modern design standards and regulations, the cemetery also incorporated ramps for wheelchair accessibility. On 19 July 2010, almost 93 years since the very first 'experimental' war cemetery was created in France, and on the 94th anniversary of the Battle of Fromelles, an opening and dedication ceremony was held for the Fromelles (Pheasant Wood) Military Cemetery.[47]

CHAPTER 5

Colin St Clair Oakes

In observing the monuments and memorials erected after the Second World War, the greater public and even design critics often fail to fully comprehend the unsettled post-war context in which they were conceived and built. Unveiled through carefully orchestrated ceremonies of solemnity and pageantry, the accommodating public and news media focused on the grief and sacrifice that these memorials were intended to represent. In these circumstances, conveying the tragedy and sacrifices extracted by the conflict through those buried within or inscribed upon stone walls takes precedence over the many who served and returned. And in doing so, remembrance occurs without fully comprehending or appreciating the sacrifices of the many participants entrusted with the arrival of that day.

Above all, unsettled conditions confronted private individuals without the financial or social means, and this was particularly true for many of the architects who had served. Without benefiting from an injection of state resources into post-war development and construction programmes, such as social housing for example, these architects had to resume their practices and often careers from the very beginning. Then there were those who returned to find their positions in design practices made redundant, if indeed the firm itself was still solvent and operating. Unemployment and queuing for welfare assistance became a necessity. Others, such as Colin St Clair Oakes, were more fortunate in being able to quickly secure employment, but in his case, it involved having to take two jobs. A similar scenario applied to Sir Frederic Kenyon's corps of young architects, many of whom returned home without secure employment prospects and were eager for the work afforded by the Imperial War Graves Commission; they were employed directly by the Commission and served as assistants to their more eminent principals.

Principal Architects such as Sir Edwin Lutyens and Sir Herbert Baker, on the other hand, were by the 1920s and 1930s nationally prominent figures, on whom the British establishment would bestow countless accolades and knighthoods. Their prominence accompanied the prestige and significant attention that their planning and architecture of New Delhi and efforts with the War Graves Commission had received. After creating the Memorial to the Missing of the Somme, Lutyens would be described as having 'become a popular social figure, much in demand for lunch and dinner parties because of his flippant unorthodoxy and humour'.[1] Louis de Soissons, son of a French count, had a large architectural practice undertaking numerous town planning projects and private housing estates. His office would be responsible for the design of over 50 war cemeteries and memorials for the Commission after the war. Sir Robert Lorimer and Sir Hubert Worthington were also enmeshed within society's elite. For such eminent architects well ensconced in the social and political circles of the period, private and public commissions would flow in, thus assuring their financial security and social standing.

Oakes was one of over five million British servicemen and servicewomen demobilised at the war's end in 1945 and having to re-assimilate into civilian life. Returning home after four years in sub-tropical north-east India and Burma, he would be greeted by the upheavals and uncertainties of life back on the home front. British society was slowly emerging from the daily rituals of lining up for limited produce, evening blackouts, air raid shelters and the widespread death and destruction wrought by the German Luftwaffe during the

Blitz. Fuel shortages and food rationing were also in place and would not be lifted for a considerable time. And while accounting for these severe deprivations, Oakes's priority was to urgently reunite with his family, for whom correspondence, though plentiful, had frequently been lost in transit during his absence. Married in the late spring of 1939 and residing in a small village in the rural county of Sussex, his wife Nancy Lea and two young children had, like millions of others, found themselves on the front lines of the war with Germany. With the capitulation of France in July 1940, and along with thousands of others living on that coastline who had somewhere to relocate, they departed for north Wales, staying with Oakes's relatives, well away from the uncertainties of the daily air raids and the seaborne invasion anticipated for the south-east coast of England. It would be almost a year, following the end of the Blitz, before Nancy and the children could return to Sussex, where in *Burmans*, a small cottage purchased and moved into just before the outbreak of war, Oakes's family would be reunited. In this historic, rural countryside set along the coast of the English Channel, Oakes would set about finding work in the desperate economic climate and resurrecting a career the war had placed on hold.

Recollecting on those early years of the turbulent post-war period, Oakes's children offer an invaluable insight into the distractions and difficulties architects such as their father encountered upon returning from the war. For one, food and money were always in short supply. Rationing, in place since 1939, saw limited availability of staple supplies such as sugar, bacon, milk and bread, along with petrol and meat. Fresh vegetables and fruit though not rationed were limited. It would be July 1954 before the last of the remaining rationing was ended and the country returned to some semblance of its pre-war past, though the effects of deprivation would linger for many years to come. In his three-month-long tour of Asia at the behest of the Commission soon after arriving back, and a second tour two years later, Oakes would appeal to the Commission requesting that his fees be forwarded directly to his wife back home in *Burmans*.[2] Along with a third child on the way, he

95

was acutely aware of the duress the family situation was under. Then there were the two jobs that he managed to secure upon returning in early 1946, in a part-time teaching position at the Architectural Association (AA) and in private practice with his former AA colleague and fellow veteran, Raymond Brown.[3]

All this occurred whilst Oakes was trying to re-establish a semblance of normal family life. Taking to working at a large, polished timber desk within the confines of the library, Oakes found himself overlooking a well-tended garden and small swimming pool under construction by German prisoner-of-war labourers.[4]

It was at *Burmans* that Oakes produced the initial sketch designs of many of the war cemeteries and memorials for the Commission, including the Singapore Memorial at Kranji. Michael, his eldest son, seven years old at the time, would later reflect on the initial designs of Kranji, his father explaining how the shape of the memorial was to resemble that of an aeroplane from the view of the front elevation and plan above, the central 'tail fin' clearly visible from the side. Over the years, it would often find itself mistaken for a submarine conning tower. Frequent visitors included by then close friends Brown and William Holford, the latter of whom had been prominent in the war effort at home and at that time headed the Ministry of Town and Country Planning. Impromptu design critiques by an open fireplace would be a regular occurrence.

This image of Oakes sitting in his library in a small county village and designing the war cemeteries and memorials in faraway India, Burma or Singapore brings home the extent to which the British psyche had been altered by the war. Not only narrowing the once great gap between the classes but broadening that between the soldiers who went to war and their families, friends and former colleagues who stayed behind on the home front. For all intents and purposes, Oakes the architect for the Kranji Memorial was a representative of the Far Eastern theatre of the conflict; but who he was and what brought him to that point is a story as much about his life before the war. By taking a critical look at the timeframe in which Oakes was raised, educated, worked and then fought, we are able to distil the many influences that shaped his outlook on architecture and were in turn reflected in his designs. While his early education followed a somewhat traditional path, the exposure he actively sought out in his formative years through extensive travelling and working in Scandinavia, the Mediterranean and South Asia undoubtedly contributed to an ideology rooted in the sensibilities of a classical past but conscious of and indebted to the implicit freedoms of the modernist agenda – an agenda progressed along by the war and its aftermath.

Early Years

Born on 23 May 1908, in the village of Tanyfron in north Wales, Colin Sinclair Rycroft Oakes was the second child of Leonard Rycroft Oakes and Mary St Claire. A sister, Elaine, was born two years earlier.[5] Leonard, an architect trained at the Manchester School of Arts, was articled to the Arts and Crafts exponent William Cecil Hardisty.[6] He would establish himself designing schools and public housing for the Middlesex County Architects Department, providing for London's booming population growth at the turn of the century and the city's expansion outwards to its fringes. Like many of his generation, Leonard experienced first-hand the tragedy that was the Great War, as an infantry officer on the Western Front

Leonard Rycroft Oakes and Mary St Claire with Elaine and Colin, 1908

and the Battle of the Somme through to the Italian campaign in the Alps. His outlook upon returning reflected the greater social changes that were taking place against the entrenched class system. His views would harden against those of privilege who perpetuated a conflict that decimated a generation of young men.[7]

This was also a time when the British Empire was at its peak and held sway over almost one quarter of the world's population and land mass. The Edwardian era, a period in which style was being influenced by the art and fashions of continental Europe, was coming to an end. In his book *The Edwardian Turn of Mind* (1968), the American author Samuel Hynes described this period as one 'when the rich were not ashamed to live conspicuously, and the sun really never set on the British flag'.[8] But it was also the period book-ended by the achievements of the Victorian age and the catastrophe that would befall the country with the outbreak of the First World War, the horror and destruction of which would accelerate the rejection of the certainty of Enlightenment thinking and a gradual repudiation of religious beliefs.

British architecture was caught between the late Victorian period, the free Renaissance eclecticism favoured by Lutyens and the shift to a neoclassical mode at the turn of the century: a retreat from the stylised treatment of the 19th century to a pared-down, homogenised classicism based on Georgian exemplars. This approach had many followers within the architectural fraternity, notably Herbert Baker and Reginald Blomfield. The first decade of the 20th century was also notable for the decline of the Arts and Crafts movement followed by the advent of new attitudes to function and style through internationalism. Emerging as a reaction against the world before the war and the historical architectural styles, it would evolve into the International Style, otherwise known as modernism.[9]

It was the onset of modernism, shaped by the development of modern industrial society and the rapid growth of cities and their urban citizenry, that would have a profound influence on young Oakes. Following in the footsteps of his father and greatly inspired by the adaptive classicism of Lutyens, Oakes sought an artisan path, setting his sights on becoming an architect. Living in London and completing his early education at the Harrow County School, he applied to the

Northern Polytechnic School of Architecture and was accepted.[10]

Founded in 1896, the Northern Polytechnic, under the terms of its Royal Charter, catered mainly to the poorer and working classes of north London, with an emphasis on providing industrial skills and general knowledge.[11] The architecture programme, competing against the orthodoxy of the established universities and their public school intakes, was only recognised by Royal Institute of British Architects (RIBA) in 1925. This coincided with the earlier appointment in 1922 of the British abstract artist and pioneer of modernism, Cecil Stephenson, as Director of Arts. The school would prove an inspired selection for Oakes, who enrolled in 1927 for a three-year programme. It would instil a cosmopolitan outlook in an impressionable young man and steer his design career towards contemporary trends.[12]

By the end of 1929, Oakes had completed his undergraduate training with two outwardly dissimilar yet analogous examples of his rigorous approach to design methodology. On the one hand, his entry submission for the annual Tite Prize, conducted by the RIBA, drew an honourable mention and brought his name to the attention of the design establishment.[13] Named after Sir William Tite, a former President of RIBA and Member of Parliament, the annual award was intended to promote the study of traditional Italian architecture. Oakes's design scheme for a private yacht club on the Mediterranean exhibited an early appreciation of a pared-down classicism that would eventually evolve into a preference for modernism.

Having spent the better part of 1928 travelling the length and breadth of Britain, the following May saw Oakes submit his thesis, 'The Development of Church Towers in England from AD 950 to 1500'.[14] His detailed pencil drawings of almost a hundred Norman and early Gothic churches and cathedrals underscored an early appreciation of what can be comfortably described as an English mediaeval. They also reinforced his understanding of how the built form was a product of scientific and mathematical judgement, something that would be valued in the functionalist modernism of his later war cemetery commissions.

After a short period articled to the London firm of T.P. Bennett, Oakes made his first foray outside the British Isles. In April 1930, he departed for Finland to work in the Helsinki office of Jarl Eklund.[15] Originally trained as a sculptor, a young Eklund would, in joining the practice of Gesellius, Lindgren, Saarinen, come under the tutelage of Eliel Saarinen, recognised for his Art Nouveau style.[16] It was a time in which Finnish architecture was evolving from the traditional Jugend-stil characterised by flowing lines and the incorporation of nation-alistic-mythological symbols, and returning to a so-called Nordic Classicism. This had been influenced by architect study trips to Italy and closer to home, Sweden, in particular the architecture of Gunnar Asplund.[17] On establishing his own office in 1905, Eklund made his own study tours to Germany, France, Spain and Italy, returning heavily influenced by the continent's shift to a functional modernism. In this atmosphere, Oakes gained invaluable experience understanding the Nordic aesthetic through working on a school in Kotka and a public library in Abo on the fringes of Helsinki. A young Eero Saarinen, son of Eliel and a fresh graduate from Yale University at that time, would a few years later return to Finland and similarly undertake his architec-tural internship under Eklund.[18]

Upon his return to the UK and following a brief stint with H.M. Office of Works as Architectural Assistant, Oakes enrolled in the Royal Academy of Arts at the beginning of 1931 to again study architecture. During this period, Baker, Sir Giles Gilbert Scott, Wil-liam Curtis Green and Lutyens were all teaching architectural design. Lectures were also provided by Harold Chalton Bradshaw.[19] With the likes of Blomfield (1914), Lutyens (1921), Baker (1932) and de Soissons (1953) having instructed at the school as visiting Royal Academicians, it would prove a veritable pathway to working for the Imperial War Graves Commission. But it turned out to be a short-lived tenure as Oakes was preparing for his next phase. He had put together an appli-cation that would change the course of his career. He subsequently won the prized Rome Scholarship in Architecture, which offered a one-year opportunity to live and study at the British School at Rome.[20]

British School at Rome

A series of carefully taken black-and-white photographs discovered in Oakes's personal papers and drawings reveals a group of young individuals living and studying in pre-war Rome, each image offering a glimpse of the unencumbered continental lifestyle found far from home. The photographs capture three unidentified shirtless young men and a woman in bathing suit reclining and baking on a rooftop; an overhead view of the architect Robert Hubbard all consumed in rendering a classical plan; a young scholar taking a dip in the courtyard fountain designed by the sculptor John Skeaping; students in shirts and ties enjoying breakfast; a relaxed William Holford staring into the camera whilst seated in a garden; and the sculptor John F. Kavanagh moulding his bust of young Oakes. It was a time of experience and opportunities afforded a selected group of talented artists and artisans, many of whom would go on to make their mark in their chosen disciplines.

John Kavanagh sculpting the head cast of his *Portrait of Colin St Clair Oakes* at the British School at Rome, 1932. The bronze head would be exhibited at the Royal Academy in 1934.

An unlikely pathway for a young architecture graduate immersed in the burgeoning modernism finding traction in 1930s England, Oakes's stint in Rome would prove enduring throughout his lifetime. For although the school's students were immersed in the history and culture of the western Mediterranean through fine art, archaeology and classical architecture, it was the interdisciplinary nature of its programmes and the friendships and connections formed whilst there that shaped Oakes's future career direction. Notable amongst these were the Rome Scholar for 1930, William Holfold (later Lord), and the school's Chairman, Sir Fredric Kenyon. Kenyon, although not present during Oakes's tenure, was influential in recommending him to the Commission after the war.

Adorned with a conspicuous neoclassical facade and originally designed by Lutyens as the British Pavilion for the 1911 International Exhibition of Art, the British School at Rome exuded an imperial confidence born of empire. With a Royal Charter issued in 1912, Lutyens's pavilion was granted in perpetuity by the Italian state to the British nation on condition that it be used exclusively as a British research centre. Its mandate was thus to promote knowledge of all aspects of the archaeology, art, history and culture of Italy by scholars and artists from Britain and the Commonwealth.[21] Students who entered the school by way of an architecture scholarship were required to undertake detailed studies of classical architecture. During the term of Oakes's residency, it was British archaeologist and academic Sir Ian Richmond, himself a former student, who headed the school.[22]

Oakes, upon accepting his scholarship, soon found himself travelling to the historic cities of Belgium, Germany and Austria before extensively touring Italy. Detailed measured drawings were produced of Roman temples and other classical buildings from archaeological surveys at Tivoli and Ostia. Further drawings would emanate from Siena, Florence, Vicenza, Vienna and Nuremberg. Indeed, Oakes's rendering, 'Restoration of Temple on the Acropolis at Lanuvium', would a few years later be selected for the Royal Academy Exhibition of 1934. The detail and quality of his work would also guarantee him an extension of a second year at the school. It was further opportunity to explore an architectural direction whilst also collaborating with fellow students on projects outside his discipline, notably painting, sculpture and archaeology.[23]

This period also provided Oakes an opportunity to undertake his first private commission, a small house and garden for the American

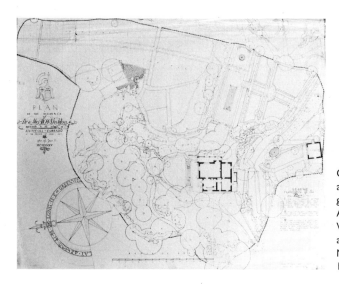

Oakes's design of a small house and garden for the American sculptor William Sheldon and his artist wife Noel in Anticoli, 1934

sculptor and teacher at the British School, William (Bill) Sheldon, and his artist wife, Noel. Situated just outside Rome in the northern hillside commune of Anticoli, the cottage was a modest cube of two levels with a separate studio some distance away. Working within the existing contours of the hilly site, Oakes introduced a rambling, informal landscape of local trees, shrubs and flowers, intercepted by formal grounds before the sweeping vineyards below. It was a clever insertion of the English garden sensibility, as often created by the horticulturist Gertrude Jekyll, within the dry, traditional Roman landscape of the region. The Sheldons would go on to become lifelong friends and a sounding board to the design ideas of a young architect.

By Oakes's second year in 1932, the British School was encountering severe challenges. On the one hand, funding problems had become acute through the Great Depression affecting the UK and the devaluation of its currency.[24] At the same time, the rise to power of Mussolini and his Fascist party had created for the school an atmosphere of isolation and dread. A single photo by Oakes captures this atmosphere succinctly: a group of young men in uniform are marching provocatively outside the academy's main entrance, bearing flags and singing the 'Giovinezza', the official hymn of the Italian National Fascist Party.[25]

It was a prelude to the turmoil that would engulf Italy and the rest of Europe less than seven years later.[26] It would also prove to be Oakes's last year in Italy before departing for home and a teaching position at the AA.

Architectural Association

After two years in Italy, Oakes returned in June 1933 to a Britain in the throes of a severe economic downturn, with great unemployment and its world trade falling by half. Taking what limited opportunities arose, he found work, alongside his father, as Chief Assistant at the Middlesex County Council, designing private and social housing. At the same time, Oakes commenced teaching part-time at the AA in London.[27] This proved to be the first of two appointments at the association. Indeed, for all his restlessness as a young architect, the war years to come and his subsequent work for the Commission, it was Oakes's embrace of the AA and his association with colleagues from wider Europe that would reinforce his design direction and prove his most enduring professional influence.

Long the vanguard of an independent architectural education in the UK, the AA had begun retreating from the Arts and Crafts and its short-lived dalliance with the Beaux-Arts by the turn of the 20th century. The early 1920s saw the school curriculum draw influence from the nascent modernism emerging through architectural developments in the Netherlands and Scandinavia. German and French modernism had also infiltrated design thinking at a time of conflicting ideals both within architectural education and the profession proper. By the late 1930s, the AA had become the country's first modernist school, discarding the last vestiges of its classical formalism and fully adopting a continental curriculum, emphasising teamwork, the metric system and a design teaching approach founded upon modernist ideals and theories.[28]

The student who once traversed the far reaches of his homeland, sketching and writing on the development of English church towers, would fully discard any lingering tendency to an aesthetic rooted in the past and return for a second time as Fifth Form Master after the war. Oakes's involvement with the ideological direction its design programme provided and the cohort of young architects emerging gave him an immense sense of self-satisfaction. This was amply demonstrated during the AA's centenary celebrations in December 1947. It was also the setting for French-Swiss architect Le Corbusier's concluding lecture on his theories of harmony, proportion and the Modulor, along with the presentation of his design drawings of the Unité d'Habitation in Marseilles and the United Nations Headquarters, New York.[29] Curating the accompanying exhibition of past works of the AA, Oakes with the assistance of his students would allocate a single studio and two rooms within Bedford Square to the past, whilst dedicating the entire upper floors to the contemporary works of the Association.[30]

Oakes's enthusiasm for the teaching of modern design was also no less due to the school's charismatic principal, Raymond Gordon Brown. Appointed upon release from army service in 1945, Brown was an active member of the Modern Architectural Research Group (MARS) and a decorated former Major of a parachute regiment who took part in the D-Day airborne assault of Normandy.[31] He would become Oakes's partner in private practice and, along with William Holford, one of his closest confidants. Returning to the UK and bringing with him many of the 1930s generation of students as staff, they were instrumental in the rapid

Raymond Gordon Brown

increase in student numbers and fostered an intensely creative environment. It was a mixture of school-leaving and mature students recently decommissioned from the services with the considerable experience only wartime could provide. Brown would subsequently bring his ideology and Scandinavian design staff with him to his next appointment

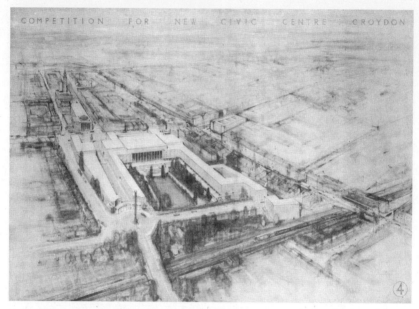

Oakes and Maxwell Allen's entry for the Croydon Civic Centre Competition, 1935

as the first Professor of Architecture at the University of Hong Kong, influencing a generation of young modernists in the Far East.[32]

After a year with his father at Middlesex, Oakes left to join the firm of Robert Furneaux-Jordan and Maxwell Allen as their Chief Assistant, having met Furneaux-Jordan, a prominent art critic, academic and broadcaster, at the AA, where he also lectured part-time.[33] Furneaux-Jordan, a significant figure in the modernist camp, would go on to become principal of the school, and is best known for his seminal books, *Le Corbusier* (1972) and the *Concise History of Western Architecture* (1984).[34] It was to prove a most productive association as by 1935 the economy was improving along with the sentiment for new commissions. In May, Oakes was awarded First Honorary Mention in the Croydon Civic Centre Competition in collaboration with Allen. Run by the south London borough of Croydon, the competition was to come up with a design for a civic centre on the site of the original Fair Field, a green space associated with public entertainment for the last five centuries.[35] Some of the leading architects of the day participated and though the winning design was never commissioned due to the onset of the war, Oakes's submission of a contemporary design proposal would mark his professional entry into the modernist realm. Subjected to air raids during the war, central Croydon would in its aftermath become renowned for modernist concrete highways, towering office blocks and multi-storey car parks that occupied landscape which had been destroyed by the war.[36]

That same year saw Oakes receive the Arthur Cates Prize for his design for 'The Promotion of Architecture in Relation to Town Planning'. In addition, his design for a cottage in Esher was shown at the Royal Academy Exhibition.[37] This cottage, following from his earlier

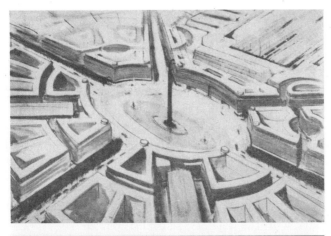

Oakes's winning design proposal for the Arthur Cates Prize, 'The Promotion of Architecture in Relation to Town Planning', 1935

Oakes's design for a cottage in Esher, shown at the Royal Academy Exhibition in 1935

domestic work at Anticoli, saw a more refined development of his modernist style, stripping the dwelling to its functional core and offsetting the standard classical elevation with an upper-level roofed balcony. By January 1936 Oakes would achieve another First Honorary Mention in his collaboration with Furneaux-Jordan in the Southern Rhodesia Houses of Parliament competition.

Yet this was all to change by the early spring of 1936, a few months before the Berlin summer Olympics. Nazism was by now well entrenched in Germany. Oakes finished up with Furneaux & Allen, resigned his appointment at the AA, and left for India as Assistant Architect to the Government of Bengal.[38] It would become his final foray overseas before the onset of hostilities. And yet, alongside his war service, this spell in South Asia would prove to have great relevance to his later recommendation and subsequent appointment as Principal Architect to the Imperial War Graves Commission.

Bengal

Bengal is a distinct cultural and historic region in the eastern part of the Indian subcontinent, cradled south of the mountainous regions of Nepal and most of western present-day Bangladesh. Calcutta, its largest city, was established as a trading post by the British East India Company, and served as India's capital under the British Raj from 1773 to 1911. It became the principal commercial, cultural and educational centre of East India, with the Port of Calcutta being the oldest operating port in the country and the centre for maritime trade to the interior through its riverine access.

The traditional architecture of Bengal, grounded stylistically over the past several centuries in the local, underwent a gradual shift during the colonial period (1858–1947). Promoted by the English-educated local gentry and the governing administration's British architects and engineers, the architecture was influenced by European forms and building techniques. This included religious buildings such as mosques, Hindu temples and tombs that were once firmly rooted in the local vernacular and influences from the surrounding empires. The

COLIN ST CLAIR OAKES

imported British architecture meanwhile was reflected in churches, mansions and public buildings, though often adapted for the tropical to sub-tropical climatic conditions. Traditional design elements in the British architecture were either included or excluded, depending on the desired image the ruling and wealthy classes wished to project.

The introduction of modern architecture in India can be traced to between 1920 and 1950, coinciding with the country's path to political independence. Jon Lang's *Concise History of Modern Architecture in India* informs that although architects in India were well aware of the stirrings in the European art and architectural scenes, as well as the influence of the Bauhaus, Le Corbusier and Frank Lloyd Wright, the modernist experimentation that did occur was largely the work of the British-trained architects and major architectural firms. While neo-classicism, Art Deco and modernist architectural theory were vying for attention in Europe, in India it was a simplified classicism and localised Art Deco that most often hinted at modernist intentions. Local Art Deco forms were often the integration of local elements and traditional Art Deco motifs in what Lang describes as a uniquely Indo-Deco architecture. What truly modernist buildings were erected in India from the 1930s to the early 1940s were few and predominantly the product of foreign architects who worked for wealthy clients with a cosmopolitan worldview. Indeed, throughout greater India and Bengal, the majority of building work was not designed by architects, but by master craftsmen known as *mistri*, who were mostly self-taught in design and construction.[39]

It was in this environment, in June 1936, that Oakes arrived in Calcutta, with its burgeoning economy, to take up his appointment as Assistant Architect within the Public Works Department to the Government of Bengal.[40] To appreciate the working context at the time, only a single architect – the Government Architect Thomas Edmondson – was found within the entire Bengal civil service. Important public commissions were routinely outsourced to British architectural firms within Bengal and greater India or overseas. Otherwise, the more rudimentary public infrastructure such as schools, police stations and hospital buildings were assigned to one of the many British-sourced senior engineers of the Public Works Department, with drafting staff assisting.

Edmondson, hailing from Lancashire, had arrived in Bengal in 1919 and by 1926 had ascended to the position of Government Architect. In January 1934, the Raj Bhavan (Government House) in Darjeeling was extensively damaged by an earthquake near the border of Nepal and Bihar. The subsequent decision to design and construct a new Government House near the site of the old would consume Edmondson for the next three years, hence the appointment of Oakes to cover the projected workload. Yet, in a twist of fate, within two months of Oakes's arrival, Edmondson would suffer a severe ailment, necessitating his leave of absence for an extended period.[41] Oakes found himself taking on the role of acting Government Architect and actively designing and administering a slew of public projects ranging from

Expansion of Dum Dum Jail, Calcutta, 1937

Artist's rendering of Sevoke-Teesta Bridge, spanning the Teesta River in Darjeeling District, West Bengal

the expansion of Dum Dum Jail and the Custom House in Calcutta to technical colleges in Dacca and Chittagong, and hospital wings, postal stations and police stations throughout West Bengal. He also assisted the renowned bridge engineer John Chambers by contributing to the design aesthetic of three bridges under construction: Cossye Bridge at Midnapore (Medinipur), Ichapur Khal Bridge (Ishapore), which crosses the Ganges River, and the iconic Sevoke-Teesta Bridge (also known as Coronation Bridge), which spans the Teesta River.[42]

During his two-year stay, Oakes also joined the Calcutta Light Horse Auxiliary Force, on account that during his young adulthood, alongside his passion for rugby and horses, he had been an active member of the Territorial Army, a branch of the Royal Engineers.[43] The experience of reservist training, time spent in India and his knowledge of greater Bengal would prove beneficial to the Army. Upon returning in 1938, he took an architecture role within the Territorial Army Branch of the War Office at Whitehall, where his talents were put

Colin and
Nancy, 1938

to use – designing barracks, drill halls, workshops and horse-riding
schools among others, in both London and the Midlands. This period
also saw him getting engaged and then marrying Nancy in April 1939,
whereupon a newly promoted Captain Oakes found himself posted to
Bengal once again. Coinciding with the onset of Japanese aggression
in the Far East two years later, Bengal would become the staging post
for an active engagement in the three-year battle along that north-east
Indian frontier and neighbouring Burma.

War in Burma
The invasion of Burma did not commence simultaneously with Japan's
7 December 1941 coordinated attacks on Pearl Harbour, the US territories of the Philippines, Guam and Wake Island, and the British
colonies of Borneo, Malaya and Hong Kong.[44] Aside from a few intermittent air raids along its border with Thailand, and the occupation of

a small airstrip near Burma's southern-most border town of Victoria Point, the first month after major hostilities erupted in Asia passed relatively uneventfully. Even the invasion of neutral Thailand, which saw fierce fighting in the south and lasted a mere five hours before ending in a ceasefire and its occupation, did not elicit great alarm with British forces headquartered in Rangoon.[45] While Japan had made its opening moves in its quest to establish the 'Greater East Asia Co-Prosperity Scheme',[46] it appeared that Burma, located to the far west of China and surrounded by difficult and roadless mountainous terrain and impenetrable tropical forest, would be spared the calamity befalling its eastern and south-eastern neighbours.

This all changed on 12 January 1942, when Japanese units from the Fifteenth Army, commanded by Lieutenant-General Shojiro Iida, launched an assault from south-west Thailand on the Burmese seaport of Tavoy. It was accompanied by a major incursion further north, with Japanese forces rapidly advancing towards Moulmein. British and local forces, under the command of Lieutenant-General Thomas Hutton, soon found themselves heavily engaged in defensive battles, all the while being pushed northwards, to avoid being encircled by superior numbers. By late February, the Japanese had forced the crossing of the Sittang River, closing in on the cities of Pegu and Rangoon. With all Allied operations now under the charge of General Sir Harold R.L. Alexander, British resistance with the support of a group of volunteer American airmen known as the Flying Tigers[47] tried to stem the tide, but on 7 March, Rangoon was abandoned. Even the introduction of two small Chinese armies, arriving over the Burma Road from China's far south-west Yunnan Province, proved unable to arrest the onslaught. With further Japanese forces arriving from their victorious campaigns in Malaya and Singapore, the inevitable was in sight. Falling back from their defence of Mandalay, the last major city still holding out, Allied forces crossed the Irrawaddy River in the north-west frontier, and blew up the bridge in the evening of 30 April. Further skirmishes and a desperate counterattack by Lieutenant-General William Slim's British Burma Corps allowed all remaining forces to cross the Chindwin

River at Kalewa, and continue their withdrawal across the mountains of north-west Burma.[48] By early May, approximately 12,000 British, Indian and Burmese survivors reached the India-Burma border, crossing through to Imphal in Manipur. This number represented less than one third of the total British forces that took part in the campaign, the remainder of which were killed or captured.[49]

Variously described as the only land campaign by the Allies in the Pacific Theatre conducted continuously from the beginning of hostilities to the end, the combination of mountainous jungle topography and the seasonal monsoons made conditions difficult to operate in. For almost half the year, from May to October, the monsoon winds originating in the Indian Ocean bring with them heavy rain, inundating the coastal lowland regions and the slopes of the Himalayan mountain ranges to the north. The rivers become swollen torrents, making passing them outside the few major bridges dangerous, whilst the populated valleys and rice-field plains become swamps. And with few all-weather roads, all other trafficable routes and trails become mud strewn and impassable, the effect being to grind transporting troops and military equipment and supplies to a standstill. Coupled with this, the Allied forces that had retreated to India under incessant fighting were demoralised, exhausted and dispirited. It would not be until the dry season of 1944 before they would consider another major operation and begin a concerted offensive to reclaim Burma.

Oakes landed in Calcutta in January 1942 and immediately took up his new appointment as Deputy Assistant Adjutant (DAA) to the Quarter Master General (QMG), the senior staff officer charged with providing supplies to the army. As a member of the Royal Artillery regiment, he was attached to Headquarters, 72nd Indian Infantry Brigade, part of the 36th British Division under the command of Major-General Francis W. Festing.[50] Over the course of the following year and a half, Oakes would be responsible for ensuring the supply and distribution of weapons, ammunition, fuel, food, medicines and other critical supplies, particularly to the north-eastern Indian frontier. These supplies shored up the fighting strength of those front-line units that had been

Oakes at the family
house in Tanyfron,
Wales, 1940

routed from Burma and were now massed from Cox's Bazar and Chittagong in the south through to Imphal, Dimapur, Kohima and Jorhat in the north. And by extension to their Allies, it would soon include US Lieutenant-General Joseph W. Stilwell's Chinese Army in India, which had crossed into Assam after retreating from the Japanese offensive.[51]

But Oakes's biggest challenge during that year and well into 1943 was in coordinating British efforts in support of urgent and regular American Lend-Lease supplies through torrential monsoons and treacherous mountain conditions to the town of Ledo in far north-east Assam.[52] With the Japanese occupation of most of north-eastern China and its seaports, and Burma now completely cut off, the need to supply vital war materials to Chinese forces to prevent their capitulation would see one of the most audacious air operations conducted. This slender link comprised a 500-mile aerial route from airstrips just outside Ledo, over a series of wild mountain ranges skirting the Himalayas in south-eastern Tibet, to Kunming in Yunnan province. Flying over mountain peaks rising to 20,000 feet with a few American-supplied Dakota transport planes, this route would be christened by those pilots who flew it as the 'Hump'.[53]

By May 1942, the Allied retreat back into India had been completed, accompanied by thousands of civilian refugees, mainly Indian and Anglo-Burmese. The pursuing Japanese forces, having reached the edges of a monsoon-swollen Chindwin River and its fast-flowing currents, halted their advance. What roads and tracks that ran between the mountainous frontier between India and Burma were rendered by this stage impassable. And yet British India Command, its Allies and their exhausted and demoralised forces feared the Japanese would soon resume their push towards India with the coming end of the monsoon. The ensuing military escalation, restriction of rice imports from Burma and rapid influx of population into the eastern provinces of Bengal, Bihar and Orrisa created an instability that was compounded by a growing widespread disorder. Acute food shortages that followed would a year later in 1943 evolve into the disastrous Bengal famine.[54]

A tentative first Allied attack into Burma after the Japanese occupation of the country, in December 1942, saw British forces commanded by Lieutenant-General Noel M.S. Irwin make minor advances into Arakan, the western coastal region. With a limited goal of capturing Akyab Island and its port and all-weather airstrip, the campaign faltered and Irwin's forces found themselves out-manoeuvred by an agile and superior Japanese offensive that had taken positions between the sea and foothills of the adjoining Mayu Ranges. Within four months, Irwin's forces found themselves cut off and fighting a desperate and vicious rear-guard retreat back through the valley. By this stage, Slim's Indian XV Corps headquarters which had been stationed in Ranchi, eastern India, were given charge of the Arakan front, shoring up what little resistance they were offering the Japanese. By 11 May, all territory gained in this short and ill-fated campaign was abandoned, with Slim's forces falling back to Cox's Bazar. The outcome would be more significant. Irwin was relieved of command, returning to Britain, and replaced by General George Giffard. Slim, promoted to Field Marshall and given command of the newly formed 14th Army,[55] set to work restoring the morale and fitness of his men and commenced planning for a major offensive a year later to retake the entire country.

As part of 14th Army's build-up for the major invasion of Burma in early 1944, Oakes was transferred to Chittagong in anticipation of an active front-line role. Meanwhile, the American-British Combined Chiefs of Staff had appointed British Admiral Lord Louis Mountbatten as the Supreme Commander of the newly created South East Asia Command, overseeing all activities in India, Burma and Ceylon. And following up on the lessons learnt from the Arakan defeat, Mountbatten wanted British forces better trained for jungle fighting. To achieve this confidence to face the Japanese in jungle conditions, another limited offensive was planned. It was decided that this offensive be again undertaken in the Arakan region, whilst Stilwell's main invasion offensive began in the north. And on 30 November 1943, three divisions of Slim's British XV Corps crossed into Burma and advanced towards Akyab, to face a heavily fortified Japanese 55th Division under the command of Lieutenant-General Tadashi Hanaya. Oakes and the 36th Division/72nd Infantry Brigade would follow soon after.

The second Arakan campaign would become a war of attrition and for a while it appeared it would suffer the same fate as the previous year's disaster. For the first two months, as British forces hammered the well-protected defences, Japanese reinforcements crossing through the mountain ranges managed to get behind British lines, cutting off both front-line divisions' communication lines. A second Japanese counterattack surrounded the 7th Indian Division, leaving isolated British units depending on emergency supply airdrops. They held their positions, though, and reinforcements from reserve were rushed to assist, counterattacking ferociously. The encircling Japanese forces soon found themselves surrounded and by 20 February were almost decimated. The pattern would continue over the following month, every position having to be bitterly fought over, with no quarter given by either side. By late March, the 36th Division had broken through the centre of Japanese lines, continuing their advance towards Akyab.

While Slim was pushing forward in the Arakan, developments further north became more dire. General Masakazu Kawabe had given the Japanese 15th Army, reinforced with troops released after the fall of Singapore, the mission of invading eastern India. On 6 March 1944, 100,000 veteran combat troops crossed the Chindwin River, with two divisions pushing towards Imphal, the third advancing further north to Kohima. This unexpected development had the effect of halting the British offensives in north Burma and the Arakan. Slim, fearing that the seizure of Dimapur on the Assam Railway would cut off supplies to the entire Allied central front, rushed all available reserves to Manipur to stem the invasion.

The 36th Division had meanwhile progressed cautiously to support the 5th Indian Division which had confronted the Japanese in the thick jungles of the hill country around Ngakyedauk and the Mayu Tunnels area. British forces had captured the small port of Maungdaw in early January, then turned their attention to two disused railway tunnels that provided a route through the hills, linking the town to Buthidaung in the Kalapanzin Valley. Engineers from the 7th Indian Division were then tasked with improving a narrow track known as the Ngakyedauk Pass across the hills so as to better reposition troops and resources for the next objective. On 5 February, Japanese forces infiltrated the front lines of the 7th Division and attacked their headquarters. The ensuing battle lasted almost three weeks, resulting in over 5,000 Japanese dead, many of whom were wounded and abandoned to die in the Japanese retreat on 26 February. Allied casualties would prove to be far greater. By late March, the 36th Division along with the 26th Indian Infantry Brigade resumed the offensive and after often fierce hand-to-hand combat, finally captured the railway tunnels on 4 April, followed by capturing the vital hill named Point 551 a few days later. The battle's conclusion on 3 May 1944 would to prove a major turning point in the war against the Japanese. Slim's XV Corps operations were then curtailed and diverted for the critical battles of Imphal and Kohima.

Major-General Francis Festing, commander of the British 36th Indian Division, decorating Major Colin St Clair Oakes with the ribbon of the MBE after the capture of Mongmit, Burma

Oakes's role in the fighting for the tunnels was duly recognised, with both Brigadier Alfred R. Aslett, Commander, 72nd Infantry Brigade, and Major-General Francis W. Festing, Commander, 36th Indian Division, recommending him for decoration. A year later, on 31 March 1945, Captain Oakes was awarded the Member of the British Empire (MBE) for his part in the campaign and promoted to Major.[56]

> During the fighting for the features covering the TUNNELS from 21 March to Apr 9, Major OAKES was always well forward, without regard to his personal safety, dealing with the problems of supply and evacuation of casualties.
>
> On no occasion have ammunition or supplies failed to reach their destination at the appointed time. That all objectives given to the Brigade were taken, was largely due to Major OAKES's unfailing energy and devotion to duty.[57]

Following the successful Arakan campaign, Slim's 14th Army moved on to the fighting in the mountainous regions of northern India, culminating in one of the most decisive battles of the war at Kohima in August 1944. Their success resulted in driving the last remnants of the Japanese Army, many of whom by that stage were suffering from disease, starvation and exhaustion, back across the frontier into Burma. The year ahead would see the army push back into Burma from the north and fight their way southwards to Rangoon – the reverse of the 1942 retreat. Subsequent battles around Imphal, Meiktila and Mandalay proved decisive in the Allied push to retake the Burmese capital. The 36th Division, after concluding operations on the Arakan front, were withdrawn and moved north to the Ledo Road area near the terminus of the Burma Road, where they would see further hard fighting around Myitkyina and Mogaung, before taking over from the remains of the Chindits.[58]

Towards the end of 1944, the by now seriously depleted Japanese forces were having to confront a reinvigorated and well-supplied Allied push across all three major fronts – the north, centre and south-west. Led by Slim's 14th Army, the final offensive to recapture Rangoon and effectively liberate Burma, code-named Operation Dracula, began in April 1945 with a concerted airborne and amphibious assault on the city by British, American and Indian forces. Lieutenant-General Hyotaro Kimura, commanding the principal Japanese headquarters in Burma from Rangoon, understanding well the futility of the senseless destruction of his remaining forces if forced to hold out to the death, ordered the evacuation of the city, commencing 22 April. Rangoon fell on 6 May, and the war in Burma that had commenced in December 1941 was effectively over.

The Allied casualties throughout the campaign would total 207,244, with British figures for killed or missing accounting for 28,878. The battles for Kohima and Imphal, through their significance as the turning point in the campaign, would account for almost 16,667 British casualties.[59] It was in this context of a gruelling campaign that turned the tide of the war against Japan that within a few years the towns of Imphal and Kohima would become sites for Oakes's most poignant war cemeteries, with comrades buried within.[60]

Yet like many who returned from the war, Oakes did not dwell upon nor talk about those experiences. Instead, he returned home in October 1945 to Nancy and his two children and embarked on the most important phase of his architectural career. For since graduating from Northern Polytechnic in 1929, his career, both by choice and circumstance, had been characterised by restlessness. Through numerous short spells working in various architects' offices within the UK and abroad. In further education at the Royal Academy, the British School at Rome and in teaching at the AA. From exploring early Nordic modernism in Finland, classical architecture throughout Italy and the reality of designing and administering a pared-down modern functionalism in Bengal, his design direction would be brought to focus with a maturity stemming from his war service.

On 2 November 1945, soon after being discharged from the army, Major Colin St Clair Oakes, MBE, ARIBA, was formally invited to undertake a three-month-long tour of the very regions he had recently lived and fought in, along with Thailand, Malaya and Singapore, on behalf of the Imperial War Graves Commission.[61] It would conclude in his being appointed a Principal Architect for the Commission, to undertake the design of numerous war cemeteries and memorials in the Asian theatre of the war.[62] This proved to be his defining body of work, bringing together all that he had learnt from his past. In accepting the position, he would follow in the footsteps of his predecessors Lutyens, de Soissons, Blomfield, Baker, Hepworth, Lorimer and Worthington. Unlike his predecessors, he would become the only Principal Architect who had served in the recent war.

CHAPTER 6

Singapore

Battle of Kranji

In the early evening of Friday, 9 February 1942, soldiers of the Japanese Imperial Guards Division, commanded by Major-General Takuma Nishimura,[1] launched a two-pronged assault on the north-western front of Singapore. It was little over two months since the invasion of peninsular Malaya and the simultaneous attack on the United States naval base at Pearl Harbour, precipitating the Americans' involvement in the Pacific War.[2] Observing proceedings from the height vantage of the Sultan of Johore's palace at Istana Bukit Serene, a mere mile from Singapore's northern coastline and now serving as his headquarters, Lieutenant-General Tomoyuki Yamashita[3], overall commander of the Imperial Japanese Army's 25th Army, could afford a wry sense of accomplishment. For not only had he correctly judged the reluctance of British forces in Singapore to fire upon Sultan Ibrahim's palace for fear of political repercussions between Johore's royal family and the British Colonial Office, but the much-vaunted defence lines of Malaya and now Singapore had so far been less than imposing.

Using specially adapted armoured landing-craft and collapsible boats, Nishimura's division crossed the Straits of Johore, the one-mile-wide body of water separating mainland Johore and Singapore island. One group landed at the mouth of the Kranji River and the other two miles to the east, where the Mandai River meets the Causeway linking

Singapore to Johore. Their objective was to establish a second foothold in Singapore after the successful landings the previous evening along Sarimbun Beach, a few miles further west, by almost 13,000 troops of the 5th and 18th divisions of Yamashita's 25th Army. This ten-mile stretch of marshy beach interrupted by numerous inlets and waterways, defended by only 3,000 men of the Australian 22nd Brigade under Brigadier Harold Taylor, was quickly overrun by the weight of numbers thrown into the assault by the Japanese. It was the culmination of a tactical ploy that had commenced with a diversionary attack on the small island of Pulau Ubin at the north-east end of the Straits, where 400 Imperial Guards had landed and taken the island two days prior, encountering minimal resistance.

The Kranji shoreline, from the mouth of the Kranji River to the Causeway, consisted of mangrove swamps and thick tropical jungle. Retreating British troops in attempting to slow the Japanese advance had on 31 January blown a gap within the Causeway, severing the sole road, rail and water connection to the mainland. The defence of this coastal stretch was assigned to the Australian 27th Brigade, under the command of Brigadier Duncan Maxwell, a former medical practitioner and veteran of the First World War. The brigade comprised three infantry battalions supported by a field artillery unit and a single platoon from the 2/4th Machine Gun Battalion that had only arrived in Singapore in the final days of the fighting on the peninsula. What numbers were available to Maxwell were bolstered by a single though inadequately trained and ill-equipped company of the local irregular militia, the Singapore Overseas Chinese Anti-Japanese Volunteer Army. Colloquially known as Dalforce by the British colonial administration, it was formed in December 1941 by Lieutenant-Colonel John Dalley of the Federated Malay States Police Force. Recruiting predominantly from among the ethnic Chinese community, it was made up of communists, nationalists and volunteers of varying ages and abilities. By the time of the Japanese invasion, Dalforce would draw upon a strength of 4,000 resistance fighters, though only a quarter of them were armed.[4]

*Sembawang
Naval Yards*

S. Simpang

*R.A.F.
mbawang*

*R.A.F.
Seletar*

Nee Soon
Rifle Range

S. Seletar

Punggol

Nee Soon

Nee Soon
Military Cemetery

S. Punggol

Pulau Ubin

seletar
e Range

S. Serangoon

SERANGOON HARBOUR

Changi

Leper Settlement

*Roberts
Barracks*

ce Reservoir

Melaik

*Mental
Hospital*

Changi POW
Cemetery
Selarang
Barracks

R.A.F.
Changi

Japanese
Cemetery

Changi
Gaol

Thomson

Wing Loong
POW Cemetery

Ritchie Reservoir

Caldecott
Hill Estate

Paya Lebar
Airfield
(Under Construction)

Bedok

Siglap

Thomson Road

Serangoon

inearn Road
es
ge

St. Patrick's
School

Singapore
Botanic
Gardens

Oldham
Hall

eorge's
urch

Kallang
Airport

Great World

Outram Road
Prison

General
Hospital

EL   HARBOUR

Pulau Brani

Pulau Blakang Mati

St. John's
Island

–·–·–·– International Border

▨ Natural Vegetation

☐ War Cemeteries

Having endured daily artillery shelling and aerial attacks since the beginning of February, intensifying in the days leading up to the invasion, the island now saw the fighting move to the ground stage. Amidst the initial onslaught, often at close quarters, the Allied resistance at Kranji proved fierce, with both sides sustaining high casualties. On the following morning, 10 February, the Japanese forces would suffer their heaviest losses in this campaign. Under sustained heavy fire from the Australian machine gun positions and mortars, the Japanese advance landing party moving up Kranji River found themselves wading through oil slicks discharged into the water body by the Allies emptying the nearby Woodlands oil depot. Ignited by the fighting, the fiercely burning oil inflicted heavy losses on Nishimura's forces, with many of his troops burnt alive. Such was the intensity of the battle and the Japanese forces' drive to accomplish their goals that Nishimura's request to call off the attack and retreat was refused by Yamashita.

Fearing being cut off by the Japanese troops that had landed at Sarimbun and further south-west at Jurong, Maxwell requested a withdrawal of his forces but was denied by the commander of 8th Division, Major-General Gordon Bennett. In the ensuing chaos and communication breakdown of that day, Maxwell ordered his soldiers and Dalforce volunteers to retreat from their positions at the Causeway.[5] Heading further south, they assumed new positions along the Jurong-Kranji defence line – a narrow ridge connecting the sources of the Jurong and Kranji Rivers and covering the strategic MacRitchie and Peirce Reservoirs. This had the effect of allowing the Japanese uncontested access to the shoreline.

Nishimura's forces, breaking out from their consolidated Kranji beachhead, now pushed forward in a two-pronged drive. One group moved towards Seletar Reservoir and Nee Soon to the south-east, the other towards Bukit Panjang to the south. Maxwell, now temporarily attached to the 11th Indian Division under orders of Lieutenant-General Arthur Percival, had new orders to counterattack and retake the abandoned positions at Kranji. Yet he claimed differing orders directing his brigade to move to recapture Bukit Panjang further west. The ensuing operation failed amidst the discipline and firepower of the strengthened Japanese forces, and what remained of the demoralised 27th Brigade retreated back to Singapore city.

The redeployment of the 27th Brigade had the unintended consequence of allowing the Japanese forces to pour onto the island, where they rapidly consolidated their gains through building up their numbers and heavy armour. Very quickly they captured the strategic crossing point at Woodlands and commenced repairs to the Causeway, which had been blown up by retreating British troops. The light Japanese tanks crossing over from the mainland unhindered, with their speed and agility well suited for the tropical terrain, proved decisive in the final push against the Commonwealth forces. Capturing both MacRitchie and Peirce Reservoirs with their water supplies intact, the inevitable was within reach. On 15 February 1942, a mere six days after the landings at Kranji, Lieutenant-General Percival, General Officer Commanding (GOC) Malaya Command and all British Forces, walking alongside his senior commanders under a flag of truce and the Union Jack, met his counterparts at the Ford Motor Factory.[6] It was here, at the foot of Bukit Batok Hill and in the presence of General Yamashita that Percival 'negotiated' the surrender of all Allied forces in Singapore. Over 85,000 British, Australian and Indian personnel would become prisoners of war. British Prime Minister Winston Churchill later called it the 'worst disaster' in British military history.

Sites of Significant Memories

Although no official policy of the Imperial War Graves Commission showed preference for sites of permanent war cemeteries that were the scene of significant battles, or had disturbing memories, the anecdotal evidence in many cases suggests an unofficial acknowledgement.[7] This tacit understanding would ensure the significance of site as an integral component of remembrance, connecting both the wider conflict and location of the fallen. It was certainly the case after the First World War when the various Commonwealth governments were tasked with considering suitable sites for their own national memorials. Those sites eventually chosen would prove significant to their men who had served and fought for their nation.

A case in point is the Australian National Memorial, Villers-Bretonneux, located within the village of the same name in northern France. Upon the end of the war in 1918, Lieutenant-General Sir Talbot Hobbs, senior Divisional Commander of the Australian Corps and a prominent Western Australian architect prior to enlisting, had been appointed to select the sites of several Australian memorials throughout Europe, prepare their designs and arrange for their construction.[8] In dedication to all those Australians who fell on the Western Front, Hobbs proposed a national memorial be erected in the Villers-Bretonneux area. The significance of this village lay in the role Australian forces played in the battle for its liberation from 24 to 27 April 1918, notably the 5th Australian Division commanded by Hobbs.[9]

In a similar vein, Colonel G. Helbert, the South African military attaché stationed in London after the war, visited France and Belgium to select a suitable site for South Africa's national memorial. Upon arriving at Delville Wood, place of the South African Infantry Brigade's first major engagement of the war in July 1916, he was struck by the scene of devastation. Once thick and dense with trees and foliage, the wood was now a desolate wasteland of craters, broken trees and abandoned trenches. Delville Wood epitomised for Helbert the sacrifice South Africa's men made for their country and the Commonwealth, suffering over 2,500 deaths in this battle alone. Fully comprehending the symbolic value of the place, Helbert on his own volition initiated negotiations for the 63-hectare Delville Wood with its owner, leading to its eventual purchase by the South African Government in 1920.[10]

Both Hobbs and Helbert clearly understood how places can convey symbolic meaning and recognised the significance in associating memorials and their subsequent commemorative services within these areas. With both men having the stature and ability to decide for their respective countries suitable sites for war cemeteries and memorials, they ran contrary to the Commission's established protocols. These were first put forward in a technical manual prepared by the Directorate of Graves Registration and Enquiries (DGR&E), precursor of the Commission.[11] Signed off by Brigadier-General Fabian Ware, then Director of DGR&E, the manual sets forth clear instructions to both management and site personnel on the procedures for establishing war cemeteries. Within Part II, under a sub-section titled 'Requirements for New Sites', the DGR&E sets out six points to guide the selection of sites for new cemeteries. They suggest minimum distances from the nearest buildings or ruins, that the site should not contaminate any water supply, should have ease of access from roadways, should not interfere with surrounding land uses, and should not obstruct existing roads and right of ways. The final point refers to selecting a site with a view to its economy – 'Where there is any choice of land, the poorer quality should be selected rather than the better quality, and arable land rather than pasture'.[12]

The selection of sites that had symbolic meaning also tended to deflect the perennial argument over the most fundamental of the Commission's principles: whether to return the remains home or leave them in foreign fields. The Commission itself had decreed from the outset that a 'higher ideal than private burial at home is embodied in these war cemeteries in foreign lands where those who fought and fell together, officers and men, lie together in their last resting place facing the line they gave their lives to maintain'.[13] Scholar Maria Tumarkin describes this connection through the war cemetery, assuming the tangible imprint left behind at a place of violent suffering, as 'traumascape'.[14] Places marked by these legacies tend to retain the awareness of this past trauma, which is often experienced and re-experienced over time. The physical setting thus provides the visual and sensory triggers that are capable of eliciting an emotional reaction from those that attend. 'It is through these places that the past, whether buried or laid bare for all to see, continues to inhabit and refashion the present.'[15]

Brigadier Obbard and Major Oakes, acutely aware of the significance of a site's history and its 'traumascape', placed it at the forefront of their decision-making process. Indeed, the Historical Section of the British Army's General Headquarters Command (GHC) in Delhi provided them directions on selecting likely sites taking into account key battles and engagements. In their 1945–46 journey across the numerous battlefields of Asia, most of the sites they recommended for permanent war cemeteries were selected in this manner. Kohima and Imphal in India, Chungkai and Kanchanaburi in Thailand, Than-byuzayat in Myanmar, and Sai Wan Bay

Brigadier Harry Naismith Obbard

in Hong Kong are the most notable examples.[16] Those cemeteries that were not selected in accordance with this ideal were inevitably the compromise as a result of ongoing conflict or inaccessibility in those locations originally preferred, or both.

Kohima, a small city in India's north-eastern border state of Nagaland, best exemplifies the recognition of a significant battle site as the location for a permanent war cemetery and memorial. It also demonstrates Oakes's considered architectural response. The Japanese offensive into India from Burma was stopped in some of the most bitter fighting of the war amongst the hilly terrain surrounding Kohima. Often referred to as the 'Stalingrad of the East', the battle would eventually cripple Japanese ambitions to occupy India along with their defence of Burma, considering their huge losses amounting to 5,746 casualties.[17] Pushing through the border town of Imphal, some 85 miles to the south, the primary Japanese advance along the Imphal-Kohima Road was confronted by desperate and besieged British and Indian troops dug in along the ridgelines. In one significant encounter, the garden and tennis court of the Deputy Commissioner, Charles Pawsey, at his bungalow high upon Garrison Hill in the centre of the city, was the setting of fierce hand-to-hand combat.[18] The opposing front lines were on either side of this 27-foot-wide court, with

Sai Wan War Cemetery, Hong Kong, c. 1956

one soldier describing the scene as the 'nearest approach to a snowball fight... [the] air became thick with grenades, both theirs and ours and we were all scurrying around trying to avoid them as they burst'.[19] Not only was Kohima selected as a permanent war cemetery, but Oakes identified the Deputy Commissioner's tennis court as a significant feature from that battle and requested its permanent preservation. The tennis court would subsequently be integrated within the overall design of the cemetery. The Cross of Sacrifice, abutting the edge of the court, was elevated on a stone plinth, allowing for a visitors' shelter beneath. Imphal, which saw the Allies' major counter-offensive back into Burma, would similarly become a permanent site.[20]

Kohima War Cemetery, Nagaland, India: The Cross of Sacrifice is elevated above a visitors' shelter, with the tennis court in the foreground.

Thanbyuzayat in Burma, and Chungkai and Kanchanaburi in Thailand, on the other hand, became permanent war cemeteries through trauma of a different sort. These three towns are associated with significant base camps that were located at either end of the notorious 258-mile-long Siam-Burma Railway, and housed the thousands of Commonwealth, Dutch and American prisoners of war forced to build it. Commencing in Ban Pong, Thailand, and ending in Thanbyuzayat, the railway was intended to provide the Japanese Army an alternative supply route to their forces in Burma, thus avoiding the vulnerable sea route around the Malay Peninsula and Straits of Malacca. Approximately 61,000 Allied prisoners of war collected from throughout the Japanese-occupied territories, along with almost 250,000 Southeast Asian civilian labourers (*romusha*),[21] were subjected to forced labour to construct this line. Completed and opened in 1943, the desperate living and working conditions along with the numerous atrocities would eventually claim over 90,000 civilian and 12,000 Allied prisoner deaths. These men were buried in the numerous prisoner-of-war

Kanchanaburi War Cemetery, Thailand: Entrance portico

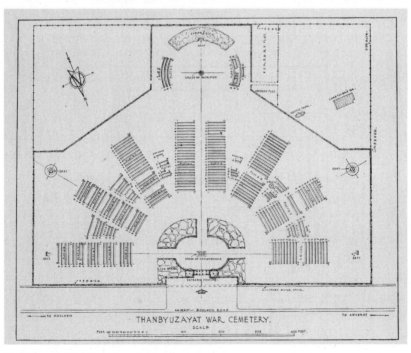

Thanbyuzayat War Cemetery, Burma: Layout plan

camps, burial grounds and lone graves dotting the entire length of the railway. Upon liberation with the end of the war, British and Australian Graves Registration Units that were rushed there began the onerous task in difficult conditions of locating and consolidating the remains. Under the command and direction of Colonel Eric Foster Hall of DGR&E, the remains of those who died during the construction and maintenance of the railway were painstakingly collected from all 144 burial sites scattered along

Eric Foster Hall

the route and brought to the three designated concentration burial grounds at Thanbyuzayat, Kanchanaburi and Chungkai. These three sites would then become permanent war cemeteries. Foster Hall's experience gained from the Siam-Burma Railway was soon directed to other former conflict areas in Asia before turning to Singapore.[22]

Singapore

Arriving in Singapore on 6 January 1946, Obbard and Oakes were greeted by the same scenario they had encountered elsewhere along the tour, namely local populations emerging from years of occupation and its deprivations, thousands of servicemen being demobilised from active duty or incarceration and awaiting repatriation home, and an accounting of the many who were either missing or presumed deceased. The most significant organisation on the ground other than the graves units was in fact RAPWI – Recovery of Allied Prisoners of War and Internees. The army had created this group to cope with the recovery of the thousands of former Allied prisoners of war that suddenly found themselves liberated. Mandated to take control of all prisoner-of-war camps and organise medical teams to take care of the ailing along with recovering any surviving camp records, they also set about apprehending enemy personnel charged with maltreatment of the prisoners. But their most critical task was to dispatch the nominal rolls of survivors to the various Allied governments to inform waiting families of the fate of their loved ones.[23]

Meeting with Foster Hall, who had recently arrived from initiating recovery operations in post-surrender Japan, Shanghai and Hong Kong, and Lieutenant-Colonel Athol Brown of the Australian War Graves Organisation, RAPWI officers briefed them on the recovery and concentration work in progress. This was being undertaken by both British and Australian graves recovery units. Brown himself had been urgently dispatched from Australia the previous day to receive them and would prove crucial in their deliberations, given the sensitivity with which the Australians had come to view the fall of Singapore and the proximity of the conflict to home. For the Australians, Singapore became the interface between their sphere of influence and that of the old empire. Meanwhile, recovery efforts and planning for war cemeteries had commenced in Borneo, Celebes (Sulawesi), Amboyna (Ambon Island), New Guinea and New Britain.

Foster Hall was a young officer with the East Kent Regiment at Ypres on the Western Front during the First World War when he was wounded by a shell and evacuated back to England. It was during a raid on German trenches in 1916 that he sustained his injuries and for which he was subsequently awarded the Military Cross. Upon recovery, he was promoted to the rank of Captain, and he returned to the front, capturing a German prisoner, witnessing the Canadian assault on Vimy Ridge and again being wounded in action the following year during the Battle of Messines. His post-war recovery sojourn in Singapore, initially as Staff Officer then Brigade-Major to the Straits Settlement Volunteer Forces (SSVF), made him an ideal candidate to head up the Directorate of Graves Registration and Enquiries for Asia upon the commencement of the Second World War. Heading the Grave Registration Units and Grave Concentration Units following the withdrawal of Japanese forces from first Burma then Thailand, Foster Hall then oversaw the efforts to locate and identify the thousands of prisoners of war who perished on the Siam-Burma Railway. Along with negotiating the difficulties encountered in the mountainous terrain of Burma, he went on to set out a series of organisational and identification lessons from the recovery work in the tropics.[24] His experience gained from Burma, Siam and Malaya would extend to Singapore, and in the early days after the Japanese surrender he organised the temporary concentration of Allied remains within existing cemeteries established by the prisoners of war during the occupation. It was a provisional solution until a decision was made as to the site of the permanent war cemetery.

Over the next seven days, with the accompaniment of Major-General Kenneth McLean, Deputy Adjutant General, HQ Far East Land Forces, and Major-General Reginald Denning, Public Affairs Officer to the Supreme Allied Commander (SAC) South East Asia, the party visited the Allied burial grounds across the island. McLean and Denning, both career soldiers, had recently led the planning of Operation Overlord and the D-Day landings at Normandy respectively, before their secondment to the Far East. They represented the Army and were the direct conduit to SAC Lord Louis Mountbatten, based in Kandy, Ceylon. All decisions regarding war graves in Singapore were suitably relayed back.[25]

War Cemeteries

The seven former prisoner-of-war and military burial sites scattered across Singapore and visited by the officers were located at Buona Vista, Melaik, Wing Loong, Changi, Nee Soon, Point 348 and Kranji. These sites had become temporary concentration cemeteries in the immediate aftermath of the surrender, accommodating the remains of servicemen collected directly from the field and other isolated graves, and were still active as more remains were uncovered throughout the island. They also accommodated the discovered remains of victims of massacres for whom an immediate identification was not possible, with classification as Commonwealth servicemen, local irregulars or civilians determining their burial requirements. As such, each site was in its own right representative of a war cemetery, making the task of consolidating them into a single or two sites all the more difficult. Obbard and Oakes, taking notes for their reporting back to London, were also morally and ethically obliged to consider the future needs of a small, land-scarce island just emerging from years of occupation and beginning its long path to reconstruction. Although no re-concentration of graves on a large scale had yet begun, their primary task was to critically assess the suitability of the existing burial sites and select one or two in which all the Allied war graves on the island could be consolidated and re-interred permanently.[26]

The western-most cemetery visited, Buona Vista, was situated high up in a cluster of small hills at Pasir Panjang, about five miles to the west of the main harbour on Dover Road. One of two British military cemeteries, the other being in Ulu Pandan, it would come to be formally known as the Pasir Panjang Military Cemetery from 1948 onwards. Along with graves from the 1907–1947 period that had been transferred from the Bidadari Christian Cemetery, the authorities had used its grounds for the temporary burials of those men who had died in the fighting for Pasir Panjang. In early February 1942, the Japanese advance on this elevated ridge-line initiated the Battle of Pasir Panjang, the final stage in the Japanese campaign to capture Singapore. Defended with a grim tenacity by the Malay Regiment and suffering heavy casualties in the often hand-to-hand fighting, the over-running of these hills and subsequent capture of Bukit Chandu (Opium Hill) nearby allowed the Japanese unchallenged access through to the Alexandra area with its British army barracks and military hospital. It culminated in the infamous massacre of civilian and military patients at Alexandra Hospital.

The scene confronting Oakes and his party as they visited the devastated terrain of the Pasir Panjang and Buona Vista battlefields was a landscape of blasted trees, but carpeted by the many wild flowers of the tropics. While noting its 'excellent views out to the sea', Oakes's initial assessment also identified its sandy clay soil and water run-off issues, which adversely influenced the layout of providing for further graves and made maintaining them problematic.[27] Over the next 30 years, situated within the wider Pasir Panjang military complex, the cemetery would serve as a reminder of the last major battles of the war before the surrender. By 1975, with the British forces withdrawing a few years earlier in 1971 and the Kranji Military Cemetery established, all its graves were exhumed and, along with those from Ulu Pandan, transferred to the north. The site reverted back to the state.[28]

The Melaik burial ground was situated within the greater Yio Chu Kang area.[29] It was the most centrally placed cemetery on the island, yet it made an 'unfortunate' choice, according to both Obbard and Oakes. Enclosed within the dense Singapore United Plantation rubber estate, it was hemmed in on three sides by building development. On the fourth side across the road, it adjoined the Mental Hospital and Singapore Leper Asylum.[30] The cemetery was in fact established by Allied prisoners of war for use primarily by the hospital and occasionally by the leper settlement. After Singapore surrendered to the Japanese, the seriously wounded patients from the General Hospital were transferred to the Mental Hospital, which had been requisitioned as the Japanese Civilian and Military Hospital. Although a great number of the mentally ill were sent off to St John's Island, where many starved to death, approximately 1,000 who remained were locked up and neglected. It was now used by the Royal Air Force from Seletar Airfield nearby to treat wounded Allied servicemen and Japanese prisoners of war.[31]

Over at the eastern end of the island, approached by a narrow, semi-private road that otherwise served the coastal village of Kampong Ayer Gemuruh and a cluster of ten grand waterfront bungalows, the Wing Loong prisoner-of-war cemetery was the second such burial ground in the immediate area. The other was located adjacent to the Changi Prison, less than a mile to the north. Small rubber and coconut groves surrounded the idyllic site, along with older Chinese and Malay cemeteries nearby. There were also the dusun[32] plantations to one side and the aerodrome's expanding runways to the other. The cemetery was within the former Wing Loong Estate, part of prominent businessman Ng Sen Choy's vast landholdings named after his High Street tailoring store. As President of the local Boy Scouts Association, prior to the war Ng had donated five acres of his land to establish a permanent campsite for the Scouts, named Purdy Camp. With the onset of the Japanese Occupation, the camp was requisitioned for burials, and prisoners of war from the British 18th Division were put to work using what materials were available from the former camp to establish the cemetery. They also built, at one end, a lychgate – a traditional entrance shelter for the bier or movable frame on which a coffin or a corpse is placed before burial and carried to the grave. While the cemetery layout was designed by Major Harper of the Royal Engineers, the lychgate was conceived by Captain Cecil D. Pickersgill and built by men from the 18th Division. By war's end, the remains of 581 British and Dutch prisoners of war and civilians would pass through this gate to be interred within its grounds. The Japanese closed the cemetery in October 1944 on account of its capacity being reached.[33] Yet for all its significance to the prisoner-of-war experience, it was the commanding sea views out to the Straits of Singapore that were its main attraction, according to Oakes and Obbard. But considering this site as a likely permanent war cemetery was predicated on the Commission gaining access rights to the extension of land across the road and additional sea-fronting land to the south. It would be ruled out due to the difficulty of acquiring this land.[34] The graves at Wing Loong Cemetery were exhumed in 1952 and reburied at Kranji, whilst the lychgate was dismantled and re-erected outside St George's Church in Tanglin Barracks.

On sloping ground facing the Seletar River estuary, about 400 yards from the main road, the Nee Soon Military Cemetery contained 350 Malay Muslim graves and a small number of Indian Christian burials. To the north-west, an adjoining plot contained the cremated remains of 400 Hindus. Across the road directly west was the Joraneu Cemetery, a larger site of Javanese civilian graves. Catering to the nearby British army base at Nee Soon and Dieppe Barracks, both of which had become prisoner-of-war camps during the occupation, the cemetery was also within the outskirts of Kampong Pengkalan Petai, a small waterfront village encircled by petai, pineapple and rubber plantations. Though both burial grounds were ostensibly for Muslims, the segregation of Joraneu from the Malay graves across the road highlighted the various social distinctions inherent in Singaporean society at the time, where the Bugis, Javanese, Baweanese, Dusun and Orang Laut among others sought separate identities.

There was also a dark history to the Nee Soon cemetery, one that involved war crimes. In January 1945, an American B-29 Superfortress bomber aircraft was shot down over Singapore and its crew taken prisoner. A few months later in July, the Japanese warship *Kamikaze* similarly shot down another aircraft, this time a PBY Catalina flying boat, with its crew of eight also imprisoned at the Seletar Naval Base. On two separate occasions, sometime between February and August that same year, the crew of the B-29 and the Catalina were taken to the nearby Nee Soon Rifle Range and executed, their bodies buried in the cemetery. Soon after the Japanese surrender, a decision was made to dig up those deceased prisoners of war and burn the remains. Although it could not be established from whom the execution orders emanated, Vice-Admiral Fukudome Shigeru, Rear-Admiral Asakura Bunji and Commander Ino Eiichi would be charged as accessories after the fact because they attempted to suppress and destroy all evidence of the execution.[35]

Oakes identified Nee Soon as both a 'pleasant and suitable' site for a war cemetery, and along with Obbard decided that rather than create the main permanent war cemetery here, given the large number of existing Muslim graves it would be better retained as the permanent Muslim War Cemetery.[36] There was one problem, though, and that was the considerable number of Hindu cremated remains buried in individual graves. Foster Hall, conversant with cremation practices through his experiences in India and Burma, would propose their removal and scattering in accordance with Hindu customs.[37]

Lying at the eastern tip of the island, somewhat centred between the 5,000 yards' distance from Changi Gaol to the south to Changi Beach in the north, Changi cemetery would become Obbard's original choice for the Combined Allied Christian War Cemetery in

Singapore.[38] Its well-tended graves told a difficult history that was well-suited for memorialisation. Established during the Japanese Occupation by the prisoners of war from the surrounding Selarang and Changi camps, it consisted of two main plots spaced 200 yards apart on a gentle slope, with a commanding mound behind it, formerly the site of a 15-inch artillery gun. The one to the south was the Australian plot, containing 150 war graves, while the other was a combined British-Dutch plot of 850 graves.

It was arguably the most symbolic of sites within Singapore, the one that best captured the ill-fated battle of Singapore and its surrender. Those interred within its grounds fell into two groups: those servicemen who succumbed to their battle wounds sustained in the final days while defending Singapore; and those who died as prisoners of war during three years of malnutrition, disease and torture. All

Watercolour painting of Changi POW Cemetery by Dutch artist and prisoner of war Henk Brouwer, 31 May 1943

these victims had passed through either the Australian General Hospital or British General Hospital units that had re-formed within the wider camp upon the surrender.[39] And unlike some of the other sites across the island that had to contend with hastily accommodating the dead during the fighting, often rudimentarily, the deceased at Changi were accorded a funeral and a marker identifying them. Each Australian grave was marked with a small concrete cross and a copper plate inscribed with only the army service number – no names – mounted on its face. British graves contained small timber crosses with the name and rank painted on.[40] The cemetery was also the site for the earliest commemoration service post-surrender. On a Sunday, 13 September 1942, staff members of the 13th Australian General Hospital and fellow prisoners of war gathered in the cemetery grounds, where Major Bruce Hunt took the parade and marched with 150 men to the gravesides. The men formed a hollow square, the commanding mound serving as backdrop, and hymns were sung after the laying of a red wreath.[41]

Indeed, the former gun mound was, in Obbard's opinion, appropriate as the site of the Memorial to the Missing, 'standing conspicuously above the cemetery and visible for many miles in all directions'.[42] Obbard would even have Denning promise to arrange for its allocation. But its location would prove limiting for further expansion. Adjoining the site to the north and east were the runways of the Changi aerodrome, which the Royal Air Force was urgently enlarging for international airways. This development would preclude Changi being considered further, and indeed the existing graves would have to be removed and re-interred.

Kranji, established within the grounds of a former prisoner-of-war hospital, was located to the north of the island, overlooking the Johore Straits. Eventually the confirmed site by the Imperial War Graves Commission, it was not preferred by those who assessed its suitability. Obbard and Oakes would not even consider the location as a possibility. 'Difficult cemetery to expand and situation not exceptional,' reported Oakes.[43] Obbard identified Kranji and Buona Vista as being

Kranji Prisoner-of-War and Hospital Cemetery, c. 1945

'surrounded by jungle and are on very sandy soil, and would be costly to construct; further ... there are no special historical associations with these two sites at Buona Vista and Kranji.'[44] It would in fact be a small yet prominent hill at the centre of Singapore island that captured Oakes's imagination. It would also meet most of the conditions necessary for its likely recommendation.

At a height of 104 feet, Point 348, also known as Bukit Batok Hill, was not the tallest hill in Singapore. That claim would go to Bukit Timah. But it was one of the tallest on an island with limited high ground. It also overlooked the Ford Motor Factory, site of the Allied surrender to the Japanese. Tall and conical in shape, it was situated centrally beside the main road connecting Singapore town with the Causeway. The summit had been levelled and a wide macadam road built to access it, along with extensive terracing, all built by Australian prisoner-of-war labour.[45] During the early days of the occupation, the Japanese used the same labour force to erect a war memorial and Shinto shrine, Syonan Chureito, on its summit to commemorate their war dead. Comprising an almost 40-foot-tall (12 metres) timber pillar with prayers for the dead inscribed along the side, the shrine allowed

143

the military and Japanese officials to worship the Emperor of Japan and the spirits of their fallen comrades.[46] And in a rare gesture to the prisoners, they would accede to their request to build their own memorial to their dead, consisting of a 15-foot-tall wooden cross behind the main shrine. After the surrender, the Japanese destroyed their shrine in accordance with their customs rather than have it desecrated, but they left the Allies' memorial intact. The British soon after completed the destruction of what remained, while also retaining the timber cross, though its whereabouts thereafter could never be ascertained. Only two entrance pillars and a series of 120 steps leading to the summit remained when the officers arrived to assess it.[47]

Yet, unlike the other burial grounds visited, Point 348 was neither a battlefield nor a cemetery, nor did it contain the remains of Allied servicemen. It was solely a place of significant commemoration to both the Japanese Army and the Allied prisoners of war alike. Indeed, such was its significance that Japanese public broadcaster NHK produced a short 50-second newsreel of the Syonan Chureito's unveiling on 18 September 1942, a mere six months after the surrender of Singapore. Featuring a Shinto priest officiating beneath the tall timber column of the memorial, partially draped in billowing fabric, officers and soldiers of the Imperial Japanese Army are seen standing to attention whilst wreaths are placed and prayers offered. This carefully orchestrated propaganda film then turns to show Australian prisoners of war ascending the main stepped axis towards the monument, then deviating to offer wreaths of their own to a smaller timber cross monument on a stone pedestal. The film ends with a combined party of Japanese and Allied servicemen standing to attention and holding a salute to both memorials, as if it was a benign annual commemorative event.[48] The significance of these two memorials on this hill, hastily destroyed by the British Army upon its recapture of the island, would not have gone unknown to Obbard and Oakes.

In his detailed report submitted to the Imperial War Graves Commission, Oakes identified Point 348 as the site most suited for the development of the permanent war cemetery in Singapore:

The site is one of the most impressive imaginable. From the summit, the views across the whole island, and to the sea beyond are superb. ... Taking into consideration all factors, POINT 348 is probably the best site for the proposed Allied Christian Cemetery. With it could well also be combined a Memorial to the Missing from that theatre of operations.[49]

The 'factors' Oakes referred to were three minor difficulties he foresaw in shaping the hill for its new role as a war cemetery. Aside from the existing levelled terracing being unable to accommodate the almost 2,500 estimated war graves, there was the 'large unsightly factory with tall chimneys, which at present disfigures the main axis and proposed cemetery approach'.[50] Both challenges were not insurmountable to Oakes. For the provision of additional war graves, he recommended levelling the lower slopes of the hill and creating further terracing. A sketch of the suggested layout was subsequently issued to the Deputy Director Graves Registration & Enquiries so as to commence filling the existing terraces. As to the 'unsightly' Ford Motor Factory, the introduction of a gently sloping carriageway winding around the hill along with suitable plantings would screen it.[51]

It was the third difficulty that would prove more problematic and ultimately insurmountable. Considering the hill's recent difficult history, Oakes noted that 'its previous association as an enemy memorial might be considered objectionable'.[52] This would also be the case with Obbard's initial reservations regarding Point 348. But unlike Oakes, who insisted on its merits from the outset and offered a design proposal for its initial preparation and the concentration of war graves, Obbard was more understanding of the politics associated with this likely site. In his initial report to his supervisors, prepared and dispatched whilst in Singapore, Obbard had determined that Changi would be the preferred choice for the war cemetery, with Nee Soon to be retained for the Muslim war graves. As to his opinion on the others, 'there are no special historical associations with these two sites at Buona Vista and Kranji'. But by the time he and Oakes reached

Colombo on their return leg home, they were informed by Foster Hall that an additional allotment of area required for establishing a war cemetery at Changi had not been secured. Instead, the Royal Air Force had demanded the removal of the existing graves in the cemetery as they were pushing on with the development of the air base. Obbard would go on to revise his recommendation in line with Oakes.[53]

> This hill forms actually the best of all the sites we saw for a cemetery. We did not suggest it in the first place because its previous use as a Japanese memorial hill might be regarded as objectionable; but, if the Changi site is not available, then we strongly recommend the adoption of this hill site, on which a most impressive cemetery can be formed, and on which also a memorial to the missing could very well be set up. The advisory architect is preparing a suggested layout on this site.[54]

And in a sign of consensus with the Australian War Graves Service, the selection of Point 348 would also be acceded to by Brown.[55]

Amidst the chaos of the first few months after the sudden end of the war, with an urgency in demobilising men, accommodating surrendered combatants and organising graves recovery and registration units throughout the region, the Commission recommended Changi as the permanent war cemetery for Singapore. This decision carefully avoided the sensitivities Point 348 would have generated amongst locals and returned service personnel. But it would be a short-lived decision, for Headquarters Air Command South East Asia had dug their heels in, proceeding with extending Changi, and would not guarantee building near the earmarked site. Kranji, an option both Oakes and Obbard had placed well down on their lists, with 'no historical association' in their opinion, was selected as a suitable compromise.

Work on establishing Kranji as the military cemetery began in April, with all available clues to grave sites in Singapore being followed up. Search work by the Graves Units dispatched from Australia and UK

Kranji Military Cemetery, 1947, with the Japanese prisoner-of-war camp next to it. The hill Bukit Mandai is visible in the background.

was continuing but with most of the fighting having taken place in the mangrove swamps and overgrown forests of the north-east, the lack of available manpower for clearing made progress slow. Large communal burial sites containing civilians and Service dead discovered within the grounds of the General Hospital had been consecrated by the Bishop of Singapore after the Japanese Occupation. These sites were being left undisturbed, awaiting a decision on their final interment. Elsewhere, returning Singaporean residents would assist the effort to locate and often identify graves and remains. It would be the end of 1946, 16 months after the Japanese surrender, before all isolated graves on the island were concentrated.[56]

CHAPTER 7

Kranji

Little more than a month after the Imperial War Graves Commission formally named their second war burial ground in Malaya[1] as the Singapore (Kranji) Military Cemetery, the site was engulfed in an international controversy. On 10 July 1947, the recently appointed Secretary-General of the Commission's Anzac Agency in Melbourne, Brigadier Athol Brown, telegraphed headquarters in London a strongly worded memorandum. It informed them that numerous local newspapers were reporting on the 'disgraceful condition [of] Kranji Military Cemetery, and that the [Australian] Government was taking a very serious view of this'.[2] The note went on to request 'strong representations be made to the War Office, firstly to ensure cemetery satisfactorily maintained secondly, to remove the Japanese P.W. [Prisoner of War] Camp from immediate vicinity of Cemetery'.[3]

Located on a small hill in the north of Singapore overlooking the Straits of Johore, Kranji cemetery also accommodated a small Japanese prisoner-of-war camp at its base, adjacent to the main access. Service personnel of the No. 61 Graves Concentration Unit resided in tents half a mile away.[4] Amidst the pending break-up of the camp and the repatriation of its inhabitants back to Japan, on three consecutive Sunday afternoons Japanese 'surrendered personnel'[5] who were otherwise employed in outside work during the day ascended the top of the hill, consumed their lunch rations, and discarded their refuse. A correspondent for Reuters-AAP[6] visiting the cemetery along with another Australian would report finding a 'couple of empty beer bottles, and scores of empty cans scattered round one section of the Australian Graves'.[7] They also went on to clarify that a party of British soldiers tasked with maintaining the general tidiness of the cemetery cleared up the debris the very next day. But within a few days, Australia awoke to the front page of most newspapers carrying such evocative headlines as 'Jap Beer Parties Among Australian War Graves', 'Japs Desecrate Australian Graves in Singapore', and 'War Cemetery Defiled'. Stoking widespread anti-Japanese sentiment, the papers paraphrased quite liberally that returning with their 'stolen' food and drink, the 'Japs were being allowed to picnic amongst the graves'.[8] Compounding the coverage, unrelated earlier incidents were introduced, further exacerbating the already inflammatory tone. In one, a former Australian Imperial Forces (AIF) army major, veteran of the Middle East and New Guinea, visiting the grave of his brother at Kranji, was challenged by a Japanese as he tried to drive through the prisoner-of-war camp to access the cemetery. His reaction was to inform the internee that should he not stand aside, he would drive right over him. Another local resident recounted how visitors to Kranji cemetery 'including women, [had] to pass within a few feet of them, where practically naked Japs [strolled] round wearing only loincloths'.[9]

Although quite incendiary in nature, in 1947, this could hardly be considered an unexpected reaction by an anxious general public, given it was just two years since the war ended. This was a nation where almost one in every seven served in the armed forces. The war against Japan had been conducted on Australia's doorstep, and was viewed as an existential fight against the belief at the time of an imminent invasion. The submarine attacks in Sydney Harbour and the bombing of Darwin only served to reinforce this intention.[10] At the same time, the fall of Singapore and capture of Malaya and the Dutch East Indies had shaken the confidence of a country well aware of the generational losses suffered from the First World War. Over 22,000 Australians would become prisoners of war of the Japanese in Southeast Asia, of whom some 8,000 would die whilst in captivity.[11] Then there were the numerous stories emerging from returning inmates of Changi Prison, those who served on the Siam-Burma Railway, combatants along the Kokoda Track in New Guinea and those who survived the Sandakan death marches in Borneo. In the popular imagination of a war-weary nation, this minor incident at Kranji elevated what would otherwise have been one of many discreet war cemeteries in a foreign land as another indelible monument of sacrifice and national identity.

Kranji Prisoner-of-War Camp

Prior to the outbreak of war, Kranji had hosted a temporary military camp, located less than a mile north of the hill which would become the future cemetery. Built by local contractors in the 1930s for the British armed forces, the Kranji Army Barracks was one of many such facilities erected throughout the island after the First World War, in light of the perceived military threat stemming from an ascendant Japan. A second camp for the Royal Navy's radio communications was established at the same time, less than two miles to the south-west, nestled between rows of rubber trees; the tributary Sungei Pang Sua off Sungei Kranji was to the immediate west and another water body, Sungei Mandai, to the east. The barracks' southern boundary abutted the Keretapi Tanah Melayu (KTM)[12] railway line to Johore where it intersected Kranji Road, with the small Kampong Kranji settlement lying to the north.

With the onset of the Japanese invasion of Malaya in December 1941, the camp was hastily appropriated by the AIF as their Battalion Headquarters and ammunition magazine. This was to prove short-lived, with its capture by the Japanese Imperial Forces early on in the battle for Singapore. The swift occupation of the island by the Japanese saw the camp's rudimentary facilities expanded and converted as a field hospital for the Indian National Army (INA) and its troops. But with the repatriation of the INA to Burma in 1944, and the increasing number of returning prisoners of war from the Siam-Burma Railway to

Changi, overcrowding the existing facilities, the impetus for an additional internment camp and hospital on the island proved decisive. As it was, on Sunday, 28 May 1944, Kranji Camp was opened when 608 British, 43 Dutch and 540 Australian patients were transferred from Changi to occupy the 'Woodlands Hutted Camp' at Kranji.[13]

By early May 1944, conditions at the Changi prisoner-of-war camp had begun to deteriorate with the influx of returnee prisoners, many of whom suffered debilitating illnesses and injuries on the Railway, prompting the Japanese to take decisive action. They began by ordering the evacuation of Selarang Barracks, which was part of the Changi Garrison and where most of the British forces were based during the battle of Singapore. Combatants were moved to the civilian gaol building at Changi, and all hospital patients and Red Cross card-holders to rudimentary huts scattered around the gaol. Given the new accommodation was insufficient for the large Changi Hospital, itself established from the onset of the occupation by British and Australian Army Medical units, the authorities ordered a new 1,200-bed hospital be established at Kranji. The Japanese policy was that all patients requiring greater than a month's medical treatment be dispatched to Kranji, thus relieving pressure on the existing Changi Hospital. Acute surgical procedures would still be performed at Changi, but all other surgical needs were to be undertaken at the new facility. A weekly ambulance transport service between the two camps would ensure both facilities operated smoothly.[14]

Describing the conditions at the newly opened Kranji camp in his *Report on Karanji Prisoner of War Camp: May 1944 to August 1945*, the hospital's Senior Medical Officer, Lieutenant-Colonel Joseph Clinton Collins, Royal Army Medical Corps (RAMC), paints a different picture from that portrayed by the Japanese. The much-vaunted weekly ambulance service never materialised; instead transfers by lorries between camps took place three times a month, slowing to twice a month, and by July 1945 they had ceased. And where the new hospital was intended to be a combined facility, Australian patients were under the care of their own medical officer, similarly for the British.

But his harshest words were left for the camp's Commanding Officer, the non-commissioned officer Sergeant-Major Yoshikawa Taira[15]: 'He ruled as a Dictator and meted out punishment in no light manner. ... To carry out his orders he had some forty Koreans. They were a band of unscrupulous and disloyal ruffians, who given authority, used it to their own benefits in a brutal and unfair manner.'[16] Former Corporal Lex Arthurson, writing in the unofficial history of the 13th Australian General Hospital, 8th Division, which provided the medical staff for both Changi and Kranji, similarly describes the harsh conditions at the latter. 'Medical supplies were limited, there being no absorbent wool. Old rags were used and rewashed after soiling, autoclaved and put back

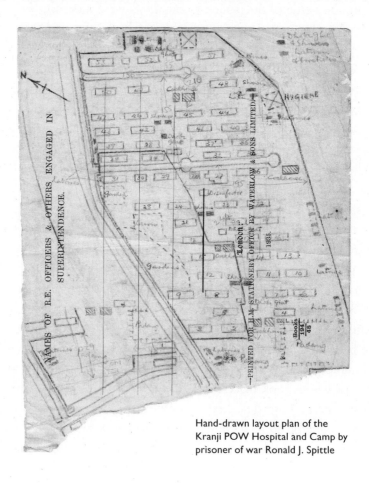

Hand-drawn layout plan of the Kranji POW Hospital and Camp by prisoner of war Ronald J. Spittle

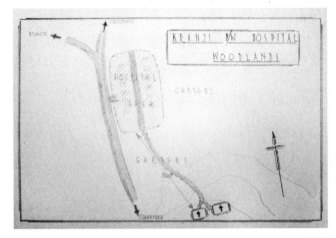

Sketch of Kranji
POW Hospital
and the nearby
cemetery, by
Lieutenant Carl S.
Flaws, AIF Malaya

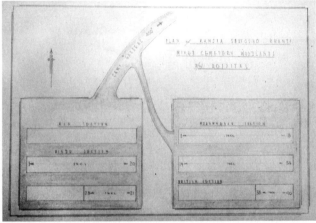

Layout plan of
the cemetery
at the POW
Hospital and
Camp at Kranji,
by Lieutenant
Carl S. Flaws

in the wards.'[17] And as with the hospital at Changi, Kranji established
nearby on Kranji Hill a small cemetery for those who died within its
care. This simple hospital graveyard would become the precursor to the
Kranji War Cemetery.

Writing in his memoir of his time spent as a prisoner of war
in Singapore, former Australian Army signalman Geoffrey Bingham
recollects being transferred from Changi to Kranji and provides an
invaluable insight into its physical state. The camp accommodation,
expanded to well over 50 huts by the time the INA vacated, was seg-
regated between the prisoners of war and the Japanese guards. Two

153

barbed wire fences and a pathway ran along the perimeter, patrolled by Korean and Indian guards. Built from local tropical timber, the huts were lined with the leaves of attap palm to their steep roofs and walls, hardwood boards provided the floors and a veranda was attached to one side. Yet for all the improvement in conditions from Changi, it was Bingham's work in the hospital that left the deepest impression. 'The convalescent hospital was for patients who were less ill than those left behind in Changi Hospital. For that reason, we did not take many of the men who had returned from Thailand. Even then we had quite bad cases ... For a time we had no chaplains at Kranji and so I had to take a burial or two in the cemetery, which was on a hill above our eastern boundary.'[18]

British Army signalman James McCormick was a member of the support staff for the British section of Changi Hospital before being relocated to Kranji. Although his main role at the new hospital was to be maintenance, his knowledge of electrics saw him go on ahead and prepare the facility for the arrival of its first patients. Recollecting years later to his daughter, McCormick described his days off from maintenance helping lay out and bury the dead, many of whom had survived the Siam-Burma Railway only to end their days at Kranji. Having dug some of the first graves at the cemetery, McCormick suggests that the location of the burial ground was chosen because of its tranquillity and the stunning view it offered.[19] Likewise, Samuel Purvis of the 197th Field Ambulance, British Army Medical Corps, was interned at Kranji and was one of the prisoners responsible for establishing the cemetery. A professional footballer for Middlesborough and Watford AFC before enrolling for military service, Purvis served as a Medical Attendant under Collins, and like McCormick, presents a positive outlook of the cemetery:

> Kranji turned out to be the worst camp of them all. Strange
> though it may seem; it was also the nicest in which to bury
> our dead colleagues. We buried them on top of a hill and
> our bugler played 'The Last Post'. He was poised right on

the crest of the hill. It was lovely and tranquil to stand and listen to his rendering. That scene always stands out in my mind. Whenever I hear a bugle playing – the tears well up in my eyes and I weep a silent prayer for those poor souls for whom the bugle played.[20]

On 12 September 1945, Admiral Lord Louis Mountbatten, Supreme Allied Commander, South East Asia, arrived in Singapore and received the surrender document of the Imperial Japanese forces, marking the significant end of the Second World War in Southeast Asia. Accompanied by his wife Lady Edwina Mountbatten, he then embarked on a tour across the island, visiting Allied prisoners of war and civilian internees at various camps. Kranji was one of those camps visited, where he addressed a group of British former prisoners of war, their mood celebratory although their physiques visibly displayed the years of malnourishment. Meanwhile, the return of command under the Allied Land Forces South East Asia (ALFSEA) saw the Recovery of Allied Prisoners of War and Internees (RAPWI) charged with repatriating Allied prisoners of war and internees, whilst the Army Graves Service was placed in temporary charge of identifying and recovering all war remains. Concurrently, the Royal Air Force had decided upon expanding the military airfield at Changi, originally built by the Japanese with prisoner-of-war labour. The RAF demands on securing and expanding the airfield for its post-war reconstruction and defence needs placed severed limitations on establishing a larger cemetery there. Faced with the need to consolidate and centralise war remains from within Singapore, the Army Graves Service, with the acquiescence of the Imperial War Graves Commission, proceeded to develop the small cemetery at Kranji into a more permanent army entity.

There was also the growing concern with identifying remains of combatants and non-combatants alike. This would prove a lengthy impasse with the Commission, which had a long-standing policy of not taking over any remains that could not be satisfactorily proven as entitled to a war grave burial. Along with those men deemed missing, nothing could be done until the War Office had completed their accounting of the regimental lists of casualties. There were also those lists prepared by the senior officers in the prisoner-of-war camps, identifying who had died whilst interned and who had been taken away, never to be seen again.[21] This would prove particularly difficult with the local population and their often-informal involvement during the war with the numerous local militias. Furthermore, across the Causeway in the post-independence Federation of Malaya, an Emergency had been declared in mid-1948, when communist guerrillas commenced an insurgency against the Commonwealth forces. The priorities of the local armed forces and colonial administration were suitably distracted. These conditions, set within the wider framework of post-war Asian independence movements seeking sovereignty from colonial rule, would set the course for contention and delays. Involving the Army, War Office, Imperial War Graves Commission, Colonial Office and subsequently the Singapore Government, it rendered the development of a proper war cemetery at Kranji a temporary casualty.

Founding a War Cemetery

All these issues had yet to materialise on 1 March 1947, when Colin St Clair Oakes was formally appointed Principal Architect and given instructions for the design and development of Kranji War Cemetery.[22] It was almost two years since his initial tour of Asia and Singapore, where his report on suitable sites for the permanent war cemetery had all but ruled out Kranji. In his report from the same tour, Harry Obbard, now a Brigadier and stationed in New Delhi as the Commission's Chief Administrative Officer for India and Southeast Asia, had similarly not recommended Kranji.

The design of Kranji would not materialise quickly. Oakes instead concentrated on designing the war cemetery in Taiping, Malaya. Then with the Commission under increasing pressure from the Indian Government to expedite their cemeteries and memorials for their fallen, he found himself committed to those sites confirmed in Imphal, Gauhati, Kohima and Digboi in north-east India. Singapore was pushed back,

'White Crosses at Kranji', 1947

though not without creative interventions necessitated by evolving circumstances.

One such intervention that involved an early design decision coincided with Oakes being in Singapore during his second extensive tour of the region from early November 1947 to late February 1948. It came about through the Commission's public relations response to a number of newspaper reports on 'disgraceful conditions' that emanated from Singapore and were soon carried in the UK and Australian press. Writing to *The Straits Times* on 27 December 1947 under the headline 'An Ex-PoW on War Cemeteries', the unidentified contributor suggested that the relocation of bodies of Allied servicemen from Changi Cemetery to Woodlands (i.e. Kranji) Cemetery compared very unfavourably with the cemeteries of the First World War that he had seen and was not a credit to the War Graves Service or Singapore.[23]

Very few ex-prisoners of war appear to know that the cemeteries of Changi, which throughout the occupation were carefully tendered by half-starved prisoners of war unfit for heavy duties, and were left by them with trimmed grass graves, lawns, paths, hedges, flowering trees and shrubs, are now just torn-up weed-covered wastes, and that the remains of their comrades have been transferred to a bare, neglected-looking hillside.[24]

He then went on to report, '[the] last time I saw the British and Netherlands cemetery at Changi some months ago the wooden lychgate ... was still standing amid desolation.'[25] Whether this letter reflected the contributor's ignorance of the workings of the Commission and the lengthy, detailed process involved in establishing a war graves cemetery, or a calculated provocation, the emotional diatribe inflamed returned servicemen and the wider general public with the idea that remains of the fallen were being disrespected, and by association, their sacrifice diminished. Protests by local residents to the various newspapers were quickly forthcoming. Similar protests overseas also carried negative undertones directed at Singapore.

Obbard, quick to appreciate the gravity of the negative sentiments and the impression of Singapore being portrayed through the article, sought an urgent containment. On 6 January, the Commission's Director of Public Relations, Colonel Royston Oliver, published a calculated reply in *The Straits Times*. Under the headline 'White Crosses at Kranji: A Singapore Cemetery', Oliver's response was an impassioned defence of everything the Commission stood for; it was 'not necessary to make explanations and contradictions but ... very wrong of people to assume that the present generation or, in particular, the public of Singapore, are of the kind who would neglect their duty to those who died in the fighting'.[26] The article then proceeded with a forthright and detailed explanation of the work of the Army War Graves Services prior to handing over to the Commission, followed by the process required to design and then create a military cemetery of a standard befitting those undertaken in the past. And in parting, the 'final design for our cemetery here will include the lychgate erected by prisoners-of-war of the 18th Division in their temporary burial ground at Changi. It has been carefully removed and stored for safe-keeping until required at Kranji.'[27] A gesture designed to appeal to public sentiment at home, it was neither run past Oakes, nor would it eventuate in the completed cemetery. It would only serve to confirm Obbard's increasing personal interest and active involvement in Kranji's initial design.

True to Obbard and the Commission's public statements, a lychgate was eventually provided at Kranji War Cemetery, but not in accordance with their original intentions. Neither was it the original lychgate that marked the entrance to Wing Loong Cemetery outside the Changi prisoner-of-war camp. With the closure and relocation of the Wing Loong cemetery's graves to Kranji, this small pavilion-like structure was carefully dismantled and placed in storage until 1952, when it was re-erected outside St George's Church, the Anglican parish church within the British army garrison at Tanglin. Here it would remain undisturbed, until the final withdrawal of British forces from the island in 1971, when it was again dismantled and shipped to England. The lychgate at Kranji was in fact a careful replica, one of two

The Kranji lychgate, modelled after the lychgate designed and erected by the prisoners of war at Changi for their POW Cemetery. Its whereabouts post-redevelopment of the war cemetery remain unknown.

that were eventually constructed, the other being dedicated in 1984 and now standing on the site of the original, outside St George's. At the end of the war, the Singapore Government had asked local architecture students to design gates for the Kranji war cemetery, and the selected proposal was a replica of Pickersgill's design for Changi.[28]

Designed by Captain Cecil D. Pickersgill of the Royal Engineers, the lychgate was based on the gate at Holy Trinity Church in Startforth, Yorkshire. Pickersgill, a trained architect, had his own practice before joining the Territorial Army and being called up for service on 3 September 1939. After serving in France and being evacuated from Dunkirk, he was posted to Singapore, where he was taken prisoner at Raffles Hotel and sent to Changi. Believing that there should be something for dead servicemen to pass through as a Christian mark of faith, he set about designing a lychgate. With permission from the Japanese commandant, his fellow prisoners of war at Changi rummaged for bits of teak and pieces of barbed wire for nails, and it was soon erected.[29] Not long after, Pickersgill would be one of the thousands dispatched to the Siam-Burma Railway and eventually one of its many casualties. With no known grave, his name now adorns the Singapore Memorial's wall.[30]

By the end of February 1948, and following the Commission's impassioned response to the negative stories circulating, Kranji as the 'confirmed' site of a war cemetery in Singapore was still a tenuous proposition. After the Chief of General Staff's visit to the cemetery in October the previous year, the Australian Army issued a memorandum to the Prime Minister's department in February outlining their concerns about the condition of the grounds and its physical suitability.[31] Compared with the layout of Yokohama War Cemetery, developed by the Commission's Anzac Agency, Lieutenant-General Vernon Sturdee's personal opinion was that the 'most satisfactory solution is to pick another site, get it ready and move all the graves'.[32] Sturdee had been satisfied with the cemetery at Changi, but felt that there was 'no sentimental aspect of the present site, it merely was a piece of ground under temporary control, and so the Cemetery was located there'. The memorandum went on to suggest that recommendations be made to the UK Government to either relocate the cemetery or remodel it after Yokohama, in particular copying the manner in which each Dominion has its own small section quite distinct from the others.[33]

Alerted to the prevailing sentiment by the Anzac Agency, an urgent conference was called with representatives of the War Office's Graves Registration and Enquiries (GR&E) unit to seek clarity and direction. It would ironically be Obbard, who had previously not recommended Kranji, who would urgently write to the Commission headquarters with an argument to retain it. Advising on the imminent take-over of the cemetery on a staged basis, and suggesting the site wasn't as problematic physically as suggested, he pointed out that 'there can be no question of moving this cemetery, nor would any more suitable site be available'.[34]

The Commission also sought out the opinion of Oakes, who like Obbard, reversed track and concurred that 'the site will make a very good permanent cemetery'.[35] In a letter of response to Brown, and by association to the Australian Government, the Commission spelt out the reasons for retaining Kranji as the site of the preferred war cemetery. Addressing the original list of issues, along with Oakes's recommendation, they also stressed the land tenure as having been fully secured, with action having commenced for its permanent acquisition with the Singapore Government. It was also highlighted that 'the original cemetery at Changi and its removal was necessitated by construction of airfield'.[36] Kranji was retained and a formal request was placed with the Singapore Government to organise a detailed topographical survey of the hill for the design to commence.

By that stage, Kranji Military Cemetery contained the remains of 893 Australians, 1,360 British, 535 Muslims, 174 Dutch, 69 Chinese, 5 Gurkhas and 764 unknown servicemen.[37] It had not yet been handed over to the Commission and was still under the responsibility of the Army. The Graves Concentration Unit, following the Army's established guidelines, developed the somewhat rectangular cemetery into two sections on either end of the summit, with an open clearing between them. North of the summit, along the gently sloping ground falling towards the coast, British, Australian, Dutch, Gurkhas and unknown Empire soldiers were laid in 34 regular plots, either side of a 38-foot-wide central axis. Each plot, measuring 40 feet by 60 feet, was separated by 5-foot-wide turfed pathways. The exceptions were two larger Dutch plots framing the axis to the summit. To the immediate south, falling sharply and constrained by the boundary, were four Indian servicemen plots, 40 feet deep by 75 feet wide. A small mass grave containing the remains of 67 Chinese members of the Commonwealth forces was sited adjacent to the Gurkha plot, to the far southwest, within the clearing.[38] Whilst the clearing was 175 feet long and spanned the full width of the cemetery, its position encompassing the summit of Kranji Hill allowed for favourable views towards the coast. It was, in Oakes's view, a suitable location for the Memorial to the Missing. What he could not have foreseen were the delays that would arise from the challenges confronting the Commission and Singapore in reconciling the thousands of servicemen and civilians dead and those missing, presumed dead.

The Chinese mass grave would prove contentious in the negotiations for the Commission to take over the cemetery. Whereas the European and Eurasian civilian and Malayan casualties were recorded as belonging to volunteer formations such as the Straits Settlements Volunteer Force (SSVF), the Federated Malay States Volunteer Force (FMSVF) and the Hong Kong Singapore Royal Artillery (HKSRA), this was not the case with the Chinese victims of the Sook Ching massacre.[39] Located and unearthed in the immediate aftermath of the end of war on 12 September 1945, they were assumed to have belonged to the SSVF and Dalforce, but this could not be readily confirmed. Only two Chinese remains were formally identified as members of the local militias. The Commission's policy position of excluding non-servicemen from war graves treatment was invoked, to the distress of the local community.

It was Governor Sir Franklin Gimson, after a joint visit to Kranji with Obbard on 10 September 1947, who requested an allotment or burial space be made available for these Chinese servicemen within the Kranji Military Cemetery[40] – an area with its own memorial where the community could suitably commemorate their own, on par with the Commonwealth personnel. Gimson, the first Governor of Singapore and a former prisoner of war of the Japanese in Hong Kong, had read the mood of the populace in the post-war climate and was adamant that the Chinese community, who had suffered immeasurably during the Occupation, be accorded the dignity of a 'site which is in no way inferior to the site on which the military cemetery stands'.[41] This was the first known occasion where the sentiments of the local populace were considered in the otherwise 'Imperial' project the Commission was planning in Singapore for the remembrance of their dead. It also considered their cultural traits, making it clear that 'since Chinese culture demands that burial grounds should be on as elevated a site as possible, sites outside our cemetery areas would be considered very much inferior to ours'.[42]

Gimson's position on the matter was quite forthright and his intention in meeting the leading members of the Chinese community soon after to offer them a suitably significant site caught the Commission off-guard, requiring an urgent response. Obbard, recounting the site visit with Gimson back to headquarters, supported the Governor's stand and stressed the considerable advantages to be gained for the Commission through rousing local interest in the cemetery area.[43] Amidst the ensuing lengthy and procrastinating discussions, it would take a phone call from Andrew B. Acheson, Head of General Department and Defence for the Colonial Office, to the Commission's Senior Administration Officer, Brigadier John Kirkland McNair, a month later to force an outcome to the simmering issue.[44] Critical of the fact that the Colonial Office had not been consulted on the Commission's decision on eligibility for war graves treatment, he pointed out the obvious – 'that the Commission have not yet acquired the legal rights to the cemetery and that if the Government of Singapore chose to allot an enclave in the cemetery to the Chinese they were within their rights in doing so, and [the Commission] should have to accept the resultant position'.[45] Furthermore, he suggested that accepting some of the Chinese victims may have been British subjects, the majority probably would have belonged to a class known as 'British protected subjects'.[46]

It had the desired effect of breaking the stalemate. During Obbard's tour of Singapore later that year in November, a final decision appeared imminent. Arranging to meet at Kranji at short notice, and without the knowledge of the General Headquarters of Far East Land Forces (FARELF), Gimson and Major-General Lionel Howard Cox, General Officer Commanding (GOC), Singapore District, put forth their firm view on the final stumbling block – that no physical boundary should separate the Chinese mass grave from the military cemetery. Obbard subsequently reverted to London, agreeing with the sentiments of the Governor and GOC, but with the proviso that a boundary was still necessary, though its design should be such that it avoided any impression of forcible exclusion of Chinese visitors from the war cemetery.[47] The Commission finally acceded to the request, but on the condition that the Chinese mass grave plot have a low boundary wall, albeit porous to interconnect with the main site, and its architectural treatment be strictly controlled.[48]

Whilst the Chinese memorial was hampering negotiations on the acquisition of Kranji, another mass grave was discovered, this time in late 1946. The remains of over 400 casualties buried within the grounds of Singapore's main Civil General Hospital would throw up another significant quandary for the Commission and the recently convened Singapore Government.[49] The question was what was to be done with a burial site where though a fair proportion (103) of the remains were believed to be British service personnel (ascertained through what admission records remained), the degree of decomposition and lack of identity discs rendered them unidentifiable.[50]

Excavated as an emergency water reserve tank prior to the war, the open trench had never been completed. As the Japanese pressed towards Singapore town in the final frenetic days of the invasion, the overwhelming number of casualties brought in daily vastly exceeded the hospital's capacity and its ability to maintain order and cleanliness.

Faced with the ever-mounting dead of all nationalities, including civilian patients, servicemen during war operations and scores from the hospital morgue, the hospital's Chief Medical Officer, Dr John H. Bowyer, made the necessary decision to utilise this open trench as a mass burial ground. Lime was then thrown in over the corpses to subdue the smell and hasten their decomposition. Two days after the surrender, the Japanese Army Medical Corps took control of the hospital for their own servicemen and continued to bury the dead that were arriving by the lorryloads and being dumped in. It was not until almost a month later, in early March, that the Japanese finally filled in the trench, using excavated earth banked up nearby, and removed any rudimentary crosses and memorials placed by loved ones and hospital staff. And with mostly foreign medical staff interned at Changi and all civilian patients given three days to move out to the Mental Hospital in Yio Chu Kang, records of admissions were degraded and local knowledge of the site diminished. The burial ground settled into becoming a nondescript turfed field set among the medical blocks.[51] Bowyer, soon after the surrender, would be placed in charge of casualties at the Mental Hospital, before being sent to Changi Gaol as Civil Medical Officer. He was arrested by the Kempeitai in January 1944 and died in Sime Road Camp on 1 November.[52]

The Japanese surrender and the return of Singapore to colonial rule on 12 September 1945 saw the British Army requisition the General Hospital and only return it to the civil authorities in June 1946. By this stage, the burial ground had assumed a role as turfed playing field and any notification of its past use to the authorities went unheard. Indeed, the Army's War Graves Units had undertaken a trial investigation of the site and had found no evidence of any burials. Only after the Army had vacated the Hospital was any consideration given to its former use. The (Anglican) Bishop of Singapore, John L. Wilson, himself having been interned at Changi during the war and tortured by the Kempeitai,[53] was brought in to consecrate the communal grave. The medical authorities then fenced off an area approximately 350 feet long by 20 feet wide until funds became available for a permanent

Fenced-off mass burial ground at Singapore General Hospital, 1946

garden of memory with a memorial. Faced with the difficulty of keeping people off that ground, Dr T.F. Strang, the Chief Medical Officer
of the General Hospital at the time, 'started telling everyone that the
spot was a *kramat* (a Malay term for the grave of a holy person). People
started treating it with some sort of respect.'[54]

Yet for all that, the local population was quite ambivalent over
this ground – it was just one of many such mass burials being discovered across the island. And there was also the wider-known and more
infamous Alexandra Hospital massacre site and its victims to consume
the authorities. The FARELF GR&E unit erected a simple, temporary
wooden cross on a pyramidal wooden base with the names of the 103
identified service personnel inscribed on a plaque.[55] A curator from the
Botanic Gardens was approached for some plantings around it.

As to the question of permanent interment and commemoration,
the impossibility of identifying the remains of any servicemen from the
civilians, and its previous consecration, led the Singapore Government
to request that the War Office take over the mass grave as a complete
military cemetery. The Commission, identifying military remains only
through what lists and records remained of servicemen having been

admitted or sent to the hospital during the last days before the fall of Singapore, felt the number was proportionately low and could not set a precedent in accepting over 300 civilians within a war graves cemetery. Their suggestion was for the Singapore Government to arrange the enclosing, marking and maintaining of this grave site.

The issue of permanently commemorating these victims was eventually raised in February 1948. A memorandum from Governor Gimson to the Secretary of State for the Colonies, Arthur Creech Jones, would see a meeting held in London on 4 March to resolve this issue.[56] Among a long list of intractable items requiring direction, the War Office's DGR&E Brigadier Croxton Sillery Vale and the Commission's Brigadier Frank Higginson were asked to decide on the outcome for the General Hospital mass grave. (The Chinese mass grave memorial impasse was also raised.) The final resolution for the hospital was that commemoration of service personnel would be by inscription of their names either on a wall or memorial at Kranji, and that the Colonial Office and Singapore Government treat the mass grave as they wished, but to place an inscription indicating that the British service dead were commemorated elsewhere.[57]

The decision would have design consequences. Acknowledging belatedly that delegating the main burial site at the General Hospital to the local authorities removed any design control and sensibility the Commission exercised elsewhere, they sought an appeasement. Senior Architect George Vey was instructed to design a more permanent memorial in place of the temporary wooden cross. Completed in September 1950, the proposed octagonal-shaped Portland stone pedestal memorial was presented the following year to the Colonial Office for their consideration. On the walls of the memorial were to be inscriptions to both the identified servicemen and the unknown civilians.[58] This memorial was never realised, and only the original cross stands today, albeit with its pyramidal base now constructed out of long-lasting granite. On the other hand, Oakes would eventually design a dedicated stone memorial for the General Hospital dead at Kranji and position it prominently at the eastern end of the plateau for

Memorial to the General Hospital dead erected by the FARELF GR&E unit

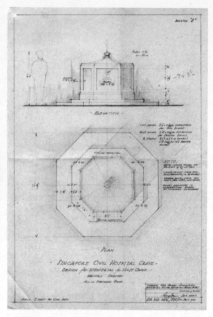

Architect George Vey's design (unbuilt) for a more permanent memorial for the General Hospital dead

the Memorial to the Missing. At the opposing western end, along the axis stands the Unmaintainable Graves Memorial, with the memorial for the Chinese mass grave adjacent. With the benefit of hindsight, this was an opportunity missed to bring the sacrifice of the Chinese servicemen within the envelope of the main commemorative structure at Kranji.

In addition to the commemorative complications the mass graves elicited, there were other challenges affecting the final cemetery layout prior to handover. Firstly, there was a need to accommodate graves of both World Wars from Singapore's Bidadari Christian Cemetery, where their permanent maintenance was no longer possible.[59] A similar circumstance prevailed for Commonwealth war graves within the Saigon Military Cemetery in French Indochina, where a rapidly escalating insurgency necessitated their urgent exhumation and relocation to Singapore. Then in September 1948, the Assistant Director GR&E

Military graves within Bidadari Cemetery. Re-interred at Ulu Pandan in 1957, they were eventually moved to Kranji Military Cemetery, adjacent to the War Cemetery.

FARELF notified the Commission that the Dutch war graves service had requested the exhumation and repatriation back to the Netherlands of all their nationals from both Kranji and Bidadari.[60] Along with the post-war haste in establishing Kranji as the permanent concentration site, it is no wonder that even the plot layouts did not conform to the Army's regulations on establishing cemetery sites, requiring a formal clarification and acceptance of this oversight by the Commission from the War Office.[61] With Oakes's visit to inspect the site now confirmed for November, and neither the cemetery handed over nor its topographical survey completed, an urgency set in. The basic design template established by Sir Fabian Ware and Sir Frederic Kenyon after the Great War for all war cemeteries was to prove at best a starting point.

Concept Design

On the original tour from November 1945 to February 1946, Oakes had assessed each burial 'concentration' site prepared by the War Graves Services. If he and Obbard deemed that location had sufficient features befitting a permanent location for a war cemetery, a rudimentary sketch design and layout would be prepared for the graves service to follow. Site contours would be adjusted and refined. Future burial plots and allocation of dedicated spaces for memorials and other facilities would be set aside for further detailed planning. This was an urgent requirement considering the ongoing recovery of remains and concentrations at the time. It was intended to prepare the sites for their subsequent handover in a condition requiring only minimal adjustments to the buried remains, and in doing so, expeditiously have the cemetery in a state of dignified readiness to receive the bereaved.

Kranji was less severe and dramatic a topography as Sai Wan Bay, Oakes's other site for a war cemetery and memorial to the missing, though both overlooked a gradual slope downwards towards a water view. With Sai Wan it was Junk Bay and the greater Hong Kong mainland as the backdrop. Kranji Hill had the Straits of Johore little over a mile to the north, and the Malay Peninsula beyond. Oakes had considered the elevated position and view over the Straits as the location's single redeeming feature. To make the most of the gradual ascent of the war graves to the summit, his opinion was that an axial approach consisting of a 'straight avenue' from the main road junction should obliquely meet the main cemetery grid: 'There are trees all along the side of the road towards the cemetery and the "avenue" would break through this and reveal the cemetery, which is otherwise hidden.'[62] In this regard, a direct and formal avenue from the nearby Woodlands-Kranji Road junction to the cemetery entrance gates was seen as a key element in framing the cemetery's formal layout. Falling outside the demarcated site boundary, this proposed alignment would necessitate the Commission formally requesting further land acquisition from the Singapore Government. And very aware of the land scarcity Singapore faced for its own post-war redevelopment, the government's position on the matter was scarcely accommodating. Initially viewed as a design intransigence by a stubborn architect, it would turn out to be a contentious issue that dragged well on into the design period.

Obbard, keenly aware of the physical condition of the cemetery through his more frequent visitations, had wanted to retain the existing roadway. This rough but serviceable gravel track, established when the site was an encampment and then hospital, also came off Woodlands Road, but further along from the corner and entering perpendicular. It then turned sharply before aligning itself to the main axis from the small car park and cemetery entrance gates. Mahogany and yew trees planted earlier, and by now well established, formed an avenue or *allée*, emphasising a formal arrival to the cemetery. He believed that rather than fighting the Singapore Government with a request for additional land acquisition, the architect should incorporate the existing access and its landscape into his scheme. Writing to Higginson, Obbard strongly opined that the proposed axial approach is 'ideal from an architect's point of view, but frankly I do not think the expense involved would really be justifiable ... The existing oblique approach is amply good enough for the purpose.'[63]

This design debate over the access avenue proposed by Oakes coincided with a growing awareness in Singapore and greater Malaya that Kranji War Cemetery was becoming a significant place. Whereas newspaper accounts on the cemetery were few in the early post-war years, by 1950 there were 14 articles covering topics such as ceremonies, maintenance and visits by prominent people. Remembrance ceremonies, previously conducted at the Cenotaph[64] at the Padang in downtown Singapore, were now being shared between this memorial originally dedicated to the First World War, and the war cemetery at Kranji. Reporting on a visit to Kranji by the Australian Major-General William Bridgeford in August of that year, the cemetery's caretaker Mr Tan Tong Toh was complimented on its pristine state – in contrast to its 'disgraceful condition' reported only three years earlier. With 20 labourers keeping the gardens trim and tidy, Tan recounted that an average of two to three persons a day were now making the 14-mile drive out from the city to pay 'homage to the war dead'. And having risked his life smuggling food, money and clothing into the prisoner-of-war camps during the Occupation, Tan also proudly pointed out his Certificate of Commendation, signed by Lord Louis Mountbatten, war-time Supreme Allied Commander of Southeast Asia.[65]

To further reinforce its growing stature, the airlines Qantas and British Overseas Airways Corporation (BOAC) had begun organising tours to Kranji War Cemetery for passengers in transit. This was one of many such tours offered, others being visits to the 'infamous' Changi Prison, the former Japanese Memorial at Bukit Batok, and Happy World.[66] It therefore came as no surprise that along with active interest from the local Ex-Services Association, the Singapore Commissioner of Lands had changed his outlook on any requests for further land acquisition, and was now favourably inclined to consider Oakes's recommendation on the access road.[67] It was now only a matter of obtaining a consensus between Oakes and Obbard. And by August 1952, almost two years since the issue of access first arose, the impact that any further delays would have on finalising the land acquisition and the likely additional costs involved saw both men willing to compromise.

The access had been narrowed down to two options – Route B was what Oakes preferred, from the main corner, while Route C was the perpendicular road. An earlier idea, or Route A, of reforming an existing dirt track leading to the caretaker's cottage from the west, was ruled out, due in part to its lacking the formality such a significant site demanded. Writing to the Commission's Area Superintendent in Penang, Obbard instructed him to personally proceed to Singapore and discuss the by now 'preferred' approach road Route C with the Singapore Government: 'In discussing this you should stress the great advantage of Route C over the existing approach road from the point of view of both architectural design and of the impression made on visitors to the cemetery. You should further stress that this cemetery is the major cemetery of S.E. Asia and will include, in addition, a large memorial to those who lost their lives but have no known grave, in the operations in S.E. Asia.'[68]

Resigned to the fact, Oakes acquiesced to Obbard's decision that Route C was the better alternative, and by the following month he was actively working on the memorial concepts. 'The layout on the summit, which represents the architectural "piece de resistance" I am not yet satisfied with and am now working on a third scheme.'[69] This

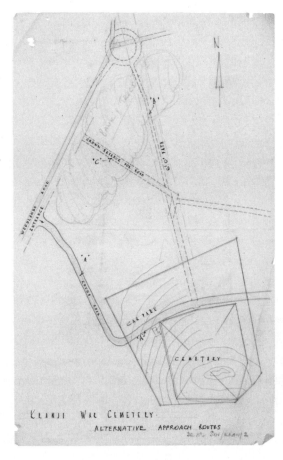

Sketch plan indicating the various access routes debated for Kranji. Oakes preferred the straight avenue from the main road junction (Route B), whereas Route A was the original service entry through the caretaker's cottage and nursery. Route C, Obbard's preferred choice, was the practical and accepted alternative, according to the IWGC.

third scheme would become the present-day memorial, yet not without its challenges to the architectural orthodoxy so ensconced within the Commission.

Memorial to the Missing

The air forces of the Commonwealth during the last war had seen an unprecedented expansion of their operations, significantly contributing to the Allied victory. They had also seen an unprecedented number of airmen killed and missing, presumed dead, in all theatres of the war. Yet commemoration of the missing as opposed to those who could not be identified necessitated a different type of memorialisation, given the deaths occurred far from any accessible location. There was no possibility of loved ones visiting the sites of where the airmen fell or were presumed to have fallen. In this regard, the air force had precedent established by the Royal Navy after the First World War. Writing in *The Unending Vigil*, Philip Longworth suggests that having been against the idea of commemorating missing sailors in the manner of soldiers 'near where they were supposed to have fallen', the Admiralty acceded to allowing the names of their missing sailors to be inscribed within memorials at significant ports where they had set sail. Consequently, the three manning ports of Portsmouth, Plymouth and Chatham were selected for identical memorials unmistakeably naval in form. Seamen of the colonies and other Dominions would similarly be commemorated in their own countries of origin.[70]

Given the need for each of the military services to preserve their separate identities, it was inevitable the air force would require its own series of separate memorials. On 20 February 1948, at a meeting of the Air Council Memorial Committee and Air Chief Marshall Sir Arthur Longmore, representing the Imperial War Graves Commission, it was proposed that the Commission 'proceed with plans for the commemoration in memorials of the names of the Royal Air Force (RAF) missing in the 1939/45 War, with a general inscription to cover the dead'.[71] With this mandate, the Air Council requested the Commission submit details and sketch designs for four separate memorials, to be located in the United Kingdom, Malta, El Alamein in the Middle East and in the Far East. Singapore, it was decided, would serve as the location to commemorate airmen killed in the Far East theatre, of which there were approximately 3,000 names. It would be the Canadians, though, through J.P. Sigvaldason representing their High Commissioner, who stated the obvious – that for all the decisions agreed upon for the memorials, they were after all for the RAF and there was no mention of those airmen representing the Dominion air forces. The Commission thus decided that those airmen of the Dominions who had been stationed in the UK and served the RAF would be included in the proposal. It wasn't quite the comprehensive offer the fellow

Commonwealth nations had hoped for, and eventually both the Air Ministry and Commission came to a compromise and also opened the memorials to those airmen who whilst engaged with their own air forces were declared missing. And in a further compromise given the many outstanding war cemeteries the war generated across the world, the Air Council offered that if 'the Commission feel that these memorials could, appropriately, be associated with any Army memorials in these areas, then the Council would wish that the RAF Memorials should be separately distinguishable'.[72] Oakes, in considering the design options for his most memorable structure in his war graves work, would duly respond with an iconic reference to the airmen.

Yet a memorial to the missing was not a fait accompli for Kranji. It was only on 20 January 1949 at the Commission's 311th meeting that a resolution was put forward approving a Memorial to the Missing for Kranji and Sai Wan Bay in Hong Kong.[73] This would be subsequently expanded with the inclusion of further memorials for Port Moresby, Lae, Rabaul, Ambon, Labuan and Bourail war cemeteries, all falling under the design direction and execution of the Anzac Agency. They would eventually be part of the 200 memorials of various sizes and types the Commission erected since its founding. And in a significant change of position, the Commission confirmed they were not restricted solely to airmen, but were for all 'the fallen of the 1939/45 War, who have no known grave'.[74]

Sitting atop an oval plateau on Kranji Hill, the Singapore Memorial commands the highest point of the cemetery. Affording views in all directions, its positioning and alignment with the central north-south axis ensures the structure and its visitors overlook the Johore Straits. This same axis, on a gentle incline with the graves to the fallen on either side, provides both a visual and pedestrian link between the Cross of Sacrifice sited at the base of the memorial and the Stone of Remembrance at the cemetery's formal gated entrance. The memorial itself is aligned with the rear boundary, creating a slight tilt off the east-west axis.

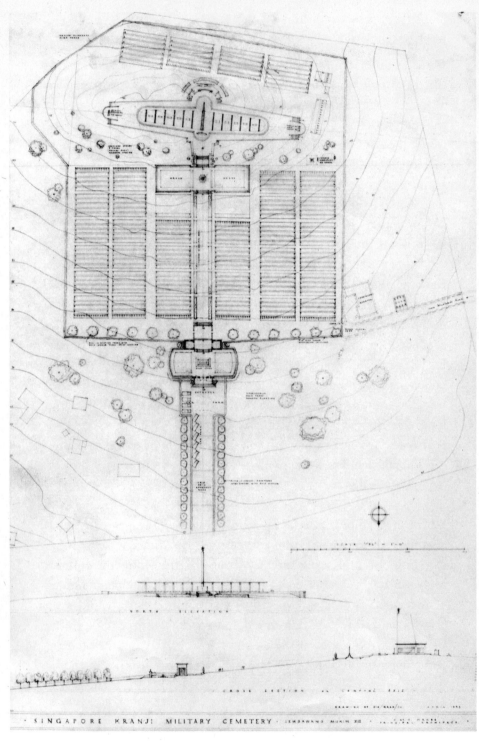

Oakes's final design proposal, 1954: Masterplan and section

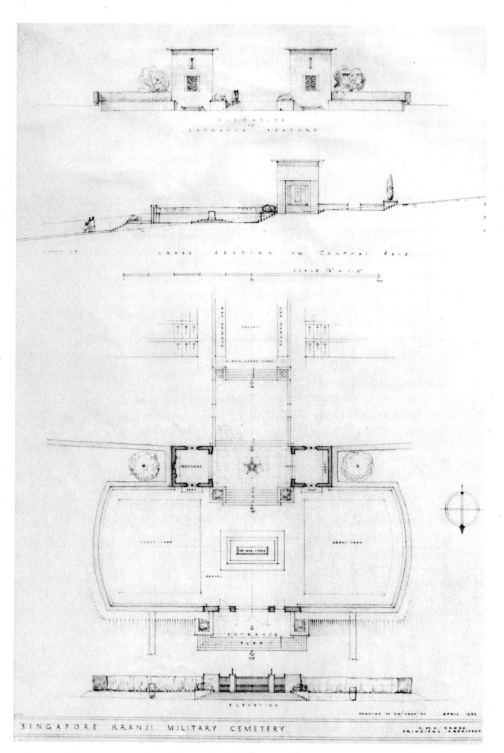

Entranceway and forecourt layout

It is in fact four memorials integrated within a single structure. The walls along the central body, lined with Portland stone, are inscribed with the names of over 24,000 soldiers and airmen who died in the war with Japan and have no known grave. Along the southern, or rear end, a curved wall over 10 feet in height and of similar stone forms the Cremation Memorial. It commemorates the over 800 war dead, predominantly from the British Indian Army, who were cremated according to their customs. At either end along the length of the memorial are two similar structures, the Hospital Grave Memorial[75] to the east and the Unmaintainable Graves Memorial to the west. The latter is dedicated to the more than 250 servicemen who lost their lives in Malaya, and whose graves were located in civil burial sites where permission to relocate to Kranji was not afforded.

Oakes would write that the shape of the hilltop influenced the design. Yet his original intention as a dedicated memorial to the missing airmen, unmistakeably aeronautical in form, clearly had an impact on the design development. Consisting of 12 'spar walls' emanating from the centre outwards with diminishing lengths, the accompanying slender flat roof closely resembles the wings of an aeroplane. Indeed, it uncannily mirrors the silhouette of the Hawker Hurricane, which along with the Supermarine Spitfire proved their mettle during the Battle of Britain and subsequently became symbols of a dogged British determinism. An 80-foot-tall central tower, otherwise referred to as the Memorial Column, surmounted with a star and domed light fitting, arises through this roof, with its tapered rear wall and ridge-line shape resembling the tail unit of a plane. The light fitting, accessed via a concealed shaft with ladder within the central spar wall, is not unlike an aircraft's tail navigation light, and was incorporated by Oakes to mark the tower's height and position for inbound air traffic using the nearby RAF Base at Tengah.[76]

Approval

The design of the cemeteries and memorials in the post-war era was changing, especially in the Far East and Australasia. Earlier proposals by the Anzac Agency for war cemeteries in Papua New Guinea had been met with cautious apprehension by the Commission. In the example of the Port Moresby Memorial within the Port Moresby (Bomana) War Cemetery, the Commission's Artistic Advisor Edward Maufe deplored its pared-down architectural features – a rotunda of cylindrical pillars enclosing an inner circle of square pillars, the lack of inflection at the top of the columns and their non-alignment with the entablature. 'This was a modern notion and how far the younger generation should be allowed to indulge it, he did not know.'[77]

Oakes would formally submit his final sketch designs for Kranji to a full meeting of the Commission on 16 July 1953. As part of the evaluation process, a 'Form A' was earlier circulated to all vested parties within the Commission for comments on the design. Form A's were the Commission's stripped-down administrative summary of its many projects and consisted of a sketch plan, a preliminary estimate and reports on the design for the cemetery construction. They were passed around selected departments of the Commission for their feedback, following which they would be discussed in one of the monthly meetings and approved or sent back for adjustments. It was a way of providing final feedback to the Commission on the proposal's architecture by its in-house Senior Architect[78], horticultural treatment, land acquisition, finance and construction works. Furthermore, specialised advice was also sought from the Commission's Botanical Advisor and final certification by its Artistic Advisor. It included the preliminary estimated construction cost of £122,830 and the approved permissible cost of £120,000. Prepared by the Finance Department and based on the bills of quantity used for the Taiping War Cemetery, also designed by Oakes and completed a few years earlier, it would prove insightful.

Major-General John F.D. Steedman, Director of Works, describing the scheme on behalf of the Chairman, voiced his concern about the cost estimate exceeding the allocated budget.[79] Acutely aware of the need to be careful with expenditure and to avoid any public perception of grandeur, he concurred with Maufe's advice and proposed that the 'total cost could be reduced by £10,000 by reducing the height of the memorial approximately by one-tenth, with corresponding reductions in other parts of the scheme'.[80] This value he proposed had been reflected in a request from the Finance Department. Although the difference between the estimate and budget was not substantial, they were concerned with the many unknown factors inherent in building in a such a distant location. Maufe would articulate this consequence architecturally, suggesting the spar walls of the memorial, those pillars accommodating the inscribed names of the missing, be reduced from a height of 16 feet 6 inches to 15 feet. The corresponding tower would likewise be lowered from its designed height of 80 feet. And when these reductions had been made, the memorial would be amply large enough.[81]

As for the central Memorial Column, Maufe contended that 'as an architect he thought it was interesting, but from the point of view of sentiment he thought it was doubtful'.[82] It was Longmore, Chairman of the Commission and a decorated former naval aviator,[83] who having visited Singapore and appreciated the location voiced his support for it. Enquiring whether the tower was to draw attention to the cemetery from the main road, and aware of the site himself, it was his opinion that it 'needed something striking to draw attention to the site'.[84]

Even the location of Lutyens's War Stone was questioned. Throughout the hundreds of war cemeteries completed by the Commission, the Stone, as a primary component of Kenyon's design principles, was with rare exceptions always placed within the burial compound. In Kranji, Oakes had proposed the Stone be positioned outside the main entrance gates and shelters. Maufe, when asked whether it was desirable to bring the War Stone inside the cemetery, replied that 'he would much prefer it to be inside. He felt that it should be visible from the graves: at present it was hidden from them by the shelter. However, he did not want to press the point because he liked the design as it stood.'[85]

And in an act of moral solidarity with Oakes's modern design, support would come from those members of the Committee best able to appreciate the similar direction the Commission's Anzac Agency had taken. The design of Kranji War Cemetery and Memorial was formally proposed by W.H. Bunning representing the High Commissioner for Australia and seconded by Walter W. Mason[86] representing the High Commissioner for New Zealand. All members accordingly expressed their approval of the design, subject to the reduction in its height as proposed by Steedman.

With the formal design approval now obtained, there was still the issue of securing the land upon which Oakes's vision would be realised. It would take another three years of negotiations before a final calculation of land area required for those presently buried and the possibility of future finds was settled upon. This was then followed by the formal acquisition of that land from the Singapore Government by the Commission for the exclusive use in perpetuity of the cemetery. Eventually measuring 13 acres, 3 roods, 14 poles (approx 5.39 ha), the Memorandum of Transfer assigning that land to the Commission would only be signed in late 1956.[87] It would be almost 11 years after the Japanese surrender that the Kranji War Cemetery and Memorial would be unveiled by Singapore Governor Sir Robert Black, on 2 March 1957, in an official ceremony.

Nanyang Siang Pau coverage of the unveiling of the Singapore Memorial at Kranji, 3 March 1957

CHAPTER 8

Building a War Cemetery

In the annals of the hundreds of unveiling ceremonies conducted for the Imperial War Graves Commission, the conduct of the event as it unfolds tends to reinforce the social and political hierarchies in place at the time. The military, politicians, clergy, grieving widows and survivors, all have a role to play in the commemoration and memorialisation process. Occasionally, the architect is feted for the completed work, recognised for its timeless value and respected for how the design portrays the suffering of the fallen. Rarely is any formal acknowledgement given to the construction of the memorial or cemetery and the many unseen hands that forged its design into reality.

In the case of Kranji, there was the additional hierarchy of language and culture overtly conspiring against such recognition. The English-language media coverage of the day's events focused on the ceremony and its many dignitaries, the majority of whom, whilst either local or from overseas, were predominantly European. The architect and his design were mentioned merely as a footnote. As for the contractor, there was nothing whatsoever. Instead, it was the local Chinese-language newspaper, *Nanyang Siang Pau,* that dared appropriate some semblance of those 'hidden hands' and their significance for the

圖示總督于揭幕典禮舉行完畢後，前往與在場員攝。貴建築該紀念碑之何木記建築公司主人何穆基握手所

The contractor for the Memorial, Ho Bock Kee shaking hands with Governor Black at the unveiling ceremony

local Chinese community. In a small black-and-white photograph set within a wider full-page spread of the coverage, a smiling bespectacled Chinese man in a white suit, standing amongst other attendees, is captured shaking hands with the Governor. It was due recognition accorded him for the effort he and his workers had put in that past year to realise Oakes's design of the Singapore Memorial. And in this small gesture, the newspaper managed to elevate, for a fleeting moment, this migrant from China onto the same pedestal as his colonial rulers.[1]

Born in 1905 in a small village in Hui An, within the mountainous province of Fujian, Ho Bock Kee's (何穆基) early life reflected the many challenges facing the working populace of China at the time – a prolonged period of dire economic conditions and political instability. The eldest of four children to a carpenter father and housewife mother, daily life growing up in a small rural community was hard and poverty was an everyday reality. By the time he turned six, the unstable Qing dynasty had collapsed and after a brief rule as a republic by the charismatic Sun Yat-sen, the succeeding army regime and insurrectionists established dictatorial fiefdoms throughout the provinces. Amidst this turmoil, the proximity to the greater prefecture of Quanzhou and its Near East trading routes, along with an abundance of granite quarries, saw Hui An become an established stone-cutting and carving centre for greater China and the nearby regions. It ensured its economy was centred around construction, with skilled labour readily available. A grounding in this industry would prove critical in Ho's future prospects. For unlike the impoverished and unskilled Chinese immigrants, who after heeding the lure of easy fortunes to be found in Southeast Asia and then finding themselves serving as indentured labour, Ho's arrival in Singapore in 1929 as a qualified carpenter proved otherwise.

Ho Bock Kee

The expansion of the British military presence in Singapore after the First World War and well into the 1930s saw Ho initially subcontract his labour to other builders working on numerous army camps and military facilities across the island. These early connections to the building industry were made through his involvement with the Hui Ann Association, one of many such similar cultural associations, which offered his fellow Hui An countrymen support, friendship and business networking. Through continuous work and a frugal lifestyle, Ho would, within a few years of arriving, bring out his siblings and eventually his mother. Though the Japanese occupation of Singapore curtailed much of the building work, he kept a low profile, slipping in and out of Malaya doing odd jobs where possible and above all avoiding the attention of the authorities.

The return of the British to Singapore in late 1945 and the subsequent post-war demand for reconstruction saw the new military authorities actively seek out contractors able to do their work. Seizing this window of opportunity, Ho established his own firm along with his brothers, and took up where he left off, repairing and rebuilding old army camps and bases, including those used for internment. A listing on the preferred contractor panel for the Public Works Department soon followed, and over the next 30 years Ho Bock Kee Construction was awarded numerous public and private contracts, including the Ngee Ann Kongsi school at Balestier Road, Singapore Broadcasting Corporation Centre at Caldecott Hill, Bedok Reformative Training Centre, Mount Vernon Crematorium, and the National Library at Stamford Road. In a quarter-page 'advertorial' appearing in the pages of *Nanyang Siang Pau* on the day of the unveiling, amidst extolling the quality English stone, Hong Kong pebble wash render and reinforced concrete structure, Ho proudly proclaimed to the Chinese community his most definitive work till then as the main contractor for the newly completed Singapore Memorial at Kranji.[2]

Advertorial by Ho Bock Kee Construction for the unveiling of the Singapore Memorial

Finalising the Burials

It had been two years since the Commission's formal approval of Oakes's design when, in October 1955, an open tender calling for the construction of the Kranji War Cemetery and Memorial was accepted. This followed an official public announcement in May 1952 informing that the military burial grounds at Kranji and Taiping in Malaya were to be redesigned so as to become permanent war cemeteries.[3] A year later, in October 1953, the Commission informed that a Memorial to the missing airmen was to be erected at Kranji. As it was, by the time construction commenced, the Commission had had charge over the site for more than five years. Then, having secured the Singapore Government's commitment to maintain the new access road, the topographical survey and draft memorandum for the transfer of the land to the Commission were prepared. Ho Bock Kee Construction was awarded the contract for the permanent works, with completion scheduled for January 1957.[4] In February the following year, like thousands before them, Blomfield's Cross of Sacrifice and Lutyens's Stone of Remembrance were carved from stone extracted from an approved Portland quarry, carefully placed within robust timber crates and loaded onto a freighter to be shipped to Singapore, where they were delivered undamaged to the site, waiting to be erected.[5]

However, this preceding period could not be described as static, awaiting only the formalities of the design and construction process to unfold. Unlike the traditional war cemeteries of the First World War, located as they were close to or upon the very sites where those interred had fallen in battle, Kranji was complicated by distance and the recovery and consolidation of remains from throughout a vast region. In this instance, the design layout was subject to numerous changes on account of unforeseen circumstances arising from both the war itself and the political dynamics of the region. The impact was felt mainly in the ever-changing burial allocations, one significant example being the Dutch contingent. In September 1948, the Netherlands War Graves Foundation (Oorlogsgravenstichting) formally requested the Commission exhume and repatriate the remains of their servicemen located within both Kranji and Bidadari. Transferred initially to a Dutch war cemetery in Sumatra, the Indonesian government's subsequent requirement for the consolidation of foreign war remains saw their final resting place within one of the seven permanent war cemeteries established in Java, as part of a total of 3,049 burials relocated from throughout Burma, Thailand, Malaya and Hong Kong. The 174 exhumed from Kranji constituted two plots, significant in their central position along the main axis fronting the site of the Memorial.

Then there were further mass graves discovered on Singapore island long after the war and the retrieval of battlefield remains had ceased. In September 1951, mass graves were discovered in the Siglap and Bedok areas, which upon excavation contained the remains of almost 1,300 soldiers, volunteers, and civilians (mostly Chinese) who had been massacred by the Japanese on 22 February 1942, at the onset of the Sook Ching. Locally known as the 'Valley of Death' due to the location's undulating terrain, it was eventually determined that 200 of these victims were military deaths requiring internment at Kranji.[6] In other scenarios, buried remains within Kranji itself would be contested for their numbers, often contradicting those figures originally recorded, requiring exhumation and re-interment where necessary. This was the case with the partially skeletonised remains of ten British soldiers who had been reported killed within the Perseverance Estate on 15 February 1942. Buried as six 'unknowns' in April 1946, fresh information four years later would see them not only identified but requiring re-interment in ten individual graves.[7] By early 1952, the ground beams had been cast and the headstones to be erected over them had begun arriving from Britain fully inscribed. Complicating matters further, two years later, in early 1954, there was a need to urgently accommodate 18 relocated Dutch military graves from Saigon on account of the increasing instability in Indochina and the Netherlands' growing rancour with its former colony Indonesia, impeding their reburial there. The works would only be completed by March that year.[8]

The State Cemetery

Kranji today is neither a village nor a town. It could not even be considered a suburb in the traditional sense, though the amalgam of low-density housing estates has gained traction in recent years, encroaching stealthily on the otherwise sprawling industrial estates. Reclamation of the swamps alongside the nearby estuaries, beginning from the early 1960s, yielded almost 250 acres of additional land and eventually accommodated sawmills and related industries.[9] But unlike many other settlements closely identified with their war cemeteries, notable examples being Villers-Bretonneux and Colleville-sur-Mer in France, Ypres and Passchendaele in Belgium, and Gallipoli in Turkey, the precinct of Kranji does not evoke similar connections to a tragic past.

With Kranji Reservoir to the west, an arrival at the local elevated rail station is greeted by an expansive concourse leading directly to the Singapore Turf Club's racecourse to the immediate south. The only horse track in Singapore, the Kranji Racecourse opened in 2000 after the closure of Bukit Timah Race Course, which pre-dated the Second World War and at one time provided early turfing for the cemetery. To the local population now, it is Kranji Racecourse that is synonymous with Kranji's identity. The reservoir itself, formed by damming Sungei Kranji in the early 1970s and cutting it off from the Johore Straits, is the same estuary the Japanese crossed to invade the island over 70 years ago. The war cemetery, situated less than a kilometre to the south-west, is identified today through directions on the station's precinct directory board, on a single street sign on the adjacent roadway, and at the immediate bus stop route guides. Indeed, taking the local bus to navigate two stops to an isolated and somewhat rural station at the base of Kranji Hill, the visitor is greeted by thick foliage on either side of the roadway, and a short bitumen track to the main entrance proper. Oakes's original proposal for the accessway, to which Obbard had objected and which was later discarded by acquiescing to the politics of the day, now makes eminently more sense.

For visitors to the war cemetery, the majority of whom arrive at the bottom of the hill and then traverse the rest on foot, the approach establishes a hierarchy, intentional or otherwise, of how once-colonial space is negotiated within an independent, post-colonial country. An unshaded roadway, carved through the base of Kranji Hill and offering no views beyond the immediate grassed embankments on either side, eventually comes to an incongruous white gateway, framing within its sights the Cross of Sacrifice and the Singapore Memorial in the distance. This towering memorial arch through which one must pass was designed by the architect Tan Beng Kiat from the Public Works Department (PWD), notable for his contribution to the modernist design of Singapore's National Stadium at Kallang and the International Airport at Paya Lebar. Spanning a clear open width of 16 feet (4.8 metres) and tapering upwards to a height of 40 feet (12.2 metres), this white concrete portal, with squared edges crowning its apex and 10-foot-high solid walls on either side, marks the entrance not to the war cemetery, but to a preceding burial ground founded in 1970.[10]

Newspaper reports from that time suggest that Singapore's State Cemetery was to be styled after Arlington National Cemetery, which lies across the Potomac River from Washington, D.C.[11] Planned for Singapore's most eminent citizens, it was intended to be the State's tribute to those who made important contributions to the country's progress during their lifetimes. Its origins stem, however, more from an unexpected event rather than long-term strategic planning. In April 1968, whilst President Yusof Ishak (1910–1970) was on a sea voyage to Australia, he suffered a serious heart condition that required his urgent hospitalisation in Melbourne. The medical prognosis was not encouraging, offering him a few months at best, and upon returning home, he was placed under constant care.[12] It then became apparent to the Government of the day that not only would this become the first state funeral after independence, it was a matter of the utmost urgency. And given the emotional sensitivity and time constraints such an enterprise would generate whilst the head of state was still alive, the selection and development of a suitable cemetery was placed under the direct oversight of the Prime Minister's Office.

In the first instance, Arthur George Alphonso, the Director of the Botanic Gardens, and Tan Beng Kiat, Senior Architect heading the Special Duties Department at PWD, were seconded to assist in the selection of a suitable site and develop its design into a stately cemetery befitting its intended. The search identified that the land granted to the Imperial War Graves Commission in December 1956 for their exclusive use as a war cemetery incorporated two smaller portions to the north, on either side of the main access driveway and car park. Both plots were not being utilised and in fact were surplus to the Commission's needs. Given their position adjacent to the War Cemetery (the Military Cemetery would only be established in 1975), it was decided they could offer the solemnity and dignity required for the proposed national cemetery. The Botanic Gardens was then tasked with making overtures to the Commission for their return back to the State.

These two small plots to the west and east of the accessway measured 103,000 square feet (2.3 acres) and 84,500 square feet (1.9 acres), respectively. The land which the accessway runs through amounted to 11,500 square feet (0.2 acres), and was to be also considered in the transaction. After a year of protracted negotiations, the Singapore Government finally acceded to the Commission's requirement of an uninterrupted right of way through the accessway parcel of land and the protection of the amenity of the war cemetery beyond. This paved the way for those portions to be returned to the State for the development of the national cemetery, whereupon on 28 October 1970 a Memorandum of Surrender between the President of Singapore and the Commonwealth War Graves Commission was finalised.[13] Yusof Ishak died less than a month later, on 23 November. After lying in state at City Hall for thousands of mourners to pass by and offer homage, he was buried according to his Muslim faith at the State Cemetery two days later, in the early evening of 25 November.

The haste in locating a suitable site and making preparations for its acquisition by the State made it inevitable that the design and final landscape of the cemetery would be delayed. Only in early January 1971 was the final design layout issued to Prime Minister Lee Kuan

IN HONOUR OF WAR HEROES

Yew (1923–2015) for his personal review and approval. Indeed, the priority leading into the latter half of 1970 was to ensure that at the very least the turfing within the plots was suitably maintained in readiness for the inevitable state funeral. And yet this was no ordinary accomplishment, for since 1963 Singapore had been experiencing severe water shortages due to an unprecedented drought and inadequate natural supplies.[14] Into this equation was the predicament the Government and its Ministry of Health found themselves in: anyone caught using potable water for non-critical activities was to be prosecuted. For whilst washing one's car or watering plants was not permitted, that same scarce water was necessary to maintain the landscape of the new State Cemetery. Neither was the Commission's War Cemetery spared, having no piped-in water for irrigation since its inception.

It fell upon the tact and ingenuity of an unlikely source to secure a permanent water supply to both cemeteries. At the instigation and cost of Singapore's intelligence services, not only were two new water meters and associated piping installed, they used the water board as agents and a front to undertake the works. Reporting directly to the Prime Minister's Secretary, the entire operation was cloaked in secrecy lest anyone detect that 'drinking water had been laid on and authorised for the state burial grounds'.[15] It would only be detected months later through the confusion arising in attempting to correct the low pressure emanating from its piping. It emerged that an inadequately sized pipe had been connected to the meters.

Yet for all its stature and intended national significance, within its ground as of today there lie only two inhabitants, Singapore's first and second presidents, Yusof Ishak and Benjamin Henry Sheares (1907–1981). Singapore's third president, Devan Nair (1923–2005), died in Canada and was interred there according to his Hindu customs. The fourth president, Wee Kim Wee (1915–2005), in connecting with his grassroots support, requested his ashes be placed in Mandai Columbarium, like many of his fellow citizens. In doing so, this marked a clean break from what would otherwise have appeared as social stratification in a nation devoted to meritocracy. This limited use of the State

Cemetery could therefore be viewed as the final barrier against colonial influence. By not using the State Cemetery for the Chinese heads of state, the government inadvertently ceased any lingering deference to the colonial presence. And with the majority of the local Chinese and Indian community opting for cremation in the land-scarce island, most of the remains of Singapore's post-independence leaders now reside at Mandai Columbarium. This also includes Singapore's first Prime Minister, Lee Kuan Yew, who passed away in March 2015. After a private wake at Sri Temasek, the Prime Minister's official residence in the Istana grounds, lying in state at Parliament House and a state funeral at the University Cultural Centre, his remains were similarly brought to and interred at Mandai. It creates somewhat of an anomaly, in that the various races that were once united in defiance of unilateralism and created a multiracial nation could now not find a way in death to share a common burial ground. Notwithstanding, it is telling that in order to access the graves of those servicemen who died for the British Empire, one must pass those of two men synonymous with modern Singapore's political separation from that same Commonwealth.

Kranji War Cemetery

The distance between the memorial arch and the iron gates of the formal entrance to Kranji War Cemetery is a mere 60 metres. Oakes in his original design had allowed the existing 15-foot-wide access road from the main roadway to merge into a 34-foot-wide (10.3 metres) avenue, lined on both sides with fern trees (*Filicium decipiens*) before a small car park at the entrance gates.[16] Today, this spatial separation, bereft of any landscape against the harsh tropical sun, consists of a bitumen roadway with angled car parking either side. From here, glancing further west beyond a walkway lined with local casuarina and rosewood trees and past the caretaker's cottage, one observes the carefully arranged rows of regimental headstones facing towards you. Immediately identifiable as military, yet unlike the crisp, white Portland stone synonymous with the war graves, they are instead a grey granite, their weathered and textured state revealing their previous history. Flanking both the State and War Cemeteries to the west, the Kranji Military Cemetery is a sizeable non-World War site comprising 1,422 burials of former servicemen and their families. It was developed and consecrated in 1975 when the need arose to relocate graves from their former locations in Pasir Panjang and Ulu Pandan which were required for urban redevelopment. Pasir Panjang was cleared first, in 1974, with 674 of its graves reburied in this new ground, followed by another 748 from Ulu Pandan Military Cemetery in late 1975. The latter site, occupying 2.5 hectares, would become a much-needed wooded park in a country encountering a booming population and their recreational needs. Distinctive in its perpendicular orientation to the main War Cemetery, this new burial ground, separated only by a cluster of trees at either end and rows of low hedges and planters, is otherwise indistinguishable. Compounding this similarity, it would later be confirmed that 11 of those interred were in fact war-related deaths and reclassified accordingly.

It is with some relief from the elements that one arrives at the entrance shelters, designed by Oakes and acting as silent sentinels over Sir Edwin Lutyens's Stone of Remembrance. Accessed by an upwards flight of stone steps, the Stone occupies the geographic centre of a semi-rectangular forecourt, its width terminating in circular arcs. Their curvature of 60-feet radius emanates from the centre of the Stone itself. Partly paved and turfed, with a gravel pathway along its internal perimeter, the forecourt is completed by a low wall adorned in a finely crushed pebble finish and an accompanying manicured green hedge above. By maintaining a low perimeter height, a visual connection with the Stone is ensured from throughout the greater part of the cemetery and in particular from the base of the Memorial atop the hill. A second flight of steps completes the entry forecourt, bringing one up between two shelters, which together frame the main axis to the Memorial beyond. An embedded stone and concrete star on the ground between these edifices marks the spot.

Rising almost 23 feet above the courtyard and measuring 16 feet by 16 feet in plan, these two stone-clad and rendered shelters offer

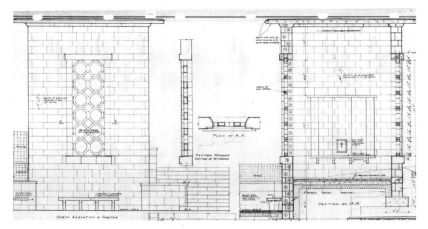

Details of the entranceway shelters with their precast octagonal screens

sanctuary from the elements, which in the case of Kranji is often the glare of the tropical sun and the occasional thunderstorm. Rectangular apertures set high upon their walls allow glances of sunlight and light breezes to penetrate their interior depths. Precast concrete screens comprising 12 octagonal elements resembling the shape of the ancient Chinese *bagua* sit within the openings, offering direct views through to both the Stone of Remembrance and the Singapore Memorial. It may suggest a conscious understanding of the local fengshui principles that often underpinned the design of local architecture prevalent throughout the overseas Chinese communities of Singapore and Southeast Asia. Having earlier completed the Stanley and Sai Wan Bay War Cemeteries and Memorial in Hong Kong, Oakes was aware of their significance. An essential tool in the teachings of fengshui, the *bagua* was traditionally used for burial sites.[17] While the east shelter accommodates the register box and book listing all those interred within the cemetery, the west shelter has a solitary timber bench. It allows for a reflective moment within the walled silence to gather one's thoughts before tackling the cemetery proper, often an emotional journey for relatives and loved ones.

Standing between the entrance shelters and looking upwards to the Memorial on the hill, one takes in the wide turfed expanse of

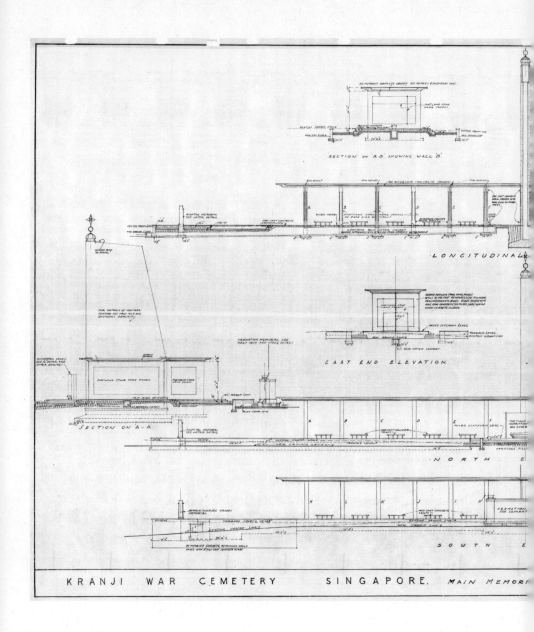

SECTION ON 'B.B' SHOWING WALL 'B'

LONGITUDINAL

EAST END ELEVATION.

SECTION ON A-A.

NORTH E

SOUTH E

KRANJI WAR CEMETERY   SINGAPORE.   MAIN MEMORI

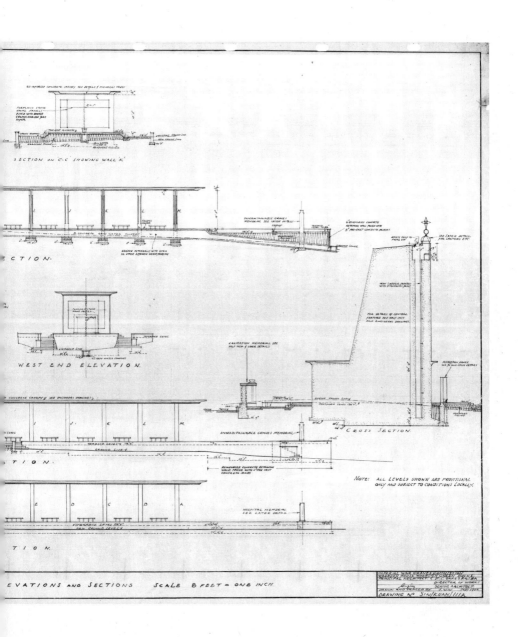

Detailed elevations and sections of the Singapore Memorial

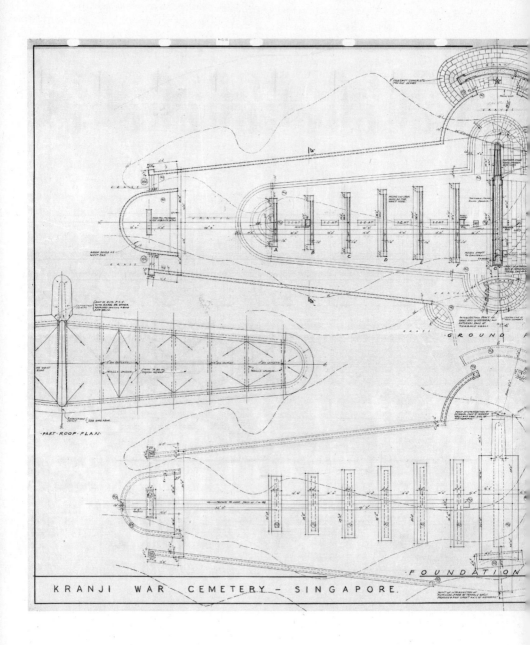

·PART·ROOF·PLAN·

KRANJI WAR CEMETERY - SINGAPORE.

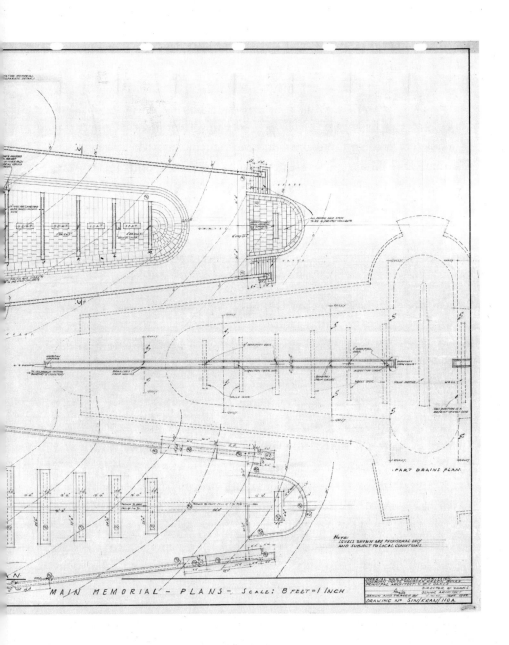

MAIN MEMORIAL - PLANS - SCALE: 8 FEET = 1 INCH

·PART DRAINS PLAN·

NOTE:
LEVELS SHOWN ARE PROVISIONAL ONLY
AND SUBJECT TO LOCAL CONDITIONS

Detailed architectural plans of the Singapore Memorial

the main war cemetery. Within this consecrated ground, spanning approximately 450 feet by 350 feet, lie the buried remains of 4,461 Commonwealth casualties of the Second World War, of which 3,692 were identified.[18] Walking slowly upwards through the lines of uniform headstones, spaced equally apart, their inscriptions face towards you, each one portraying a simple story of name, rank, regiment and faith. For some, a short verse or phrase underlines their identity, a personal choice offered to loved ones, more often than not the parents. For others, the Biblical phrase 'Known unto God' – selected for the Commission by British poet Rudyard Kipling – is their only mark.

Here at the equator, the tropical sun casts deep shadows into the earth, and quickly disappears with the onset of twilight. An understanding of how sun and shadow play across the ground in the tropics makes one appreciate Oakes's design better. At the apex of the hill stands the Memorial, shaped as it was to resemble the wings of an aeroplane. Its height and north-south orientation allow the 12 stone-clad 'spar walls' to cast shadows equally at sunrise as at sunset. With each wall diminishing in length the further away from the central 'tail fin' pylon – all of which are inscribed with the names of missing servicemen, 24,307 in total – the sense that sunlight can penetrate even the deepest recesses becomes more apparent. No inscription is allowed to linger in prolonged darkness. As the local breezes pass through the parallel spars unfettered, stone benches afford the visitor an idyllic and peaceful station by which to commemorate those on the walls.

Walking past the inscriptions of the missing, engraved as they are within 3-inch-thick Portland stone panels embedded in the walls, the clear visibility of the names is no coincidence. When the architect-cartographer-graphic designer MacDonald Gill was approached to design the lettering for the standard war graves headstone, the Commission insisted on a specific angle for the incision of the letters.[19] This angle differed from that used by stonemasons within regular cemeteries. The angle and measurement of the inscriptions was designed to ensure their visibility and legibility as one walked along the rows of headstones. In the case of Kranji, Oakes further amplified the presence of the inscription panels by offsetting them with a 2-foot-wide border along both sides, above the floor level and beneath the soffit of the roof structure above. Their grey rendered finish provides an additional textural contrast with the polished white of the stone.

Whilst each spar wall's thickness measures 1 foot 6 inches, the thicker central (or 'thirteenth') spar strikingly resembles an aircraft's tail fin, with a 'rudder' extension to the south. Flanked by the Dedicatory Inscription Panel to the north and the Cremation Memorial to the south, its full presence is better realised from afar rather than within the Memorial proper. Its apex is adorned with a finial comprising a glass domed lantern and four-pointed star. Access to this crown is through a cleverly concealed shaft, its one-foot radius accommodating only the modest in girth. With its entrance from an adjacent floor-mounted panel, avoiding the need to disturb the inscription panels with an unsightly door, one must descend beneath the podium before climbing a cat ladder almost 80 feet to the apex. This more substantial central wall similarly bears the names and regiments of the many who have no known grave, but no benches are provided on either side of it. Instead, a small rendered masonry enclosure takes their place, its top honed smooth with an eggshell finish. Embedded with a bronze registry box containing names, ranks, regiments and dates of death, these two silent pillars serve as guards to all those the Memorial represents.

Along the northern perimeter of the Memorial's podium, the external face of a low terrace wall provides two axes, which meet the short axis through the length of the central spar. All three then intersect the centre line of the main approach to the cemetery. What previously appeared as a slight tilt of the Memorial's plan in relation to the formal symmetry of the war graves is in fact a considered 4.5° rotation. Neither in the drawings nor Oakes's personal notes is an explanation for this angle provided. Was he considering some form of magnetic declination to Singapore, making a reference to a far-off significant location or was it a matter of fengshui, the local Chinese geomancy? Maybe time will reveal the significance of this small detail.

Details of the glass dome and bronze finial, fabricated in a UK foundry, that cap the central tower of the Memorial. Note the access via a concealed shaft.

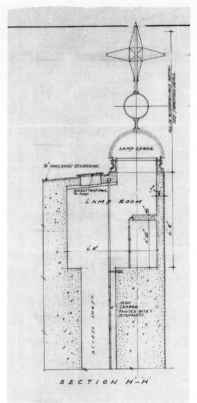

SECTION 'H-H'

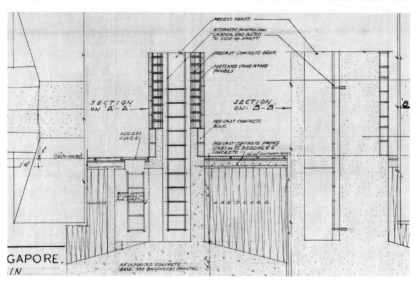

Detailing the Design

The Imperial War Graves Commission first announced to the general public their intention to erect a Commonwealth Air Forces Memorial at Kranji in a small article in *The Straits Times* on 7 October 1953.[20] The last of four memorials to the missing airmen of the Second World War – the others being in England (Runnymede), Malta (Valletta) and Egypt (El Alamein) – it was suggested that it would be similar to but less elaborate than its counterpart overlooking the River Thames in Runnymede, Surrey.

Designed by Sir Edward Maufe, the Runnymede Memorial commemorates over 20,000 airmen and women who were lost in the Second World War during operations from bases in the United Kingdom and northern and western Europe and who have no known graves. Officially opened by the Queen on 18 July 1957, its neoclassical architecture of pitched roof cloisters embracing an internal courtyard and two-storey shrine of white Portland stone evokes similarity to the control towers that aircrew would have seen when returning to base. The shrine itself is adorned with three stone figures by the noted sculptor Vernon Hill representing Justice, Victory and Courage, whilst its engraved glass and painted ceilings were designed by the artist John Hutton. The roof of the tower is surmounted by an Astral crown of blue and gold.[21] There appear to have been no limitations placed on the design of Runnymede, unlike Oakes's Singapore Memorial, which was physically scaled back 10 per cent to fit a modest budget. Sir Hubert Worthington's Malta Memorial suffered a greater cost-cutting fate of 20 per cent, coincidentally also with Maufe as Artistic Advisor, who advocated the Memorial's adornment of 'bronze eagle and ball' being reduced in height from 11 feet to 7 feet 6 inches.[22]

It was left to Oakes, who whilst working in private practice after the war had considerable experience in designing to limited budgets, to draw on his practical sensibilities. The modernist stripping back of architectural adornment, along with the advancement of contemporary building materials and construction methods, contributed greatly to his cause. Pioneer of the Modern Movement in architecture, Ludwig

Mies van der Rohe's adage, 'Less is more', is suitably apt for the Kranji Memorial.

Notwithstanding the advances in construction detailing, the Commission had tended to maintain the course in the use of building materials for the vast majority of the war cemeteries and war memorials since the First World War. Stone as a building block was by far one of its most consistent selections. Minor variations to the origins of the stone did occur in regions where the England-extracted Portland limestone was ill-suited to the terrain and climatic conditions or proved challenging to transport. Few examples departed so considerably from the norm as Lutyens's Thiepval Memorial, with its extensive use of facing brick. Over time, however, the French bricks would prove problematic, with constant spalling – owing as much to their composition and forming as to the rain and frost.[23] Yet throughout the British Isles, continental Europe, North Africa and the Middle East, the association of the Commonwealth war cemetery with the white headstone, the name of the dead etched upon it, was more often validated than not. And that included the method by which its structures were erected, with traditional load-bearing stonework during and immediately after the First World War, evolving to a greater use of stone cladding on reinforced concrete substrates thereafter. This was certainly the case for many of the war memorials and cemetery structures in Asia after the Second World War.

Oakes's working experience in India had introduced him to the many possibilities and limitations in constructing otherwise British edifices in Asia, from the access to and quality of local building materials to the labour skills available in any one country. Following the war cemetery examples built by the Anzac Agency in Borneo and Papua New Guinea, he also understood how the tropical climate, heavy rain and seismic activity made for unstable soil conditions. Whilst Worthington was concerned with desert winds and shifting sands in North Africa, and Sir John Burnet with seismic activity on the Gallipoli peninsula, Oakes's primary concern was with rain and flooding. This was particularly the case in some of the low-lying cemetery sites in

Southeast Asia. Recognising that Kranji was prone to ground movement given the poor quality of the soil and occasional tropical deluge,
Oakes from the outset recommended that in lieu of the Commission's
upright headstones erected in their millions across the former European theatre, they provide a ground-embedded version constructed in
concrete, with the epitaphs cast on bronze plaques and mounted over.[24]
Concurrently, all memorial walls were to be formed in reinforced concrete, using thin slabs of Portland stone as cladding only. This method
had been utilised successfully in Thanbyuzayat and Kanchanaburi War
Cemeteries, which were nearing completion.

Oakes had precedent in his proposal for an embedded plaque and
pedestal design in lieu of traditional headstones for the Asian war cemeteries. At their September 1948 monthly meeting, the Commission
had been tasked with approving a design proposal by the Anzac Agency
to adopt this alternative headstone and inscription for war cemeteries within their sphere. The proposal was in three parts, the first of
which was to accept a bronze plaque, with inscription and service
badge embossed. The second was to consider the low concrete pedestal design that would be embedded upon a submerged concrete plinth.
And finally, to decide what pedestal design should be used in any other
cemeteries where the bronze plaque was adopted. This was due to the
Australians having proposed two designs, on account of the two types
of ground conditions they were encountering across the south-west
Pacific. In this instance, they proposed one pedestal for general use
in island cemeteries, and the other for those cemeteries afflicted by
frequent seismic activity. Lieutenant-Colonel R.W. Bateman, the Commission's Director of Works, who introduced wooden models of the
two pedestal designs, subsequently produced a further design intended
for use in cemeteries outside the Anzac Agency area, ideally suited to
Oakes's intentions and sites.[25]

After considerable deliberation, the Commission accepted the
Anzac Agency's proposals, and approved their use in selected sites both
inside and outside their area of responsibility. This allowed Oakes the
opportunity to use them in his Siam and Burma sites. Yet when it came

to Singapore, the Commission rejected Oakes's recommendation of this alternative option, insisting instead on the retention of the traditional headstone.

This cleared the way for the first large consignment of finished headstones, with their epitaphs machine-engraved back in England, to be shipped off, arriving at a Singapore dock in early 1952 for onward transport to the cemetery. An early contract awarded for their installation on recessed concrete beams would see the final war graves component of the cemetery completed by the end of that year. Throughout this period, an agent from the Commission's regional office in Penang was dispatched to supervise that the correct heights, row lines and uniform spacings were achieved. And in the Commission's archives, captured in a series of black-and-white progress photographs, the unidentified officer, with local labourers in the background, can be seen lowering small wooden caskets of servicemen's remains into freshly excavated plots, completing the war graves.

Oakes detailed all the structures at Kranji in either reinforced concrete masonry blocks or in-situ poured reinforced concrete. The Singapore Memorial spar walls and the surrounding Hospital, Cremation and Unmaintainable Graves memorials were all built in this manner. The same methodology was also extended to the boundary walls, main entrance gateways and shelters. Cladding of the memorials, though, remained in the traditional Portland stone. For all areas with carved inscriptions, Oakes allowed for 3-inch-thick stone slabs. Sheets of paper with the names to be inscribed, marked out at full scale, were arranged to determine the number of stone tablets required. It also allowed Oakes to verify that the entire list of names could be accommodated on the walls. Only after confirming the layout were the stones cut and inscribed at the Commission's approved facility in England. Like the headstones before them, the Memorial's engraved tablets would then be shipped out to Singapore, to be assembled as in a jigsaw puzzle and erected in the corresponding wall relief. Stone cladding that was without inscriptions would be of thinner material, 2 inches thick. The use of solid stone was left to the curved Dedicatory

Remains of servicemen arranged and awaiting reburial

Portland stone headstones unpacked and awaiting erection

Erection of the Cross of Sacrifice

Inscription Panel fronting the Memorial, in keeping with construction methods from an earlier period.

It would be another design decision, though, that highlighted Oakes's understanding of the Asian aesthetic and the need to incorporate it. In all areas of the cemetery and memorial that were not clad in stone, including reinforced concrete structures, Oakes specified a Hong Kong rendering finish. Hong Kong render, more commonly referred to as Shanghai plaster, is a cement-based granolithic plaster coating, particularly used on walls and columns, that leaves a fine textured pebble finish. This technique had its origins in Hong Kong and had spread throughout Malaya and greater Southeast Asia in the 1920s, reflecting how the overseas Chinese constructed their cultural identity through architecture, especially during those interwar years. It also came to symbolise an early regional building modernity.[26] Oakes first encountered the coating in Malaya whilst undertaking the Taiping War Cemetery and subsequently used it on the Memorial and ancillary structures within the Sai Wan Bay War Cemetery in Hong

Construction of the Singapore Memorial

Kong. Applied extensively on most of the non-stone surfaces, it acted to reduce the glare reflecting under the intense tropical sun and protect the substrate from frequent torrential downpours.

In providing octagonal screens and a local render finish, small as these design gestures may appear, along with the more significant placement of the Singapore General Hospital Memorial and Chinese Memorial around the Singapore Memorial, Oakes was not without moral if not explicit support. As far back as September 1947, Obbard, through his position overseeing the Commission's work throughout South and Southeast Asia, had written to headquarters highlighting the concerns of the Singapore Government with respect to sentiment among their local Chinese population. Although his correspondence was ostensibly related to providing an allotment or burial space for massacred Chinese personnel, he relayed his concerns on more than one occasion on the sensitivities of the local culture and the need to be conscious of it. This included acknowledging and making accommodations for the spatial requirements that Chinese burial customs required.[27]

Aerial view of Kranji War Cemetery and Memorial

Landscape

British horticulturist and garden designer Gertrude Jekyll, one of the most influential advocates of the Arts and Crafts movement through her involvement with Edwin Lutyens from the late 19th century onwards, would become synonymous with the gardens of the war cemeteries. Trained originally as an artist, Jekyll's influence by the painter J.M.W. Turner and Impressionism carried through to her landscape design and planning of some 400 gardens over her lifetime, many of which were in collaboration with Lutyens and Robert Lorimer. Her use of colour, texture and an appreciation of how plants present, would become the intrinsic template by which the war cemeteries came to be identified. And yet Jekyll's ideas spread far beyond the timeframe of Lutyens's work. Writing for *Garden History*, Sarah Joiner suggests that while the Commission archives have no mention of her collaboration with the organisation, her influence and techniques were well known among the leading horticulturists and Kew- and Royal Horticultural Society-trained gardeners who were serving at the Front.[28]

While working alongside Lutyens on seven British war cemeteries for the First World War in northern France, notably in Gézaincourt, Fienvillers, Auchonvillers, Trouville and Warlincourt,[29] Jekyll would imprint in her gardens a concept of English landscape and 'English-ness'. This sensibility carried though in her garden designs for the War Cloister at Winchester College and Delville Wood Memorial, both designed by Herbert Baker. Scholar Kristine Miller in her book, *Almost Home: The Public Landscapes of Gertrude Jekyll,* suggests that it was Jekyll's

> common desire that the cemeteries reproduce the image of the English landscape and, in particular, the English garden. The symbolic power of the English garden to portray the British Empire as strong, stable, and enduring cannot be overestimated. The garden signified 'rootedness' as it linked 'nation and soil'. The cemeteries as gardens depicted a 'pre-industrial past' and suggested the naturalness, timeless-ness, continuity and health of the English countryside and by association, the British Empire.[30]

Emerging from England in the 18th century, the English garden, or landscape garden, supplanted the more formal, symmetrical *jardin à la française* developed in 17th-century France, whilst spreading across Europe. Inspired by the landscape paintings of Claude Lorrain and Nicolas Poussin, and by the classic Chinese gardens of the East described by European travellers during the period, the English garden presented an idealised view of nature. Set amongst the picturesque architecture of the rolling countryside, the English landscape garden was centred on the sensibility of the English country house.[31]

Scholar Mandy S. Morris in her oft-cited essay 'Gardens "For Ever England"' argues that during and after the First World War, the tra-ditional English garden was mobilised as an essential ingredient in the iconography of British war cemeteries. Alluding to the opening verses of Rupert Brooke's 1915 poem, 'The Soldier', the gardens of the war cemeteries were quite 'literally meant to represent an unambiguous "corner of a foreign field / That is for ever England"'.[32] The enduring image of the war cemetery across the world would thus become one of the English county churchyard, more by default through the selection of architect and landscape designer than a formal edict issued by the Commission.

In spite of this prevalent sentiment, perceived or otherwise, the Commission had taken great strides to carefully consider the land-scape within the context of each site. For cemeteries outside Britain, particularly those with varying concentrations of non-British remains, they would wherever the climate permitted be actively infused with a variety of trees, shrubs and flowers native to the dead soldiers' origins. Morris highlights Australian graves adorned with wattle, Tasmanian eucalyptus and blue gums, while Chinese graves were interspersed with the maidenhair tree, otherwise known as the gingko biloba, which has historically been associated with Buddhist temples.[33] Philip Longworth recounts that whilst landscaping the First World War cemeteries of northern Europe with perennials such as variegated roses between the headstones, and thorn, hornbeam and beech hedges along the boundaries, wherever possible, Indian irises, marigolds and cypresses, Canadian maples, and New Zealand olearia would be cultivated and planted. It was only the West Indian, African and Malayan native plants that could not acclimate. And yet, citing A.W. Hill's 1920 essay, 'Our Soldiers' Graves', to 'preserve a special English feeling, daffodils, snowdrops and crocuses were allowed to grow up through the grass in some cemeteries'.[34]

The tropical climate of the Far East was far removed from that of the temperate English countryside. It wasn't as forgiving on nurturing the sense of 'Englishness' so described by Jekyll and Morris. Neither were the sentiments of former British colonies inclined to appreciate an overtly nostalgic English aesthetic within their modernising socie-ties. After all, horticultural maintenance of the war graves before their handover to the Commission, and after their permanent landscape schemes were implemented, fell to a local population of gardeners and groundskeepers. In the case of Kranji, it would be bolstered by the readily accessible plantings propagated by the Singapore Botanic Gardens for a tropical environment, and, in a significant way, by Obbard's increasingly active intervention to ensure the retention of the existing native plantings.

Oakes's ideas of how landscaping could embrace the site and interact with the architecture differed from the long-standing orthodoxy of fellow architects and designers a generation prior. Faced with addressing the very real concerns of local conditions, he was prepared to adapt the design and construction methodology accordingly. Unlike his predecessors and fellow Principal Architects, he was not tied to a formal 'English' past and was comfortable in an Asian landscape of deep shadows and vivid colours. This was suitably displayed at Taiping, his first project completed for the Commission.

At almost 2,000 feet above sea level and in a region where the rainfall is the heaviest in Malaya,[35] the Taiping War Cemetery is situated within an amphitheatre-like enclave, surrounded by a dense, verdant tropical jungle. Consulting the Royal Botanic Gardens in Kew, the advice to Oakes was to rule out European plantings and instead use species that thrived and grew in Taiping, famous as it was for its century-old rain trees. *Mesua ferrea* (Sri Lankan ironwood), *Cassia javanica* (Java cassia) and *Calophyllum pulcherrimum* (bintangor gasing) were recommended.[36] Oakes eventually settled on local palm trees, carefully embedded at regular intervals amongst the plots, to create simple relief for the white Portland headstones. This was in keeping with the original edict that although 'the cemetery would have the appearance of a small park or garden' it should be viewed unmistakeably as a war cemetery. And with no traditional rose bushes planted, the local ground cover and shrubs lining the headstone planting beds proved that tropical plantings could also produce the strict formalism so desired by the Commission without detracting from the standards required of such a site.

With Kranji, on the other hand, the topography did not lend itself to the kind of planting scheme adopted in Taiping. Nor was it like the featureless flat terrains of Kanchanaburi, Thanbyuzayat and Chungkai, where the sites were framed within clearings carved out of the surrounding jungle and separated only by a low fence. Instead, Kranji's position on a hill was more in keeping with Sai Wan Bay in Hong Kong and the hilltop of Kohima. Their gentle contours sloping downwards towards the sea (Sai Wan Bay) and the surrounding urban city (Kohima) would become their defining landscape elements. The siting of the memorials and monuments would direct the visitor in experiencing the nature of the site and the views it afforded. What landscape was provided would seek to complement rather than create the setting.

In the case of Singapore, the advice of the Botanic Gardens was eagerly sought from the outset, partially in response to the initial complaints on its condition by the Australian government. Having the Australians commenting on its poor shrubs, soil washing away and the poorly trained local gardening staff, along with the original reports by Oakes and Obbard which had painted the site as unexceptional, the Commission decided to redevelop the entire site and consult a local horticultural expert.[37] Obbard, by now transferred to Penang to head the Commission's work in Southeast Asia, would play a significant role in the landscape redevelopment and planting scheme. Through his frequent visits to Singapore, he would make numerous requests to London recommending the retention of various existing trees and native plantings. Accompanying Obbard on one such visit to the cemetery in April 1948 was the then Director of the Botanic Gardens, Professor Eric Holttum[38], whose advice the Commission had sought on improving the poor soil quality and recommending suitable plantings that could best be sustained under the conditions. Holttum, a renowned English botanist and author, had himself been interned within the Gardens during the Japanese Occupation and was favourably inclined towards the successful development of Kranji.

It would be a year later, in May 1949, that a comprehensive levelling and grading scheme was finally drawn up for the permanent ground works to commence. The final stage of the handover had been completed earlier in March, with the Commission formally taking over

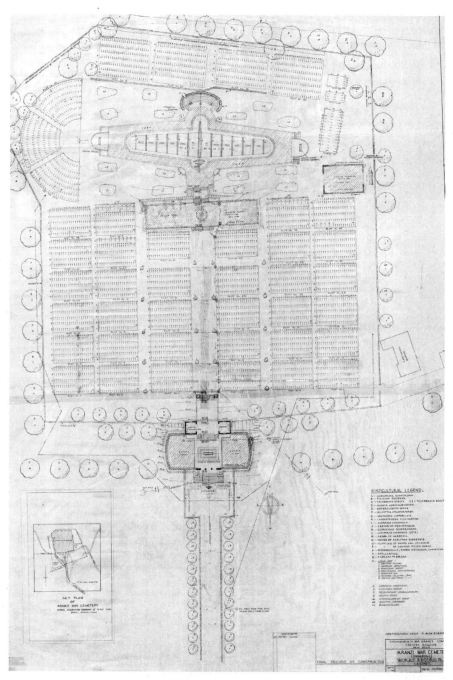

Landscape drawing for Kranji War Cemetery

the cemetery from the Army's War Graves Service on 1 April 1949.[39] Earthworks were by now well under way and the Singapore Botanic Gardens had made provision to supply all the trees necessary to implement Oakes's design intentions.

Over the next three years, whilst Obbard and Oakes differed on the position and importance of the main accessway to the cemetery, they would eventually concur in retaining the significant number of existing mahogany and yew trees that lined it. These native trees had been planted as part of a temporary scheme established when the site was still an army hospital and had been supplemented and enhanced by the War Graves Unit that took over after the war. By now tall and mature, they would be integrated into the final design scheme. Oakes, having wanted more colour in the plantings, would also settle on this evergreen effect. In one area where both architect and administrator agreed, it was that protecting the views from the elevated Memorial towards the coast was paramount.

The final detailed landscape plans, incorporating the temporary plantings, were issued in May 1953. Oakes, Obbard, and the Commission's Botanical Advisor and Director of the Royal Botanical Gardens Kew, Sir Edward Salisbury, would review them and agree on the intended outcome, though some level of dispute between Oakes and Obbard on plant retentions would linger. In any case, by the time construction and final horticultural works commenced three years later, both men would no longer be actively involved. Oakes, having relinquished his appointment with the Commission, returned to private practice, whilst Obbard retired. Even so, with the permanent landscaping confirmed and the Kranji War Cemetery drawings approved in July, there was still confusion as to the final intention. In a proposal emanating from Penang, it was revealed that the main avenue in the cemetery would be planted with trees from every country in the British Commonwealth. Holttum, by then Professor of Botany at the University of Malaya, however, reappeared to debunk the notion: 'It is out of the question ... not a single tree from Britain or Canada would grow in this climate, unless in an air-conditioned greenhouse.'[40]

As with all major horticultural projects, not all the landscaping was successful. In a horticultural site report prepared for the Commission later that year, it was identified that the combination of the original turf taken from the nearby racecourse and the *lalang* grass was struggling under the moist conditions. It was recommended that a local carpet grass better suited to the moist, low-fertility soil of the site replace the existing. And in a rebuttal of the earlier contentious scheme of retaining the existing mahogany trees, not only was their rapid growth beginning to obstruct the desired views from the Memorial, but they had all been attacked by white ants. The Commission would go on to approve their replacement with the native yellow saraca. With these flowering trees interspersed along the avenue with the remaining yews and cypresses, Oakes's original scheme of a colourful approach was being realised.

Kranji War Memorial on the day of its unveiling, 2 March 1957

CHAPTER 9

Post-War

As Governor Robert Black stepped forward upon the circular dais of the Singapore Memorial to place his official wreath at the foot of the Dedicatory Inscription Panel – the multilingual inscription 'They Died For All Free Men' peering back from its concave stone face – an elderly Chinese woman, dressed in the traditional *samfoo* of her generation, emerged weeping from the surrounding crowd and stumbled up to the Cross of Remembrance, a few metres away.[1] Among the onlookers, consisting of official guests, military officers and presiding clergy, was Australian journalist Nan Hall, who was attending the event on behalf of the local newspaper, *The Straits Times*. In her coverage the following day, Hall recalled that the woman

> sobbed loudly and rocked her head in her hands – oblivious to the sea of concerned faces turned towards her. Two men tried to draw her aside but it was not until Major-General John Steedman, of the Imperial War Graves Commission, gently put his arm around her shoulders that she stopped weeping. His row of medals clinked against her wrinkled old cheeks as he led her away and found a chair for her in the background under the shade of a tree.[2]

When the formalities of the ceremony were over, Hall approached this elderly woman, seated alone amidst the slowly dispersing crowd. In the ensuing conversation, she proceeded to produce papers and photographs identifying herself as Madam Cheng Seang Ho (alias Cheong Sang Hoo, 郑双好), an 81-year-old Singaporean war-time heroine. Cheng and her husband, Sim Chin Foo (alias Chum Chan Foo, 岑振扶), had joined an irregular band of army and civilian fighters formed by Lieutenant-Colonel John Dalley of the Federated Malay States Police Force on 25 December 1941. Colloquially known as Dalforce, this guerrilla unit within the organisational structure of the Straits Settlements Volunteer Force, recruited from the ethnic Chinese community of Singapore, had acquitted themselves honourably in the battles against the Japanese invading force.[3] One of the letters in her hand was in fact signed by Dalley himself, stating that 'Madam Cheng fought gallantly and risked her life by going to the front at the battle of Bukit Timah where her comrades died one after the other'.[4] Unable to contain the advancing Japanese, Cheng along with a few other survivors had subsequently escaped through the jungle, emerging some time later in the Malayan hinterland. Her husband Sim meanwhile had slipped into Singapore city. Briefly reunited and working as labourers in Singapore a few months later, Sim would be eventually captured by the Kempeitai, the Japanese military police, and tortured to death. His name, along with 132 fellow Chinese volunteers of Dalforce who died in the campaign, was engraved on the very memorial being unveiled.[5]

It was a poignant moment that perfectly captured the emotional toil borne by those who survived the war and came that day to remember the many who didn't. For the survivors, Kranji would take on a special meaning in their recollection of those three and a half years under the occupation of the Japanese. And in doing so, the memorial would become the setting for further narratives of a country's history. Kevin Blackburn and Karl Hack in their book, *War Memory and the Making of Modern Malaysia and Singapore*, describe in detail this scene of Madam Cheng within the context of local Chinese war heroes and the search for a Malayan identity. In doing so, the struggle united a disparate social, cultural and economic group, otherwise collectively seen as the Overseas Chinese, through their common hatred of Japanese aggression against the motherland China. And by 1957, after a decade of communist insurgency and the Malayan Emergency, this had evolved into a 'wider struggle to define what the "Overseas Chinese" were, who most deserved to lead them, and what sort of postcolonial state was desirable'.

Amidst all the pomp and circumstance, the presence of Madam Cheng at the unveiling ceremony was but one such reminder of those local survivors for whom Singapore and now Kranji War Cemetery and Memorial held strong memories. The Australians attending that day were another such group, consisting of survivors of the Japanese internment, bereaved family members who had lost sons and husbands in the fighting, and those who had managed to escape the fall of Singapore and make their way back to the relative safety of home. In addition, ten British widows of servicemen whose names were inscribed on the walls of the Singapore Memorial had also been flown to Singapore for this day. Their presence at the unveiling, at the bequest and funding of the Imperial War Graves Commission, would offer the general public back home, listening in on the national radio broadcast and reading the news correspondent's dispatches, a small yet recognisable connection to how the war had affected them all.[6]

Writing in the 27 March 1957 edition of *The Australian Women's Weekly*, war correspondent and staff writer Dorothy Drain provided Australia's only extensive print account of the Kranji Memorial unveiling ceremony. Through the first-known colour coverage of that event, it brought home in pictures the serenity of Kranji to the faraway families and friends of the deceased.[7] For the Australians, little-known Kranji had come to represent their doomed efforts in the fall of Singapore, the British Empire's so-called 'impregnable fortress'. In the public imagination that day, listening in on the Australian Broadcasting Corporation's (ABC) national radio feed and reading dispatched accounts, Kranji's transformation into a war cemetery and memorial came to

TO HONOR THE 24,000

• "To my darling son" . . . "For my beloved husband" . . . "To Dad." These messages of simple intimacy were attached to hundreds of wreaths laid on the Singapore War Memorial at its unveiling on March 2.

THE SINGAPORE WAR MEMORIAL, the largest in South-east Asia, at its official unveiling. Christian, Moslem, Hindu, and Buddhist priests prayed for the dead, and jet-fighters of the Royal Australian Air Force flew overhead in salute. The Memorial has 12 granite pillars.

MORE than 3000 people, including 40 Australian relatives of men honored by the Memorial, attended the ceremony, which was performed by the Governor of Singapore, Sir Robert Black.

The Memorial, in the Kranji War Cemetery, overlooking the Straits of J o h o r e, commemorates 24,000 members of the British Commonwealth Forces w h o d i e d in the Japanese theatre of World War II. Most of the men whose names are carved on the 12

granite columns have no known graves. Others are buried in the cemetery.

Built by the Imperial War Graves Commission, the Memorial stands on a hilltop in the area where Australian troops made their stand as the battle for Singapore entered its final stages in January, 1942.

The official Australian contingent at the unveiling was led by Lieut.-General H. Gordon Bennett, who commanded the Eighth Division in Malaya.

AUSTRALIANS PAY TRIBUTE. Left: Lieut.-General H. Gordon Bennett, who commanded the Eighth Division in Malaya, and his aide, Capt. L. Logan, at the Memorial. Above: Sister Vivian Bullwinkel, survivor of the Banka Island massacre, at the ceremony.

THE AUSTRALIAN WOMEN'S WEEKLY – March 27, 1957

Page 8

Australian Women's Weekly coverage of the Singapore Memorial unveiling

signify a war on its doorstep that accounted for 45,843 casualties out of a 1945 population of almost 7.43 million.[8] Kranji alone accounts for 1,049 Australian burials (almost 1 in 3) of a total 3,702, and 1,639 inscriptions of the missing (almost 7 per cent) out of 24,304.[9] For a country that had scarcely recovered from the atrocious losses sustained in the First World War, these numbers were significant. Few families back home had been spared the grief of a loved one reported deceased, injured or missing. The news of the unveiling ceremony brought them some measure of comfort if not closure. It offered a necessary pause to a nation that had until a few years prior seen involvement in Korea and was already turning its attention to the unfolding unrest in Indochina.

In a prequel article titled 'Singapore Memorial' written a month earlier, Drain had unveiled an artist's drawing of Oakes's Singapore Memorial and announced the official party attending the ceremony on behalf of the Australian government.[10] Led by Lieutenant-General Gordon Bennett, commander of the 8th Division in Malaya during the war, the small Australian contingent was accompanied by Brigadier Athol Brown, Secretary-General of the Anzac Agency of the Imperial War Graves Commission. This party of 15 had been carefully selected to represent the majority of Australians back home and comprised service personnel, representatives of various Services organisations and family members who had loved ones interred in the cemetery or inscribed on the memorial. And for each member, the significance of being present in Singapore, at Kranji, with the memorial being unveiled, was acutely personal. The party included Bennett's aide, Brigadier Harold B. Taylor, who had commanded the 22nd Infantry Brigade which defended the north-west corner of Singapore near Kranji, and Group Captain R.H. Davis, representing the Royal Australian Air Force.[11] Taylor and Davis had both been captured, and after a brief spell in Changi they were sent to Formosa (Taiwan) and then Manchuria. It was whilst interned at Changi that Taylor established and ran an educational programme for his fellow prisoners of war which came to be dubbed 'Changi University'.[12]

Among the civilians present was Sir Albert Ernest Coates ('Coates of Thailand'), who had served as the Senior Medical Officer for the 8th Division. Coates had performed hundreds of operations with primitive and improvised equipment, saving numerous lives on the Siam-Burma Railway. Indeed, Coates was that rare breed of citizen-soldier who whilst excelling as a student had in 1914 enlisted as a medical orderly to serve in the Gallipoli campaign followed by France and the Western

Front. With the onset of the war in Asia, Coates was again pressed into service and appointed Lieutenant-Colonel and Senior Surgeon to the Second Australian Imperial Force in Malaya, followed by the 2/10th Australian General Hospital in Singapore after the Japanese invasion of the peninsula. During the evacuation from Singapore to Java, his convoy was bombed, and in the ensuing journey on to Sumatra he found himself a prisoner of the Japanese. In May 1942, Coates would be sent to Burma to work on the notorious 'Death Railway'.[13]

Representing the ex-Services organisations was Sister Vivian Bullwinkel, who had been attached to the 13th Australian General Hospital in Malaya which relocated to Singapore with the invasion of the peninsula by the Japanese. With the imminent fall of Singapore, Bullwinkel and her fellow nurses, along with wounded servicemen, were ordered to evacuate on the Royal Navy steamship SS *Vyner Brooke*. Two nights later, on 14 February 1942, Japanese aircraft attacked the convoy, and sank the ship in the Bangka Straits, east of Sumatra. Surviving nurses who managed to swim ashore to nearby Bangka Island were met by a Japanese ground force which after rounding them up took them back into the sea and set upon them with machine guns. Bullwinkel, feigning death, would be the only survivor of the massacre. After the Japanese left, she managed to scramble to shore, where she encountered a seriously injured soldier from an earlier massacre, whom she proceeded to care for until his death. At that point Bullwinkel gave herself up and was interned for the remainder of the war.[14]

Then there was the father from North Wagga, New South Wales (NSW), whose two sons were killed in Malaya at the onset of the war and who feared the renewal of grief 15 years after that event; a wife from Earlwood, NSW, widowed when her pilot husband was lost in a reconnaissance flight over Kota Bharu in February 1942; a mother from Prahran, Victoria, whose two sons died in Malaya; and another father from Narrandera, NSW, whose two sons were commemorated on the Memorial's walls.[15] These were some of the civilians who had taken the opportunity offered to be present, each standing in silence as the ceremony progressed, fully comprehending and appreciating the small act of grief by an elderly local woman. Yet for many in this group, Kranji was a relatively ambiguous setting, its rows of uniform war graves and names inscribed on the memorial providing the sole emotional connection to the war.

To the majority of Australians following the war in Asia from their living rooms back home, it was Changi Prison that had become synonymous with the disastrous surrender of the Allied forces upon the fall of Malaya and Singapore. Its status as the site of mass incarceration of Australian prisoners of war and their inhumane treatment was assured upon the return of those who survived, with the harrowing stories that emerged. What public understanding that the passage of time had afforded the disaster of the Gallipoli campaign[16] almost 30 years prior was undone by the sense of vulnerability that the capture of almost 30,000 Australian soldiers produced. And yet if there was any positive outcome from such a tragedy, it would be that the many trials and tribulations of its prisoners, the scenes of 'mateship' forged under difficult and trying conditions, fostered another view of this aspect of the war in Singapore – a view that was co-opted into a nation-building exercise many years later.

The physical remnants of Changi, on display along with Kranji War Cemetery for holidaymakers during stopovers in Singapore, would go on to become an informal Australian transnational heritage site. It is 'informal' in the sense that whilst its demolition in 2004 saw considerable opposition from the Australian Government, various heritage bodies and ex-Services organisations, there was an inability to constrain a sovereign nation's right to manage its own heritage sites.[17] Kranji, without the intense history that sites of difficult memories offer and being established only 'after' the war, does not have that similar cultural resonance. Where Villers-Bretonneux War Cemetery became synonymous with Australian involvement on the Western Front and Lone Pine Cemetery with the Gallipoli campaign during the First World War, both having tangible long-term connections with their local communities and national narratives, Kranji War Cemetery and Memorial remain identified solely as sites of remembrance. Unlike the Siam-Burma Railway, Changi, Sandakan, Ambon and Kokoda,[18] Kranji's lack of identity somewhat precludes it becoming anything more.

The unveiling of what was the last of the four dedicated memorials to the missing airmen of the Second World War, accompanying the completion of one of the final war cemeteries in Asia, was variously accounted for by the print media throughout the Commonwealth. A great many more newspapers had earlier that year reported on the upcoming event, often displaying the Commission's official photograph of the architectural model of Oakes's memorial, along with a few salient points such as the 24,000 inscribed names of those missing. The *Singapore Free Press* in its emotive piece, 'A Moving Dedication at New Shrine', couched their coverage in biblical idioms, and Singapore that day became a 'hallowed' place for the Commonwealth, with many old servicemen and relatives making a special pilgrimage to see their comrades and loved ones laid to rest. The *Northern Daily Mail* in the UK highlighted the significance of the inscription 'They Died For All Free Men' on the Dedicatory Inscription Panel, written in English, Urdu, Hindi, Chinese, Malay and Gurmukhi.[19] Sir Robert Black was quoted as saying: 'That simple sentence tells us why this multitude of men and women, of differing faiths and races but united in the service of their King, were faithful unto death. The traditions they so worthily upheld live on in the hearts and minds of those who follow them.'[20] In Australia, the *Canberra Times* devoted its coverage to the almost 3,000 Australian war dead buried in the cemetery and inscribed on the stone-clad walls of the Singapore Memorial. Although nominally a national tribute from Australia, the service had taken on an Anzac tone on account of the 76 New Zealand casualties and the various groups of New Zealand servicemen deployed in Malaya and Singapore, many of whom were among the crowd that day. Canada offered only a single entry about the day – a few lines from January in the regional *MacGregor Herald*, Manitoba, indicating the upcoming unveiling and that the names of 197 Canadian airmen were among the 24,909 inscribed on the walls of the Memorial.[21]

And yet, for all the coverage seemingly available, the sense that many of the major broadsheet papers had chosen to ignore this event could be viewed as testimony of the time taken to arrive at that day. Of the other memorials to the missing airmen, Runnymede had been unveiled in 1953, El Alamein and Malta both in 1954. It also inadvertently exposed the general public's fatigue with the Second World War, by then a good 12 years after General Douglas MacArthur had taken Japan's unconditional surrender. The previous decade had seen unprecedented turbulence in the political and social landscapes throughout the Far East and Southeast Asia, with the Malayan Emergency (1948–60), Indonesian War of Independence (1945–49), Korean War (1950–53), First Indochina War (1946–54) and the beginnings of the second conflict in Indochina otherwise referred to as the Vietnam War (1955–75). It most certainly put paid to the notion that peace and an era of stability would prevail throughout the region after the years of Japanese aggression and occupation.

Indeed, the insurgency in Malaya, ongoing during the unveiling, had seen former allies and resistance fighters now arrayed against the Commonwealth forces. Japan, once the common enemy, was now a staunch ally against the growing threat of an increasingly belligerent China. Although private trade was resumed with Malaya from as early as August 1947, Japanese citizens, albeit only those seeking business connections, were only allowed back into Singapore in 1953, following the signing of an official peace treaty in 1951 and the arrival of the first post-war Japanese Consul-General in November 1952. This followed the Singapore Government's decision in March 1952 to approve the opening of a Japanese Overseas Trade Agency and the effectuation of the San Francisco Peace Treaty a month later in April 1952, whereupon Japan regained its sovereignty. By May, Singapore lifted the ban on the landing of Japanese merchant seamen. But a comprehensive rapprochement only occurred with the bilateral signing of a Commercial Agreement with the Federation of Malaya in 1960 and the signing of the Singapore-Japan Tax Convention the following year. And although only Japanese diplomats and their families were initially permitted to reside in Singapore, by the latter half of the 1950s this condition had been relaxed, bringing this former enemy fully back into the fold of the post-war Southeast Asian economies.[22]

Beyond the official acknowledgement of the day's occasion, any significant and in-depth coverage of the unveiling ceremony and its human element fell to two of the more unlikely sources – the *Australian Women's Weekly* and the local Chinese-language newspaper, *Nanyang Siang Pau*. The *Weekly*, through its correspondent Dorothy Drain, presented three separate articles looking at those who were affected by the war and attended the unveiling ceremony in its own right, and then interestingly two years later in January 1959, followed it up with a postscript take on its connection to Australia. In 'Poignant Link with Australia', the article sought to reaffirm Kranji's connection to the Australian story, lest it be dulled or forgotten in the relatively short period that had passed. In a somewhat melancholic reflection on the intervening years since the war's end and the unveiling of the Singapore Memorial, Drain also captured some of the many views of those who had visited, through their handwritten notes in the visitor's book. 'A poignant memory,' wrote one Australian woman who made no claim to kinship with any serviceman buried there. 'Visited by us in gratitude to them who died, we hope not in vain,' wrote another. Drain, who through covering the Korean War earlier that decade had been challenged by the human cost of war, surmised in what proved a self-reflective yet succinct observation that 'coming back, seeing the ages on the headstones, I remembered that time has marked all of us, the living, but here is a little city where scarcely anyone is over 30'.[23]

The *Nanyang Siang Pau*, one of Singapore's oldest and most respected Chinese-language broadsheet newspapers, took a similar approach as the *Women's Weekly* to its coverage. From the perspective of the local Chinese population, it captured not only the formality of the event itself, but also, fleetingly through photographs and their captions, those who otherwise were on the margins or simply invisible to the English-language press coverage of the day. One such image depicts Ho Bock Kee, the Fujian-born carpenter-turned-contractor tasked with

Nanyang Siang Pau's coverage of the unveiling, showing two elderly Chinese women laying a wreath at the Memorial

building the memorial, being congratulated by the Governor for his efforts. The other depicts two elderly Chinese women laying a wreath at the steps of the Memorial. Where its local competitor *The Straits Times* highlighted the minor drama Madam Cheng's interruption created through the filter of an English-speaking journalist, the *Nanyang Siang Pau* instead selected two seemingly ordinary local women commemorating their loved ones. The caption, as translated, describes 'a scene of those survivors left behind by the Malayan Chinese soldiers who were killed in battle, placing a wreath in front of the war memorial'. As with those families who had come over from Australia, standing nearby and preoccupied with their own thoughts, the focus was on those left behind rather than those who died.

If the major newspapers were somewhat judicious in their coverage, tending to focus on both the ceremony and those for whom the memorial was intended, then the design fraternity locally in Singapore and in the United Kingdom was indeed shameful in its lack of interest in the new architectural structure at Kranji. With the exception of the *RIBA Journal* including Oakes's design proposal for Kranji within an overarching feature of the many war cemeteries and memorials planned for Asia and the Far East in its October 1953 issue, its completion was greeted by the architecture community in Malaya and Singapore with silence. Neither the *Quarterly Journal of the Institute of Architects of Malaya*, published between 1951 and 1958, nor its successors, the *Journal of the Society of Malayan Architects* (1958) and *Rumah* (1958–69), the dedicated journal of the Singapore Institute of Architects, carried any descriptive or critical analysis. Indeed, *Rumah* would a few years later in 1963 provide in-depth coverage of the design competition for the Memorial to the Civilian Victims of the Japanese Occupation. This may in part be attributed to the rising sense of national identity within the local architecture community, in no small part a reaction to the loosening of control that foreign, mainly British, architects had in the past. Through their ascendency of primary positions in the civil service such as the Public Works Department, and their outsized allocation of significant projects of national interest, what commemorative spaces were afforded the local population were filtered through colonial representation.[24] And yet for the nascent modernism being experimented with throughout Malaya in the 1950s and early 1960s, to not consider the Singapore Memorial within this greater design discourse was an unfortunate aberration.

Against the background of the new memorial, the immediate years after its unveiling saw the war cemetery and this new structure settle into a pattern of official yet somewhat inconspicuous biannual ceremonies. It was inconspicuous as it was only covered in small news articles after the event, and the majority of the general public had no inkling of either the event or its importance, or even that Kranji had hosted them. Organised by the local British and their fellow Commonwealth member state communities, the annual Remembrance Day ceremony initially observing Armistice Day had morphed into Remembrance Sunday, in recognition also of the Second World War and later conflicts, and was observed at 11 a.m. on the Sunday closest to the original date of 11 November. Indeed, Kranji by the mid-1950s had supplanted the Cenotaph at City Hall as the official site for the annual Remembrance Day service. The other significant ceremony Kranji held each year was Anzac Day, this time organised by the Australian and New Zealand High Commissions and conducted through a dawn service on 25 April. Then there were the occasional visits of foreign diplomats, dignitaries and school groups who whilst passing through the country would often attend Kranji and lay wreaths. As Brenda Yeoh and Hamzah Muzaini identified, Kranji and its memorial could not find the emotional resonance to figure in the local collective imaginings.[25]

And yet this was hardly to be unexpected, given the tenuous self-governance state in which Singapore found itself in the post-war period. With its autonomy within the British Empire only achieved in 1959, Singapore's merging a few years later with the Federation of Malaya in 1963 proved calamitous. Communal tensions and racial riots against the backdrop of deep political and economic differences saw its ejection from that same Federation in 1965, culminating in it becoming an independent and sovereign state. The situation was compounded by the extreme post-war migration influx, where in the decade prior to the unveiling Singapore saw over half a million people arrive, all searching for opportunities, placing great strain on housing, healthcare, sanitation and other critical services. The priorities of the state at the time differed markedly from those of its colonial rulers. From the local perspective, perhaps if the British Government at the time had been prepared to spend money on the living as well as the dead, the people might have viewed this commemoration enterprise in the north more favourably.

If any single opportunity arose in the post-war aftermath to create an ongoing legacy with Kranji, through those who survived the war, it manifested in an attempt to create a self-sustaining farming community for war widows and their dependants. Within close proximity to the war cemetery, it tellingly revealed an acknowledgement by the UK government and its Colonial Office that whilst dealing with their own devastation back home and reconstruction efforts after the war in Europe, they could afford some limited consideration for the difficulties encountered by their colonies and protectorates overseas in the hands of the Japanese Imperial Forces.

The Far Eastern Relief Fund, established by the Mayor of London after the occupation of Malaya by the Japanese, raised funds in the UK for Singapore and Malaya to relieve the distress arising from the invasion. With an initial allocation of £17,000, the Singapore committee of the Fund, working under the auspices of the Social Welfare Department, determined from the outset that the principle of its expenditure should, wherever possible, focus on providing tools and equipment to the recipients.[26] This would give some 90 families that stood to benefit from the aid the ability to earn a living, as opposed to simply receiving small sums for month-to-month subsistence. And in an attempt to expand the scope of its benevolence and in the process create a physical legacy befitting their principle, the committee also decided to proceed with the creation of what came to be known as Kranji Farm. This agricultural precinct was intended to both accommodate families made destitute by the war, and to provide them with the means to a farming livelihood.

Located less than two miles to the south of and within a visual sight-line of the Singapore Memorial upon Kranji Hill, the farm's location and purpose offered the ideal project to co-relate the tragedy of the war through both the living and the dead. In the process, this would further embed Kranji War Cemetery within the wartime history of its region, the glaring issue that Obbard and Oakes had once considered worked against the selection of this site. It was determined that at the 11½-mile stone mark of the road to Kranji, near Yew Tee village, 15½ acres of Crown land would be allocated for the erection of six semi-detached brick buildings, to accommodate 12 families. At a cost of S$50,000, or just over 30 per cent of the funding allocation, the creation of this rural community was always going to be contentious within the wider post-war reconstruction efforts undertaken at the time. Indeed, the Fund's original mandate was intended for the relief of 'Europeans and other Malayans, whether British subjects or British protected persons, who were or are permanently resident in the territory known as the Malayan Union and who have lost their homes or livelihood as a result of the Japanese invasion'.[27] This could literally apply to thousands in Singapore at the end of the war, in particular the many widows in the local Chinese community who lost their bread-winners in their husbands and sons during the Sook Ching round-up. As it were, on 31 March 1951, the foundation stone was laid by G.W. Webb, Secretary of the Social Welfare Department and Chairman of the Fund Committee, signalling the commencement of construction works.[28] Five months later, in August, with extensive coverage by the local newspapers, only six Singaporean Chinese widows and their families were finally selected from over 90 applicants to become the new settlers. A further three families, after 'careful investigation of their cases' would join them shortly after.[29]

Along with their accommodation, each family was provided with an acre of land to farm and the critical household utensils and essential furniture needed to make a home. A cash allowance of S$50 for the first six months of their tenure was also offered to assist with provisions and other sundries whilst getting started. Farming implements such as changkols and shovels, as well as vegetable seeds, were also provided, with the result that within a few months upon settling, cucumbers, *kangkong* (water spinach), sweet potatoes, tapioca, long beans and banana plants were being grown.[30] Most importantly, it was decided that all income derived from the cultivation of their farms belonged to the settlers. In an attempt to ensure its long-term viability, the Social Welfare Department even undertook to purchase what produce and crops were ready for the market.[31]

It was an experiment in social welfare that, not without precedent or untried elsewhere,[32] would always be limited in the context of the wider social issues of Singapore in the late 1940s and early 1950s. These issues required longer-term planning for the collective hundreds of thousands of its population, not just a handful, no matter what hardships they had experienced. And this would eventually prove to be the case, with the farms themselves unable to be sustained and reverting back to the state land authority, all without the media coverage their founding created. For although well-intentioned at the time, the idea that the Social Welfare Department could provide six solitary dwellings and maintain them in the long term in a land-scarce country was proven to be the fallacy that it always was, considering the acute housing shortage and almost 550,000 people living in squatter settlements and squalid shophouses. What housing for the displaced, destitute and others was being constructed, albeit limited in quantity, was the responsibility of first the Singapore Improvement Trust, and after Singapore achieved self-governance in 1959, its successor, the Housing and Development Board (HDB).

After the War Graves

Oakes would not see out the completion of Kranji War Cemetery nor attend the unveiling ceremony of his 'winged' memorial. One of the Commission's in-house architects, working alongside field officers from Penang, was assigned to take the building and final landscape works through to completion. By 1957, Oakes was 49 years old, and along with his wife Nancy and their children, had settled in Nottinghamshire, on the outskirts of the historic city of Nottingham. For Oakes, this relocation was on account of his appointment as Chief Architect for the Boots Pure Drug Company a few years prior. It would become the final, and most prolonged, stage of his varied architectural career, culminating in a maturing of his modernist design sensibility.

Oakes never attended any unveiling or dedication service for the war cemeteries and memorials he designed, nor was he ever engaged by the Imperial War Graves Commission throughout this period or thereafter. It was as if the reminder that these memorials offered someone who had participated in the very war they commemorated was too great, and that part of his life needed segregating. He wasn't alone. Like many of that generation who returned, he decided never to speak about what he had witnessed. His solitary concession to those four years of his life was an annual trip into London to attend the Burma Star Association reunion gathering.[33] A member of the Burma Star Association of veterans from the campaigns in north-east India and

Burma, he gathered with fellow veterans for an evening of dinner, drink and recollections, reflecting on those who survived and those who didn't. Amidst the camaraderie and comfort of former army colleagues, the music of 'Forces Sweetheart' Vera Lynn[34], and other bands performing in the background, they would share and relive their experiences of the Burma campaign as part of General Slim's 14th Army, the so-called 'Forgotten Army'. Oakes often stayed the night in London, returning the following day accompanied with a sadness. Recollecting her father's infrequent forays into his war-time service, Oakes's eldest daughter Sally recounted how every year on Armistice Day, he would gather his family around the wireless listening to the Remembrance Service held at London's Cenotaph. On this rare occasion, Oakes's children witnessed their father shed tears, the emotion overwhelming him.

The late 1940s was a period of great upheaval for Oakes. Without a prolonged or extensive body of design work, and having recently demobilised from years of active service, he was suddenly handed the responsibility and solemnity that the war graves work provided. Unlike his fellow Principal Architects at the Commission, all of whom were considerably older and established figures within architectural society, Oakes never quite found a similar confidence in his design direction. Whereas Lutyens, de Soissons, Worthington and Hepworth were well ensconced within the aesthetic conservatism of their generation, Oakes found himself conflicted and unable to fully embrace a definitive and distinctive architectural methodology. The projects he designed and completed between returning in late 1945 until early 1953 attest to this. Whilst displaying a strong understanding and appreciation of architecture's formal design principles, his works move between the pared-down classicism of his predecessors and the modernism emanating from the continent and slowly taking shape throughout an increasingly more confident United Kingdom. This also coincided with his new position at Boots and with their assent, his completing the outstanding war cemeteries for the Commission. It was inevitable that both parties soon began vying for his dedicated attention, culminating in his relinquishing his appointment with the Commission. And yet arriving at this position could not have been a surprise. Oakes's struggle to articulate a clear design identity could be traced back to 1946, with his appointment to the senior staff of the Architectural Association (AA) on the one hand, and accepting a partnership with the established London practice of Sir Aston Webb & Son. They could not have been more ideologically apart in their architectural principles and methodology.

Joining Sir Aston Webb & Son provided Oakes the prestige only an eminent and large practice could accord. Established in 1874 by Aston Webb and succeeded by his eldest son Maurice, the firm's association with an imperial England was assured through their significant public commissions, notably the Victoria and Albert Museum, the Victoria Memorial, the Admiralty Arch, and the remodelling of the east facade of Buckingham Palace. To critically assess their work, a significant comparison can be made with the considerably younger Lutyens, who coincidentally for a period was carrying out his practice adjacent to Webb's offices at 19 Queen Anne's Gate in Westminster. While Lutyens was able to deftly adapt this fundamental classicism without recourse to the overtly ornamental, Webb's buildings tended to be defined by these very elements and he was often accused by critics of facadism. Indeed, at the time it was considered that Lutyens's more distinctive, more original vision would carry British architecture into the future.[35]

Oakes's accomplishments within the Sir Aston Webb & Son design orthodoxy, though considerably conflicted given his past experiences, maintained the status quo of the firm's principles. Notable examples of this include the new assembly hall, accommodation wing and further extensions to Queen Mary College at the University of London. What opportunity did arise to explore his personal design philosophy came in the form of his first war memorial, though ironically, not for the Imperial War Graves Commission for which he had by then been appointed Principal Architect, but by the Royal Navy. Carved out of the chapel lobby at the Britannia Royal Naval College

Oakes's Naval War
Memorial shrine
at the Royal Naval
College, Dartmouth

in Dartmouth, the Naval War Memorial shrine was dedicated to the 529 ex-Dartmouth cadets and staff who had lost their lives during the 1939–45 war. Unveiled and dedicated in October 1949, this shrine lined with Portland stone and carrying the engraved names of those missing also consolidated those remembered from the First World War. In this small space, Oakes's design displayed an elegant departure from Sir Aston Webb & Son's trademark neoclassicism and conveyed an early modernist sensibility. A curved Art Deco window off the main lobby provides the only clue to its presence inside.[36]

If joining an established architectural practice and undertaking commissions for the Imperial War Graves Commission was intended to cement his professional standing, then accepting Raymond Brown's offer to once again return to the AA revealed Oakes's predilection for teaching. The end of the war had seen the AA experience a surge in admissions, with enrolments reaching 500 by 1949. Recent school leavers and overseas admissions found themselves studying alongside mature students returned from the war and bringing considerable experience with them. Men such as Oliver Cox, Bernard Feilden and Alan Colquhoun, all having served with the Indian Army, would go on to play prominent roles in the reconstruction of modern Britain. Patrick Horsburgh and Michael Ventris, both of whom served in the Royal Air Force, similarly benefited from their time at the AA during these more optimistic post-war conditions. This expanded student body of varying ages and experiences would be suitably described as 'fostering an extreme creative dynamic'.[37] Under Brown's firm stewardship, Oakes in his role as Fifth Form Master wholeheartedly committed himself to this progressive curriculum. In doing so, he joined like-minded colleagues David Goddard, Robert Furneaux-Jordan, Fello Atkinson, Kenneth Capon and John Summerson in espousing the modernist agenda.

Oakes's leadership traits, forged during the Burma campaign, made him a natural mentor to the students. None more so than those who shared the camaraderie only wartime could produce. When the AA commenced preparations to celebrate its centenary in 1947, the council presided by Howard Robertson approached Oakes with the task of organising the Centenary Exhibition, one of many related events scheduled for the school throughout that year.[38] While this might easily have transpired as a rudimentary or 'safe' retrospective, Oakes took the opportunity to reinforce the AA's progressive role within the broader architectural education community. With the acquiescence of the exhibition's sub-committee chaired by Roderick E. Enthoven and comprising card-carrying members of the Modern Architectural Research Group (MARS) in Brown, Furneaux-Jordan, Summerson and others, the exhibition became a statement of the school's position in the post-war climate.[39] If anything, it represented the final expunging of the conservative Victorian past by the modern future.

Occupying three of four terrace houses that accommodated the school in Bedford Square, London, the exhibition was centred around three periods in the AA's past hundred years. Within a myriad of rooms inside these Victorian buildings, Oakes and the sculptor William Stevenson, along with students from both the AA and the Liverpool Municipal School of Art, reimagined each space, providing examples of the work of the school's past presidents and principals. The library, rendered in formal decorative set pieces, would showcase work from 1847 through to 1900. In two of the members' rooms, it was the period from the turn of the century that was curated. The slide room became the AA's scrapbook – a showcase of prints, drawings, documents and photographs illustrating the life of the school over 100 years. Finally, the studios were dedicated to selected work of the School of Architecture, emphasising the modern direction architecture had evolved into. And if there was any lingering doubt about the sentiment surrounding the school's early work, displayed as it was in the cartouche-like library, it was firmly dismissed in the very review of the exhibition by *The Architectural Association Journal* the following January: 'The architecture shown in this precious and so flattering *cadre* could not I think, possibly have been worse … what a past we have! Bless our "early men"; they touched bottom.'[40]

Selected student projects on display for the Architectural Association's Centenary Exhibition in 1947, organised by Oakes

For all the politics of the AA's design education so obviously out on public display, the official opening of the Centenary Exhibition on an early Wednesday afternoon of 17 December 1947 passed off successfully. Opened by Sir Ernest Pooley, Chairman of the Arts Council of Great Britain, and attended by a who's who of the architectural and construction industry along with invited guests and representatives from the Dominions and overseas, the affair offered an opportunity to reset the role of architecture – from the catastrophes that befell the world and ceased a mere two years prior, to one where cooperation across cultures and the exchange of ideas and techniques across frontiers could no longer present barriers.

Oakes's place at this critical juncture of architecture post-war would come to define his later legacy. At a time when his attention to the Imperial War Graves Commission work precluded his further involvement with teaching, events would force a critical re-evaluation. But not before he was able to elevate the profile of a young, up-and-coming student in much the same way his standing benefited from early recognition. This came by way of his considered decision in selecting for his assistant with the Centenary Exhibition one of the more talented students attending the AA, a 22-year-old who had resumed his studies after serving with the Grenadier Guards during the war. Peter Dickinson, born into a wealthy family from Suffolk, had commenced studies at the AA in 1942, completing two years before the interruption of the war. Upon returning, he quickly re-established himself as a designer and won the fourth-year prize in 1946. Presented by the famed American architect Frank Lloyd Wright, it was the prelude to his being awarded the fifth-year prize the following year, before graduating with honours in 1948.[41] Within a few years, Dickinson would relocate to Toronto, quickly establishing himself as one of the leading pioneers developing the mid-century modern style in post-war Canada.

In young Dickinson, Oakes found a kindred spirit, and their association in delivering a highly commended exhibition capped off his final term at the school. And yet it coincided with the other significant event to befall Oakes. For on that evening following the opening, on the occasion of the President's reception being held by the RIBA, Oakes would be involved in a car accident, leaving him with serious head injuries and an extended period of hospitalisation. It proved to be the turning point in his life away from the frenetic pace of multiple associations and engagements. Whereas Dickinson would decamp to Canada and scale the heights in a short but illustrious career, Oakes would take a completely different direction. In the period taken to recover and reconnect with the war cemetery projects that had been placed on hold, he completed some of his most accomplished works. The proposed Memorials to the Missing at Kohima and Sai Wan, along with the Kanchanaburi War Cemetery, would be featured in the Royal Academy's exhibitions.[42] The preliminary designs for the Thanbyuzayat War Cemetery and the Singapore Memorial had also been completed. And by 1949, with four young children and having endured years away from his wife during the war, followed by months of travelling for the War Graves Commission, Oakes took pause of his life and like his father before him, embarked upon a final career direction. This would be as Chief Architect for the Boots Pure Drug Company.[43]

Established in 1849, the Boots Pure Drug Company expanded and grew to become by the late 1930s the leading pharmaceutical company in the United Kingdom. Involved in the research and manufacturing of drugs, it also presided over a sizeable retail network through its hundreds of high street stores and outlets. Percy J. Bartlett, head of their Architects Department between 1927 and 1949, had been responsible for designing most of these company stores across the country, in a wide variety of styles appropriate to their locations. Those few buildings not designed in-house were assigned to some of the leading contemporary architects of the day. The renowned engineer Sir Owen Williams was engaged to design one such structure, the D10 factory in Beeston, Nottingham. Hailed in the press as the 'Factory of Utopia' when completed in 1932, it is now recognised internationally as a significant icon of British Modernism.

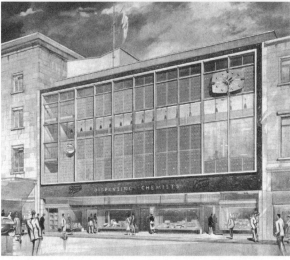

Boots buildings
designed by Oakes:
The Broadmead store
in Bristol (left), which
opened in 1955, and the
Exeter store (above),
which opened in 1957.

By the conclusion of the war in 1945, the tally of buildings within London and other cities across England that had been destroyed in the Blitz amounted to over two million. The devastation included industrial estates, dockyards and commercial centres, among which were a considerable number of Boots retail stores and production facilities.

Upon his arrival in Nottingham, Oakes's primary task and responsibility was twofold. Firstly, he was to carry on from Bartlett in designing and rebuilding those damaged and destroyed Boots buildings, notably major stores in Southampton, Plymouth and Swansea. And secondly, Oakes was to apply the design and planning principles of the modern movement to all the new and renovated work. In this instance, he would over the next 17 years follow the course exemplified by Williams in Nottingham, steering the Boots brand through its extensive and highly visible building stock into a modernist identity. Finally, Oakes had the opportunity and appropriate vehicle to fully embrace the modern movement in architecture. In the numerous Boots stores, office buildings, laboratories and factories that he designed and supervised, a distinct style emerged that would reflect the ambitions of a progressive nation of the 1950s and 1960s.

It was the era of the baby boomers and along with the end of rationing the country was experiencing huge social and economic changes. The standard of living for the ordinary citizen was improving together with consumer demand. Oakes and the design office he inherited found themselves overwhelmed by the sheer number of Boots stores requiring urgent design and construction. At times he would be away days on end, travelling the length and breadth of the country, ensuring each store's unveiling passed without incident, often working overnight to ensure the details of the interior fitouts were up to his high standards. And yet for all the demands the corporate life extracted, he was also acutely aware of the need to complete the outstanding designs for the Commission, themselves falling further behind schedule. The Commission had by now imposed deadlines by which designs had to be submitted, and projects not commenced were off-loaded to in-house architects, the most notable being the Rangoon Memorial. And yet this same heavy workload provided Oakes the distraction he needed from the personal turmoil he and his family were encountering.

Where Boots provided the professional and social support network Oakes needed in this new environment, the relocation proved more difficult for his family. For Nancy, the dislocation from the relative comforts of family and friendships in coastal and often sunny Sussex to the harsher English Midlands was a major challenge. Her health declined. And then in November 1952, she was diagnosed with poliomyelitis. Narrowly avoiding being placed in a tank respirator or iron lung, the treatment of last resort, she was nevertheless rendered partially paralysed and unable to walk for almost five months. It would be a year before she was well enough to return to her home, during which time Oakes had assumed all household duties and care for the children. Whereas Boots and the design office were supportive of his prolonged absences and an adjusted workload, the relationship with the Commission on the other hand was coming to a strained end. As it was, by December that year, without significant progress having been made in the delayed design works, the discussion of terminating his services was raised on a few occasions, with preparations being made to take over what was outstanding. It would not come to that, though. By mutual agreement, on 31 March 1953, Oakes's term as Principal Architect with the Commission came to an end.[44]

Oakes's daughter offered that her father had two sides to his personality. Oakes the architect was a charming and outwardly confident professional, attuned to the rigours of the highest standards of architectural practice. Oakes the family man, on the other hand, was someone considerably different. Very personal in his demeanour, his life was centred around his wife and children, going on annual holidays either in the countryside or by the sea. His love of music was equalled by his fondness for a drink with company, often with his closest friends William Holford and Raymond Brown, both of whom would go on to become godparents to his daughters. In spite of that, there was a darker space where others could not enter – the kind of solitude that only those who served and fought in war encountered upon their return. There was the need to keep that part of their life compartmentalised, not telling loved ones what really happened, leaving it only to those occasions when in the company of similar veterans.

In these recollections, we get an insight into a man who on any ordinary day was an accomplished architect with an expansive portfolio of post-war work for the Boots Pure Drug Company among others, contributing to the wave of modernism that swept Britain after the war. We also see someone who lived the carefree life of a young man in Rome, then became besotted with Bengal and found himself, like millions of others, fighting a war far from home. It would culminate in his designing the war cemeteries and memorials throughout South and Southeast Asia for the Imperial War Graves Commission. It can be safely inferred that he was in fact designing those sites for the men who fought, died and are now remembered within them.

Whereas the unveiling of a significant memorial or monument usually meant that the stature of its design or that of its architect grew with the publicity and public adulation it garnered, as was the case with many of the works undertaken by the Commission's other Principal Architects, this wasn't the case with Kranji nor with Oakes. Lutyens's Thiepval Memorial and Maufe's Runnymede, opened by the Prince of Wales (later King Edward VIII) and Queen Elizabeth II respectively, were celebrated in literature, architectural critiques and through popular culture and the arts. Maya Lin's minimalist Vietnam Veterans Memorial in Washington, D.C., dedicated in 1982, was steeped in controversy from the outset – the source of an aggressive public outcry and criticism, largely centred on its 'nihilistic slab of stone' and 'lack of ornamentation'. This was followed by vigorous public and professional debates and ultimately an emotional outpouring and embracing from the very people it was intended for – families, loved ones and comrades of the over 50,000 inscribed names it contains. It captured the spirit of a generation, much the same way as Thiepval did 50 years earlier. Today, both Thiepval Memorial and the Vietnam Veterans Memorial are significant landmarks for their respective countries and account for annual visitations of some 160,000 and 4.7 million persons, respectively.

The Singapore Memorial does not affect a similar significance, but interestingly, neither does any other Second World War memorial in South and Southeast Asia. Similar attendance numbers for Kranji are not possible given its distance and accessibility from the countries of origin of the fallen. The figures available are relegated to the voluntary recording of visits in the Entrance Gate's log book. But then, Kranji never aspired to achieve the level of celebration the others were accorded, each of which have come to symbolise quite strongly the human cost of their wars. Even Oakes the architect, through an honest evaluation of his design efforts, ranked Singapore behind his work in India and Burma. This is evident in the fact that his original design sketches for Singapore were for Point 348 (Bukit Batok Hill), given its significance – albeit a contentious one – as a memorial site built by the Allied prisoners of war for the thousands of their comrades who died during the campaign, as well as a memorial site for the Japanese war dead, built by the same prisoner-of-war labour force. Instead, for Oakes, it was Kohima, and his own personal involvement in that campaign in the north-east of India which turned the tide against the Japanese push westward, that pressed upon him the greatest emotional resonance, which in turn manifested in his considerate design for that war cemetery.

Oakes's stature did not grow, nor was it assured through his design of the Singapore Memorial. On the contrary, his reputation was unobtrusively enhanced through being identified as having worked for the Commission rather than the actual body of work produced. Where many prominent architects were celebrated through the filter of their national identity, Oakes was not accorded such interest in his homeland Britain, nor in Australia and Singapore for that matter, both of whom should have had an interest in Kranji and its architecture. Similarly in modern-day India and Pakistan, which collectively account for over one in three servicemen whose names are inscribed on the Memorial's walls, there was no interest extended to understanding the structure and its architect.

Indeed, when Oakes is credited with designing the Memorial at all, is often merely as a footnote to another discourse. An opportunity to make the architectural connections he forged throughout his design career in South and Southeast Asia, through shared suffering across many nations, is therefore missed. Any appreciation offered, in

Colin St Clair Oakes

the occasional trade publication or corporate journal, was inevitably confined to Britain and British architecture through his later work for Boots. With Oakes's passing on 12 December 1971, a few years after taking his retirement, a retrospective of his life and work remained wanting.

And yet this approach in remembering Oakes the architect is not unusual. It mirrors the muted silence the war in Asia received in the public imagination in the decades following the war. For the public back home in Britain, war memory was confined almost exclusively to adjacent Europe and the fight against Nazism, followed soon after by the expansion of Soviet communism. In the edited collection, *The Pacific War: Aftermaths, Remembrance and Culture*, scholar Paula Hamilton in her essay, 'Contested Memories of the Pacific War in Australia', suggests that without the 'intimate geographies of remembrance' that occur through symbolic investment of where battles actually happened, the conflict and its commemoration in these transnational spaces

248

creates an absence of 'collective memories' and thereafter 'collective remembrance'.[45] Janet Watson's contributing chapter, 'A Sideshow to the War in Europe', reflects that Britain's first series of significant events to mark the end of the war in the Pacific commenced only in 1995 – the 'war in Asia remained peripheral, an afterthought; something one might be justified in overlooking'.[46] In both Australia and Britain, there were no constant physical reminders of the war in the Pacific – the remoteness and limited size of Darwin and its bombing, along with government censorship at the time, precluded that event from capturing a wider national mood. The devastation of London and the existential fight for national survival across a few miles of the Channel overwhelmed the collective public understanding and comprehending of other campaigns thousands of miles away in far-off colonies. The exceptions are the recollections from returning participants and the occasional paraphernalia or war souvenir. The Australian War Memorial and Imperial War Museum bridge this divide and take responsibility for creating the foreign spatial connections, along with internal sites of commemoration. Sites of commemoration and remembrance outside the nation's shores become somewhat clouded with the distance. Only some smaller museums catering to a particular conflict or campaign in both countries and Singapore offer dedicated histories of the war in Asia. Australia, unlike Britain with its colonial connections and heritage, and with its long history of fighting wars overseas, exemplifies this 'Asian' amnesia, even though the fighting was on its northern doorstep.

There is no doubt that the Singapore Memorial is one of Oakes's pre-eminent works. Indeed, within the context of his war graves projects, only the Sai Wan War Cemetery and Memorial and the Kohima War Cemetery rank alongside for architectural significance. In the case of Sai Wan and Kohima, it is their layouts and pared-back designs responding to the distinct hillside topographies – overlooking the sea and town, respectively – that create the dramatic aesthetic. The Singapore Memorial, dedicated to the military casualties of a war that occurred over 70 years ago, still resonates strongly in today's society.

That this structure remains standing in an ever-increasingly land-scarce country whilst numerous national cemeteries have undergone consolidation and or removal is testament to its enduring role as a reminder of an uncomfortable past, even if its use for commemoration is limited.

And whilst the Singapore Memorial can objectively be seen as an acknowledgement of the war through those whose names are inscribed upon its walls and the thousands who lie within the cemetery beyond, its design does not signify any triumphalism. It is not a victory monument or a site commemorating a significant achievement. Its modern formalism instead acts as a marker, identifying a particular dark period in many countries' histories, not just that of the colonial power. Where many other sites of remembrance have been well-documented in films, books, music and plays, the relative obscurity of the many battles in Malaya, Singapore, Burma and north-east India, as compared to those in Europe and the Pacific, precludes similar recognition and awareness of those sites designed by Oakes. What stories these sites in Asia do tell have emanated to a greater extent from the voices of prisoners of war that survived. Similarly, the past 20 years have also seen a generation of written works appearing to explore the war through local viewpoints and national narratives. They tend to demythologise the events as once presented by an imperial military history standpoint. By looking at the dead and missing through a history of a common war cemetery, it opens new ways of exploring the past. The Singapore Memorial and its architect Colin St Clair Oakes offer an opportunity to begin this wider regional understanding.

Kranji War Cemetery and Memorial, August 1957

Notes

Preface

1. Created in 1975 and formalised by the War Graves Act 1980, the Office of Australian War Graves (OAWG) is a branch of the Australian Government Department of Veteran Affairs. Previously the Anzac Agency of the Imperial War Graves Commission, it now acts as the Australian agent for the Commonwealth War Graves Commission.

2. https://www.dva.gov.au/commemorations-memorials-and-war-graves/memorials/war-memorials

3. By way of comparison, the Gallipoli campaign of 1915–16 saw 26,111 Australian casualties, including 8,141 deaths. The battle for Malaya and Singapore saw almost 15,000 Australian servicemen captured and 700 killed. The subsequent internment conditions and forced labour of these prisoners of war, along with an additional 7,000 captured throughout Southeast Asia, would see the loss of 8,789 lives, or more than one-third. Source: AWM website.

Chapter I: Introduction

1. Involved with organising the armed resistance in North Borneo during the war, Black was captured by the Japanese in 1942. His posting to Singapore in 1955 after a spell as Colonial Secretary for Hong Kong lasted for two years. He then returned to Hong Kong as its Governor in 1958. In March 1965, Black would be appointed Member of the Commonwealth War Graves Commission, serving until July 1982.

2. John Hare through his appointment as Secretary of State for War in October 1956 automatically assumed the Chairmanship of the Commission. For a detailed account of the politics behind the decisions on official attendance at the ceremony, see Romen Bose, *Kranji: The Commonwealth War Cemetery and the Politics of the Dead,* 42–43; and Imperial War Graves Commission, Minutes of Proceedings [hereafter IWGC MoP], at the 339th Meeting 17 Jan. 1957, 10.

3. On the term 'impregnable fortress' often used on Singapore at that time, refer to Fred Glueckstein, 'Churchill and the Fall of Singapore', *Finest Hour,* 169, Summer 2015, 32–35, from the International Churchill Society.

4. IWGC's *Order of Ceremony at the Unveiling of The Singapore Memorial*, 2 Mar. 1957, retrieved from CWGC; also refer to IWGC MoP 401, 21 Mar. 1957, 2–3.

5. IWGC MoP 401, 21 Mar. 1957, 3.

6. Allowing for the goodwill offered, £200 was still a considerable amount for 1957. The equivalent today of approximately £1800 was mentioned in 'Fifteen Australians will fly to unveiling', *The Australian Woman's Weekly*, 27 Feb. 1957, 21.

7. The US President delivered this speech at the dedication of the Soldiers' National Cemetery in Gettysburg, 1863; reported in 'A Moving Dedication at New Shrine', *The Singapore Free Press*, 2 Mar. 1957, 3. Retrieved from NewspaperSG.

8. IWGC MoP 400, 21 Feb. 1957, 3. In view of the distance and reception difficulties encountered, the BBC was unable to provide live coverage. Instead, a special sound broadcast with a complete recording of the ceremony was provided on the BBC Home Service the following day, Sunday 3 March, at 3.30 p.m.

9. Bob Chaundy, 'Anthony Lawrence obituary', *The Guardian*, 26 Sept. 2013. Retrieved from https://www.theguardian.com/media/2013/sep/26/anthony-lawrence

10. IWGC *Order of Ceremony at the Unveiling of The Singapore Memorial*, 2 Mar. 1957.

11. Ibid., and IWGC MoP 401, 21 Mar. 1957, 2–3.

12. The IWGC India, Pakistan and South East Asia District, with headquarters in Delhi, was an amalgam in 1951 of three sub-offices originally conceived in 1947. Of the three remaining cemeteries in its jurisdiction as of March 1957, work soon commenced on Assam, one in East Pakistan and the third at Thanbyuzayat in Burma with the improving political conditions. See IWGC MoP 393, 21 Jun. 1956, 7.

13. Jay Winter, *Sites of Memory, Sites of Mourning: The Great War in European Cultural History* (1995), 98.

14. CWGC/1/2/H/T 571 Colin St. Clair Oakes. Handwritten note dated 27 Oct. 1945 from Sir Frederic Kenyon, IWGC Artistic Advisor to Brigadier Frank Higginson, Controller and Director of Works, IWGC, recommending Oakes for the initial tour of Asia. Oakes's military record and time spent living in Bengal were earlier highlighted to Kenyon in a letter from the Royal Institute of British Architects dated 2 October 1945.

15. Servicemen from New Zealand, Canada, South Africa and Germany are also represented. Those casualties from local Malay regiments and Hong Kong are accounted for under the United Kingdom figures. The Indian numbers represent the Indian subcontinent as they stood in 1945, including today's Pakistan and Bangladesh along with ethnic Gurkhas from within India and Nepal.

16. IWGC had required the location of permanent war cemeteries in the Far East and Australasia be subject to regular access by ship or plane for visiting relatives. It was a similar case with Burma and the difficulties involved in accessing the interior due to topography, lack of transportation networks and internal unrest.

17. CWGC: RA 41595 Pt 1 'Kranji War Cemetery Singapore'. Letter dated 11 Sept. 1947 from CAO I&SEA Dist IWGC, Brig. Harry Obbard to VC SAO IWGC HQ clarified that a considerable number of Chinese massacred by the Japanese had joined the volunteer forces or were members of special organisations (Dalforce), entitling them to be buried with war graves treatment. He also highlighted that until their military or semi-military status could be proved, they would be considered as civilians.

18. Arising from the Sook Ching massacre of February 1942, the memorial was designed by Leong Swee Lim of Swan & Maclaren Architects and inaugurated by Lee Kuan Yew, Prime Minister of Singapore, on 15 February 1967. Dhoraisingam S. Samuel, 'A Memorial for Civilian Victims', in *Singapore's Heritage: Through Places of Historical Interest* (1991), 315–317.

19. Organised by the British High Commission and the Singapore Armed Forces Veterans' League, the annual Remembrance Day ceremony is held on the Sunday closest to 11 November, and is otherwise referred to as Remembrance Sunday. The Australian and New Zealand High Commissions alternate in organising the annual Anzac Day dawn service and ceremony every year on 25 April.

20. The architectural programme was laid out in Sir Frederic Kenyon's report to the IWGC on 20 November 1917, *War Graves: How the Cemeteries Abroad will be Designed.*

21. Less than six months after the unveiling, on 31 August 1957, Malaya declared their independence. Singapore became self-governing soon after, on 1 January 1958.

22. The IWGC diligently recorded the yearly honours bestowed upon those closely associated with the Commission's work in their Annual Reports. Death notices, promotions, retirements and other significant personal milestones would also be recorded in the Annual Reports and in the monthly Commission Meetings.

Chapter 2: Writings

1. It would be a further six months before the opening of international facilities at Heathrow, London, in May 1946. Poole was one of the principal staging points for the Normandy landings.

2. CWGC SDC97, Obbard's report 'Tour of IWGC Representatives in India, Burma and the Far East'. Copy issued to Major A MacFarlane 15 Feb. 1946. Tour details and objectives were also recorded in Oakes's report as Advisory Architect, issued to IWGC HQ dated 16 Mar. 1946.

3. Andrew MacFarlane (1888–1969) was also responsible for all IWGC construction in Norway, Sweden and Denmark. CWGC: CWGC/6/4/1/2/4271.

4. CWGC: DS/UK/75 and CWGC/6/4/1/2/4933 retrieved from the CWGC Archive Catalogue, Harry Naismith Obbard (1893–1970).

5. CWGC: SDC 97, Col. Harry N. Obbard's 'Tour report of India, Burma, Ceylon, Thailand & Singapore, Nov. 1945–Feb 1946'.

6. Ibid. The party travelled to 42 cities and towns and visited 52 war cemeteries and civil cemeteries where war remains were located. This number does not account for the many burial sites along the Siam-Burma Railway that were being exhumed for concentration at Kanchanaburi, Chungkai and Thanbyuzayat.

7. Ibid. These numbers would be re-evaluated a few years later in a subsequent tour, where those deemed inaccessible or in politically unstable environments were further consolidated. War cemeteries and memorials in New Guinea, Indonesia, Borneo and the Australasian region including the Pacific Islands, and Japan would fall under the purview of the Anzac Agency of the IWGC, based out of Melbourne.

8. Jean-Louis Cohen, *Architecture in Uniform: Designing and Building for the Second World War* (2012). This publication accompanied the exhibition held by the Canadian Centre for Architecture in Montreal, April–September 2011. Hugh Casson (1910–99) and William Holford (1907–1975) both had an influence on Oakes in his early years as colleagues at the Architectural Association. Holford was also a fellow Rome Scholar with Oakes at the British School at Rome, and would go on to become the third Artistic Advisor for the Imperial War Graves Commission, succeeding Edward Maufe in 1969.

9. Ibid., 410–415.

10. Though the examples cited are in book format, writings include journal articles, academic papers, unpublished theses and online pieces.

11. Attesting to its popularity as the definitive reference on the CWGC, the book was revised and updated in 1985, and reprinted in 2003 and 2010.

12. Philip Longworth, *The Unending Vigil: A History of the Commonwealth War Graves Commission* (2010), xiii.

13. Ibid., 198, 204–205, 213. Similarly, the significant war cemetery sites of Taukkyan, Thanbyuzayat, Taiping and Kohima only elicit a single mention. Imphal in India and Sai Wan in Hong Kong are omitted altogether.

14. Oakes is also credited with the Sai Wan Bay War Cemetery and Memorial, but not mentioned for Kanchanaburi, Chungkai, Imphal, Kohima or Thanbyuzayat in Edwin Gibson and Kingsley Ward, *Courage Remembered* (1989), 163.

15. CWGC Annual Report 2006–2007, 12. Photographs for the exhibition and book were provided by photo-journalist Brian Harris.

16. Julie Summers, *British and Commonwealth War Cemeteries* (2010), 47.

17. Ibid., 48–49. Interestingly, as found in Gibson and Ward's book, Summers presents two photographic views of Sai Wan War Cemetery with the bay in the background: one taken soon after the war ended with all graves marked by wooden crosses; the other a more recent image depicting the same bay view 'obliterated by the skyscrapers that crowd around the cemetery's perimeter'.

18. *Singapore at War* is a compilation of three of Romen Bose's previous publications, *Secrets of the Battlebox* (2005), *The End of the War* (2005), and *Kranji* (2006). Oakes is not acknowledged as the architect in Bose's books, though his sketch designs of both the cemetery and Singapore Memorial are provided in the appendices.

19. Amaris Lee identifies that the war memory in Singapore is political rather than emotional. Singapore's abandonment by the British and subsequent occupation by the Japanese was used to emphasise self-reliance and the concept of 'total defence' – the importance of a strong national identity. Lee, Amaris, 'A Case of Renewed Identity: The Fading Role of WWII in Singapore's National Narrative', *AFFAIRS*, 9 Oct. 2015. Retrieved from https://spj.hkspublications.org/2015/11/09/a-case-of-renewed-identity-the-fading-role-of-wwii-in-singapores-national-narrative/

20. Brenda Yeoh and Hamzah Muzaini, 'Memory-making "From Below": Rescaling Remembrance at the Kranji War Memorial and Cemetery, Singapore', *Environment and Planning*, vol. 39 (2007): 1288.

21. P. Lim Pui Huen and Diana Wong's *War and Memory in Malaysia and Singapore*, a collection of eight essays from a 1995 workshop at the Institute of Southeast Asian Studies commemorating the 50th anniversary of the end of the Second World War, provides a good example of the various disciplines engaged in the study of memorialisation: political science, geography, Chinese studies, history, Southeast Asian studies and sociology. Note also that Lim and Wong identify that interest in the war at the Institute dates from 1973.

22. The term 'deathscape' emanated from a multidisciplinary conference in Bath, England, in 2007. Avril Maddrell and James Sidaway edited 15 papers into the 2010 work, *Deathscapes: Spaces for Death, Dying, Mourning and Remembrance*. It introduced scholarship in the cultural practices surrounding death.

23. Brenda Yeoh and Hamzah Muzaini, *Contested Memoryscapes* (2016), 95.

24. Ibid., 96; and Lily Kong, 'Cemeteries and Columbaria, Memorials and Mausoleums: Narrative and Interpretation in the Study of Deathscapes in Geography', *Australian Geographical Studies*, (1999), 5. Kong situates her study of deathscape within the field of cultural geography.

25. Ibid., and Mandy Morris, 'Gardens "For Ever England": Landscape, Identity and the First World War British Cemeteries on the Western Front', *Ecumene,* 4, no. 4 (1997), 410–34.

26. Ibid. 93–94. The difficulty in this argument is that the intentions of those who participated in the design of the war cemetery were not courted. Neither is Oakes, as the architect, mentioned.

27. Scates includes memorials and carefully tended cemeteries in his reading of traumascapes. Bruce Scates, *Anzac Journeys: Returning to the Battlefields of World War II* (2013), 3.

28. Ibid., 3–5.

29. Produced in 1982 by John McCallum and Lee Robinson, under Southern International Films, *The Highest Honour* was released in two versions – the Japanese version emphasising the Japanese actors.

30. On a mission by a team of Australian special forces to destroy Japanese ships in Singapore Harbour, the first operation, codenamed Jaywick, was a success, but the subsequent Operation Rimau was disastrous. The entire team was either killed during the action or captured and executed.

31. Philip Longworth, *The Unending Vigil: A History of the Commonwealth War Graves Commission* (2010), 213.

32. Ibid. Edward Maufe, succeeding Sir Frederic Kenyon as the IWGC Artistic Advisor, was ambiguous in his appraisal of the modern. Wary of the creeping trend to the contemporary through his reviews of the war cemeteries and memorials presented by their architects at the monthly Commission meetings, in the case of Oakes's work in Asia he was willing to support the design proposals with an occasional amendment.

Chapter 3: The Architects

1. Stephen Wyatt, *Memorials to the Missing: A Play for Radio* (2008). The play was first broadcast in 2007, followed by the printed publication a year later.

2. Ibid., 50.

3. 'Afternoon Play' is a long-running programme series broadcast every weekday since its launch in 1967. It was renamed 'Afternoon Drama' in 2012.

4. From the interior book flap of Gavin Stamp's *The Memorial to the Missing of the Somme* (2006).

5. From the correspondence with Stephen Wyatt; the tour of Arras Memorial was conducted by Stamp himself.

6. Gavin Stamp, *The Memorial to the Missing of the Somme* (2006), 72–76.

7. Fabian Ware, *The Immortal Heritage* (1937), 16. Blunden, pursuing an academic career after the war, would succeed Rudyard Kipling as the IWGC's Literary Advisor.

8. For a comprehensive account of Ware's time with the Red Cross 'flying unit', refer to David Crane's chapter 'The Mobile Unit' in *Empires of the Dead* (2013), 30–58.

9. Also known as the Norton-Harjes Ambulance Corps, on account of the American banker Henry Harjes, who donated funds and ambulances. Refer also to https://net.lib. byu.edu/~rdh7/wwi/comment/AmerVolunteers/Morse4.htm, last accessed 22 July 2020.

10. Ware, *The Immortal Heritage,* 24–25. General Sir Cecil Frederick Nevil Macready (1862–1946) was a founding member of the Commission and one of the individuals personally responsible for its existence. With the founding of the IWGC, he was appointed one of the eight unofficial Commissioners.

11. Le Tréport Military Cemetery, Forceville Communal Cemetery and Louvencourt Military Cemetery in France were the first three Commission cemeteries built after the First World War. They were designed by Sir Reginald Blomfield. Although the Commission had originally intended that each Principal Architect – Baker, Lutyens and Blomfield – design one war cemetery each, the German spring offensive of 1918 along the Western Front, or Kaiserschlacht, rendered various cemeteries inaccessible. Blomfield was subsequently tasked to design all three sites.

12. CWGC: *Twentieth Annual Report of the Imperial War Graves Commission,* 1938–1939 (1940). Appendix G: Distribution of Cemeteries, Graves and Memorials, 45–49. The Report ends 31 March 1939.

13. CWGC: *Annual Report For The Year Ended 31 March 2019.* As of the current 2018–2019 reporting period, the number of Commonwealth war dead stands at approximately 1,700,000 throughout more than 23,000 locations in over 150 countries and territories.

14. These were found by French government search parties as well as local farmers and landowners.

15. CWGC: *Twentieth Annual Report of the Imperial War Graves Commission* (1940), 3.

16. IWGC: MoP 248 (special), 26 Mar. 1943. Reference was made to letter dated 6 Feb. 1943, to IWGC from Major-General D.G Watson, DAG(A), War Office.

17. Ibid. The three experimental cemeteries of the First World War that became the template for the Commission's work thereafter had been studied as early as May 1918, six months prior to cessation of hostilities on 11 November 1918. The DGR&E was a British Army department established under Fabian Ware, with responsibility for preserving records of burials and providing the means for graves to be marked and identified. The DGR&E would merge with the IWGC in 1921.

18. The UK, Canada, Australia, New Zealand, South Africa, India, British West Indies and Newfoundland.

19. Refer to Edwin Gibson and Kingsley Ward's *Courage Remembered* (1989), in particular Chapter 8, 'Planning and Construction', 49–57, for a comprehensive explanation as to the financing of the Commission's operations.

20. IWGC: MoP, 248 (special), 26 Mar. 1943, 3–4.

21. Ibid. The minutes identified the North African area as part of the Middle East campaign. It included the coastal region approximately 1500 miles long from Alexandria through to Tobruk and Tripoli, Tunisia, Algeria and Morocco to the west and seven cemeteries in Ethiopia, Eritrea, the two Somalilands (present-day Somalia) and Kenya. Madagascar was to fall under the Commission's South Africa Agency.

22. Ibid.

23. IWGC: MoP, 249, 19 May 1943, 8. Also CWGC/1/2/4/5 and DS/UK/21 Worthington, Sir Hubert (1886–1963), architect, and Archer, John H.G. (2004), 'Worthington family (per. 1849–1963)', *Dictionary of National Biography,* Oxford University Press, retrieved 22 Oct. 2019, https://en.wikipedia.org/wiki/Hubert_Worthington

24. IWGC: MoP 255, 19 Jan. 1944, 2. In tribute to Lutyens, Principal Architect from 1918 to 1930, the Commission put forth a resolution expressing their profound regret at the loss of the man 'to whose genius they owe it that so many British dead of the Great War are buried in cemeteries or named on memorials supremely worthy of their sacrifice'. Sir Fabian Ware, as Chair, moved the resolution and given that Lutyens had designed the Villers-Bretonneux Memorial, the motion was seconded by the representative of Australia, F.T. Sprange.

25. Ibid., 1–7.

26. The Arts and Crafts movement was an international trend in decorative and fine arts between 1880 to 1920. It originated in the UK, then flourished in Europe and North America.

27. CWGC: CWGC/1/2/H/6 and DS/UK/12, also https://en.wikipedia.org/wiki/Edward_Maufe last viewed 11 Mar. 2018; also CWGC: MoP 310, 16 Dec. 1948, 7. Maufe's appointment as Chief Architect and Artistic Advisor was officially on 31 March 1949.

28. CWGC: CWGC/1/1/13/52, and CWGC: MoP 261, 16 Aug. 1944. Memmo was the Commission's sole representative in Italy since 1936. During the war, he continued to maintain the war cemeteries whilst Italy was an 'enemy power'. Upon the end of the war, he was appointed the Italian Liaison Officer, assisting the Commission in resuming its work in the country. His position and standing in Italian society, along with his understanding of Italian horticulture and local conditions, would prove invaluable to de Soissons and the Commission.

29. Ebenezer Howard founded the garden city movement at the turn of the 20th century, an urban planning methodology that advocated the human benefits of the natural environment as being integral to the built. Appointed the architect for Welwyn in 1920, de Soissons and his practice would be significantly involved in its development over the next 60 years.

30. CWGC: Id CWGC/1/2/H/7 and DS/UK/44 archive and https://www.louisdes-oissons.com/#about-us Mentioned in Dispatches, de Soissons was awarded the Order of the British Empire (OBE) and the Croce di Guerra, and made a Cavaliere of the Order of the Crown of Italy.

31. CWGC: CWGC/1/2/H/7 and DS/UK/29 archive, https://peoplepill.com/people/philip-dalton-hepworth/ and https://en.wikipedia.org/wiki/Philip_Hepworth. As with de Soissons, Hepworth would design 46 war cemeteries, alongside the Memorials to the Missing at Bayeux, Dunkirk and Groesbeek Canadian War Cemetery.

32. From 'The Task Ahead', first published in *The Herald* (Melbourne), 27 Dec. 1941, http://john.curtin.edu.au/pmportal/text/00468.html and https://www.nma.gov.au/defining-moments/resources/fall-of-singapore

33. Where the primary battles were American-led, it fell upon the United States Army Quartermaster Corps' Graves Registration Service.

34. The British Army's War Graves Service was heavily involved in India, Burma, the Siam-Burma Railway, Malaya and Singapore.

35. Jack Leemon, *War Graves Digger* (2010), 1. Leemon served as member of 10 Australian Graves Registration and Enquiries Unit, and OC of 26 Australian War Graves Unit, in locations such as New Guinea, the Siam-Burma Railway, and Yokohama, Japan.

36. Seumas Spark, *The Treatment of the British Military War Dead of the Second World War,* PhD Thesis, University of Edinburgh, 2009.

37. AWM52: 1/1/15 Headquarter Units: Director of War Graves Services (LHQ Graves Registration), Jan.–Jun. 1942, Nov.–Dec. 1942. From the War Diary. The Field Service Pocket Book (FSPB) was issued as of 1 March 1942, as Pamphlet No. 11A (Australian Edition). It was distributed to all units of the Australian Imperial Forces and Australian Military Forces. Instructions regarding the selection and layout of cemetery sites were prepared and distributed two months later on 18 May 1942, to each Line of Communication (L of C) Area.

38. Leemon, *War Graves Digger,* 1–4.

39. The Temporary War Cemetery applied to those recently liberated or battlefield locations outside Australia where final decisions pending their permanent use could not reasonably be made at the time. Similarly, in the case of multiple burial sites located within

difficult terrain or inaccessible areas, a Concentration Military Cemetery was established prior to the confirmation of its transformation into, or relocation to, the permanent war cemetery.

40. AWM52: 1/1/15 Headquarter Units: Director of War Graves Services (LHQ Graves Registration), Jan.–Dec. 1943. From the War Diary, 14 Jun. 1943, memo to Secretary, Dept. of the Army for onward inclusion in IWGC Annual Report.

41. Photographing the headstones was an important aspect of the War Graves Units. The photograph was intended to prove to the next-of-kin that their loved one had a grave and proper burial. These images, along with information on the war cemetery where the grave was located, offered a semblance of closure since the anxious families were unable or unlikely to venture to these foreign sites.

42. AWM52: 1/1/15 Headquarter Units: Director of War Graves Services (LHQ Graves Registration), Jan.–Jun. 1942, Nov.–Dec. 1942. From the War Diary, enacted 30 Mar. 1942. All notifications were to go through the Divisional Records Office (DRO). The establishment of General Headquarters, Southwest Pacific Area GHQ SWPA in Melbourne on 18 April 1942, with General Douglas MacArthur, Commander-in-Chief, saw HQ USAFIA abolished by July, its functions transferred to Headquarters, United States Army Services of Supply (HQ USASOS).

43. CWGC: MoP 265, 16 Jan. 1945.

44. Bruce had served as the eighth Prime Minister of Australia (1923–29).

45. The final Cowra Japanese Military Cemetery was established and consecrated in 1964, and contains 523 Japanese graves, including the 231 graves of prisoners of war killed during the breakout. https://www.cwgc.org/find-a-cemetery/cemetery/4007288/cowra-japanese-military-cemetery, accessed 3 Feb. 2020.

46. The CWGC website lists 644 separate entries for Australian Second World War sites alone, ranging from single-casualty sites to 748 casualties recorded at the Sydney Memorial.

47. From the Department of Veteran Affairs website, https://www.dva.gov.au/commemorations-memorials-and-war-graves/cemeteries/first-and-second-world-war-cemeteries/cemeteries#nsw; also, the CWGC: https://www.cwgc.org/find-a-cemetery/cemetery/4007288/cowra-japanese-military-cemetery

48. McNair would go on to join the Commission as their Foreign Relations Officer.

49. CWGC Archive Catalogue DS/UK/30.

50. Dictionary of Scottish Architects, http://www.scottisharchitects.org.uk/architect_full.php?id=203484 last viewed 9 Nov. 2018 and from a letter from Arthur Hutton (1891–1982) to his wife on 11 Mar. 1942, and reproduced in 'Escape from Singapore' by Shel Arensen 17 Nov. 2015, http://oldafricamagazine.com/escape-from-singapore/, accessed 9 Nov. 2018.

51. Alisdair Ferrie, 'Designing Kohima', BBA News, August/September 1995, 20. And 'In Honour of the Brave', author and source unknown. The erection of boulders is a long-standing tradition among the menfolk of the Naga tribes. Over the course of their lives they should take a boulder from the river and move it to a high and prominent position. One explanation is that this represents a measure of the stature of that man.

52. The original epigram inscription referred to 'their tomorrow' and was later changed to the corrected version.

53. AWM Photograph Accession No. 117206. Provisional captions to the photograph. The image was one of a series taken by a Department of Information photographer, Lt. R.J. Buchanan. The £100 prize was the equivalent of $1,500 in today's terms.

54. Correspondence from Australian Army Museum of Military Engineering.

55. CWGC/1/2/H/T 571 Colin St Clair Oakes. Letter dated 2 Oct. 1945 from C. Spragg, RIBA, to Kenyon.

56. Ibid. Handwritten note dated 27 Oct. 1945 by Kenyon to Brigadier Higginson IWGC.

57. Longworth, *The Unending Vigil*, 180.

Chapter 4: Architecture

1. 'The Imperial War Graves Commission: Architectural Work Following the 1939–45 War', *Journal of the Royal Institute of British Architects*, Sept. and Oct. 1953. The Commission would soon after publication reprint the combined articles with a Royal Institute of British Architects seal as its cover for its own promotion.

2. Ibid., 1.

3. John Ellis and Michael Cox, *The World War 1 Databook* (2001). Commonwealth air force casualties for WWII number over 109,700. This compares with almost 6,170 aircrew lost in combat for the UK in WWI.

4. IWGC MoP 267, 21 Mar. 1945, 5. The rocky outcrop of Gibraltar, turned into a fortress for the war, was severely limited in area for future burials. The existing North Front Cemetery contained 350 graves of WWII, and had reached its capacity, with one of its two burial plots encroaching within the safety margin of the runway, and in other cases, two burials being made in each grave. Up to October 1942, RAF burials amounted to 162. The missing presumed dead amounted to about 600.

5. Similar in significance to the Royal Navy; and like the navy, the sites of battle were not in locations accessible or practical. Runnymede by Maufe was the sole Air Force Memorial in the UK for those killed or missing in the European campaign, whereas the Malta Memorial in Valetta, designed by Worthington, was dedicated to the Commonwealth aircrew lost whilst serving in the Mediterranean. Kranji was intended for those who died in the Pacific campaign.

6. 'The Imperial War Graves Commission: Architectural Work following the 1939–45 War', *Journal of the Royal Institute of British Architects*, Sept. and Oct. 1953, 1.

7. George Esslemont Gordon Leith (1885–1965) had commenced his career working for Herbert Baker, before serving as a captain in the Royal Field Artillery on the Western Front, where he suffered the effects of a gas attack. Upon the conclusion of the war, he would become an assistant architect to the IWGC before heading back to his native South Africa to set up practice.

8. Fabian Ware, *The Immortal Heritage: An Account of the Work and Policy of The Imperial War Graves Commission During Twenty Years 1917–1937* (1937), 16.

9. Ibid., 11. Established in 1915 as the Graves Registration Commission, a British Army department under Ware, it was renamed the DGR&E in 1915, responsible for preserving records of burials and providing the means for graves to be marked and identified.

10. Ibid., 27–30.

11. Sir James Barrie's stepson George L. Davies had been killed in the trenches of Flanders, Belgium, two years prior to the tour. He was the model for Barrie's acclaimed novel *Peter Pan*. Source, CWGC Archives.

12. Ware, *The Immortal Heritage*, 31, and Philip Longworth, *The Unending Vigil: A History of the Commonwealth War Graves Commission 1917–1984* (1985), 32–33. It was Sir Charles Holmes of the National Gallery who had initially put forward Kenyon's name to Ware to consider. Respected, widely experienced, learned and well-travelled, Kenyon

had by the young age of 28 edited the first printed edition of Aristotle's Constitution of Athens.

13. Frederic Kenyon, *War Graves: How the Cemeteries Abroad will be Designed* (1918), 2. Ware's introduction to the final Report, 22 Nov 1918. Along with deciding on the architectural direction, the Commission had two further terms of reference for Kenyon, the first of which was to consult the various churches and religious bodies on questions of religion, and secondly, advise on forming an advisory committee from those consulted to undertake the agreed proposals.

14. Ibid., 6–7.

15. The Report would be updated and re-issued 14 November 1918, following modification of some of its initial recommendations. The most notable was the unanimous preference by the artists and architects for a uniform headstone as opposed to a variety based on different units or arms of service, and the selection of Kipling's proposed inscription for the Stone of Remembrance.

16. Kenyon, *War Graves*, 7.

17. Ibid., 10. While most Commonwealth countries allowed for these personal inscriptions, New Zealand was the notable exception, believing they contravened the principle of equality. Britain would impose a fee on the next-of-kin for this service, while the Australian and Canadian governments elected to cover the cost.

18. Ibid., 13. Kenyon's first decision on the horticulture design was to express preference for a levelled, grassy surface over the burials rather than separate mounds over each grave.

19. Capt. Arthur W. Hill, 'Our Soldiers' Graves', *Journal of the Royal Horticultural Society*, vol. xiv., 1919, Part 1. From the lecture delivered on 25 February 1919. Hill, a noted botanist and taxonomist, would go on to become Director of the Royal Botanic Gardens, Kew.

20. Kenyon, *War Graves*, 19. Kenyon also proposed that the young architects be stationed in France or Belgium so as to supervise the work.

21. Ibid.

22. Blomfield was also a garden designer and author, noted in particular for the controversial book, *Modernismus* (1934), an anti-Modernist polemic.

23. Kenyon, *War Graves*, 10. Kenyon's acceptance of the Stone as a central element within the war cemetery was predicated on it being more than a simple feature – that it could accommodate the commemoration processes which would undoubtably occur there. He also insisted that although it was intended as a secular object, it should be capable of religious association, satisfying the religious needs of the many without offending any.

24. Gavin Stamp, *Silent Cities: An Exhibition of the Memorial and Cemetery Architecture of the Great War*, 1977, 9. The Stone's dimensions are 12 feet long, 3 feet wide and 3½ feet high. The steps at the base add approximately another 1 foot to the overall height.

25. Gavin Stamp, *The Memorial to the Missing of the Somme* (2006), 79. In the case of Lutyens's Stone, the curves were part of a hypothetical sphere measuring 1,801 feet 8 inches in diameter.

26. 'Known unto God' was possibly taken from Acts 15:18 – 'Known unto God are all his works from the beginning of the world'.

27. From Kipling's 1897 poem 'Recessional': 'Lord God of Hosts, be with us yet, lest we forget – lest we forget!' Originally composed for Queen Victoria's Diamond Jubilee, the poem served as a note of warning of the transient nature of the British Empire (notes credited to Mary Hamer, 2008), http://www.kiplingsociety.co.uk/rg_recess1.htm, accessed 5 Apr. 2018.

28. King James Version of the Bible, Eccles 44:14. The chapter begins with 'Let us now praise famous men, and our fathers that begat us.'

29. Personal communication. The Lutyens Trust, 29 Feb. 2020.

30. Hansard Notes, House of Commons Debate, 4 May 1920, vol. 128 cc 1929–72.

31. Kenyon, *War Graves*, 11. For the non-Christian fallen, Kenyon made the distinction that their graves were to be treated in accordance with their own religious beliefs and practices, with their own religious symbol placed over them. Furthermore, the design of mosques or temples erected in Muslim and Hindu cemeteries should be in conformity with the religious customs and aspirations of those they served.

32. The Cross of Sacrifice originally came in four heights: 14 feet, 18 feet, 20 feet and 24 feet.

33. Kenyon, *War Graves*, 20. Kenyon qualified his statement to include those who were precluded from serving on medical grounds, though they would be lower down the preference order.

34. Cathy Wilson, *Architects in the First World War*, 9 Nov. 2017. https://www.architecture.com/knowledge-and-resources/knowledge-landing-page/architects-and-the-first-world-war, accessed 16 Nov. 2018.

35. Ibid.

36. Longworth, *The Unending Vigil*, 190–191.

37. Ibid., 204.

38. CWGC Archives: CWGC/6/4/1/1/35 and DS/UK/77.

39. CWGC Archives: CWGC/1/2/J/13 and DS/UK/42. Hobday would be awarded an OBE by the Queen in 1959 in recognition of his work at Brookwood Memorial.

40. Stamp, *The Memorial to the Missing of the Somme*, 164. Quoting Edward Maufe, the design works 'sweetly and is in the Lutyens manner, in no way detracting from the existing work'.

41. CWGC Archives: CWGC/6/4/1/1/300 and CWGC/6/4/1/1/84.

42. CWGCArchives: CWGC/7/3/2/1/8 Form A – Digboi War Cemetery.

43. CWGC: *Fifty-First Annual Report*, 1st Apr. 1969 to 31st Mar. 1970 (1970), 9–10.

44. CWGC: *Fifty-First Annual Report* (1970), 10.

45. Ibid.

46. https://www.awm.gov.au/articles/encyclopedia/fromelles, accessed 7 July 2020. The Battle of Fromelles occurred on 19 July 1916, when newly arrived soldiers of the 5th Australian Division along with the British 61st Division attacked strongly fortified German front lines near Aubers Ridge in French Flanders. The operation proved disastrous, with over 5,500 Australian casualties, of which almost 2,000 were killed in action or died of wounds. It was the greatest loss of life by a single Division in a day during the entire First World War.

47. https://www.cwgc.org/learn/horticulture-and-works/our-architects/barry-edwards, accessed 20 Nov. 2018. Edwards would also design the Brookwood 1914–1918 Memorial at Brookwood Military Cemetery in Surrey, unveiled in 2015. Of the 250 burials at Fromelles, 96 Australians are identified by name, a further 109 are known to be Australian, 3 are British and 42 remain unidentified.

Chapter 5: Colin St Clair Oakes

1. Gavin Stamp, *The Memorial to the Missing of the Somme* (2006), 50.

2. CWGC Archives: CWGC_1_2_H_T 571 Colin St. Clair Oakes, Letter from Oakes to the Controller, Accounts Department, IWGC, 9 Nov. 1948.

3. Raymond Gordon Brown (1912–1962) served as a Major of a parachute regiment during the war, taking part in D-Day. After the war, he became President of the Architectural Association (1945–48), followed by Chair of Architecture at Edinburgh College of Art (1949–50). In 1950 he took up an appointment as the first Professor of Architecture at the University of Hong Kong.

4. As part of the reparations demanded by the UK after the war and comprising mostly non-officers from over 400,000 prisoners of war, many of these ex-servicemen had been transferred from the United States and Canada. They would be mainly engaged in agriculture, with at least three-quarters of the prisoner-of-war population being involved. In 1947 the Ministry of Agriculture reported that their contribution amounted to 25 per cent of the land workforce. Then there was general labouring such as repairing damaged roads and infrastructure, whilst those employed in industry were chiefly in brickmaking and cement. Refer to Henry Faulk, *Group Captives: The Re-education of German Prisoners of War in Britain 1945–1948* (1977), 32, 42; Inge Weber-Newth and Johannes-Dieter Steinert, 'Chapter 2: Immigration Policy – Immigrant Policy', *German Migrants in Post-war Britain: An Enemy Embrace* (2006), 24–30.

5. Sally Thomas, *May: Family Histories 1850–2000 Book 4* (2013), 102.

6. Antonia Brodie et al, *Directory of British Architects 1834–1914 Vol. 2 (L–Z)* (2001), 278. Leonard Oakes (1879–1969) would be articled to Hardisty for four years, before moving to Nottingham and the architectural firm Messrs Brewill & Baily.

7. Thomas, *May*, 115. Leonard's daughter recounts her father as taking a stance against wearing any formal evening attire upon his return from the war – 'anything perhaps that smacked of the formal attire worn by officers during leisurely dinners, eaten at a safe distance from the front line'.

8. Samuel Hynes, *The Edwardian Turn of Mind* (1991).

9. Hasan-Uddin Khan, *International Style: Modernist Architecture from 1925 to 1965* (2009), 11–17. Khan identifies the escape from the rigours of 19th-century architectural revivals through their replacement by an attitude – Functionalism. With the 20th century having its own set of aesthetics and a single body of architecture, it would be defined by broad principles. This pan-European movement would in turn spread to the United States and Latin America.

10. Thomas, 125.

11. Northern Polytechnic would amalgamate with North-Western Polytechnic and eventually merge with London Guildhall University to form London Metropolitan University.

12. John Cecil Stephenson (1889–1965) would be Oakes's introduction to modernism. With his acquaintance with artists, architects and historians such as Piet Mondrian, Henry Moore, Herbert Read, Walter Gropius, Alexander Calder and Ben Nicholson, Stephenson was somewhat of a template for Oakes in broadening his own outlook on architecture.

13. The RIBA Tite prize extended throughout the Commonwealth to all RIBA members and students, with all winners and honourable mentions being recorded in the newspapers. Oakes's mention would also appear in the *Malayan Architect*, his first exposure to the Singapore architectural fraternity.

14. Thomas, 125. The thesis was submitted in May 1929 as part of the RIBA Final Examination.

15. Ibid., 126.

16. Biography of Jarl Eklund (1876–1962), Museum of Finnish Architecture. http://www.mfa.fi/architect?apid=3135, and http://www.mfa.fi/architect?apid=3871, accessed 2

Dec. 2019. Eliel Saarinen would go on to have an influence on modern architecture in the United States, particularly skyscraper and church design, after migrating there in 1923.

17. Roger Connah, *Finland: Modern Architectures in History* (2005), 53. Connah argues that it was Gunnar Asplund who primarily brought back to Sweden the notion of the timeless tradition that was connected to the Mediterranean. These design principles were founded on good sense, sound planning and a modest and functional response to the programme.

18. Biography of Eero Saarinen (1910–1961), Museum of Finnish Architecture. Source http://www.mfa.fi/architect?apid=3870, accessed 2 Dec. 2019.

19. Harold Chalton Bradshaw (1893–1943) designed several of the Imperial War Graves Commission's First World War cemeteries and memorials. He was the recipient of the first Rome scholarship in Architecture (1913).

20. British School at Rome: Correspondence from BSR to Oakes 15 June 1931, BSR Box 242a, file on Oakes (1931).

21. Andrew Wallace Hadrill, *The British School at Rome: One Hundred Years* (2001), 7.

22. Ibid., 80–86. Ian Richmond (1902–1965) studied at the British School at Rome between 1924 and 1926, exhibiting an enthusiasm for collaboration with architects. This set a pattern during his subsequent directorship tenure for scholars in architecture to actively participate in archaeological sites across Europe. Oakes would take this opportunity to collaborate with his professors and colleagues in archaeological surveys at Tivoli and Ostia, and the restoration of the Lanuvium excavation, south-east of Rome.

23. British School at Rome: Various correspondences, BSR Box 242a, file on Oakes (1931).

24. Hadrill, 89. Upon the gold standard being abandoned in 1931, the pound fell in value against the lira by 30 per cent, exacerbating the school's dire financial condition. Richmond's successor Colin Hardie would embark on extensive staff redundancies and winding-down activity.

25. Oakes annotated this photograph '*Giovaniezzi Fascista*', taken from the rooftop of the Pavilion.

26. Hadrill, 89–90. During the period of financial strain, the Fascist regime of Mussolini would impose pressure on the school through urban encroachment, whilst rising anti-British sentiment created an environment of uncertainty and hostility.

27. Thomas (2013),132–133.

28. Architectural Association Archives, GB 1968 AA, 'Administrative/Biographical History' and Edward Bottoms, Feb. 2010, introductory lecture to Archives For London & the Twentieth Century Society, https://www.aaschool.ac.uk/AASCHOOL/LIBRARY/aahistory.php, accessed 13 Dec. 2018.

29. Edward Bottoms, 'Corb at the AA', *AArchitecture*, Issue 4, 23–25. Based on the height of a man with his arm raised, Le Corbusier's Modulor is an anthopometric scale of proportions developed to improve the appearance and function of architecture.

30. The A.A. Centenary Celebrations, *R.I.B.A. Journal*, Jan. 1948.

31. 'Soldier Architect', *The Yorkshire Post and Leeds Mercury*, 1 Dec. 1944, 2; 'To Teach Architecture', *The Evening Telegraph*, 4 Dec. 1944, 5.

32. 'Prof. R Gordon Brown Resigns', *The Hong Kong and Far East Builder,* Vol. 13, No. 1, 53.

33. Thomas (2013), 133. Robert Furneaux-Jordan (1905–78), having trained at the AA in the late 1920s, and lectured there from 1934, would go on to become Principal of the AA between 1949 to 1951, succeeding Brown. Furneaux-Jordan would have an important influence on Oakes in his initially joining the AA and subsequent re-joining after the war.

Brown, on the other hand, become a close family friend of Oakes, both having seen active service during the war.

34. Ibid.

35. https://www.architectsjournal.co.uk/competitions/design-an-interactive-streets-cape-for-croydon-enter-the-aj-competition/10018074.article

36. https://fairfieldcroydon.wordpress.com/weekly-video-blog/home/fairfield-halls-the-history

37. Thomas (2013), 133.

38. Ibid., 133–134.

39. Jon Lang, *A Concise History of Modern Architecture in India*, (2002), 7–30.

40. *The Combined Civil List for India and Burma*, No. 119, Jan.–Mar. 1937, 483. Along with Edmondson, Oakes was a Special Appointment in the Bengal Public Works. Sir John Anderson was the Governor of Bengal between 1932 and 1937.

41. Thomas (2013), 135–139.

42. Ibid.

43. Ibid.

44. The war in Asia had in fact commenced in 1931 with the Japanese occupation of the Chinese province of Manchuria. Then on 7 July 1937, Japanese troops attacked Chinese soldiers at the Marco Polo Bridge near Peking, launching the invasion of China. By the fall of 1941, Japan had conquered most of northern and eastern China, holding all its important seaports.

45. Burma's forces in December 1941, under the responsibility of General Archibald P. Wavell, Commander-in-Chief, India, consisted of only one and a half poorly prepared and under-equipped divisions, comprising British, Indian and local Burmese units.

46. The GEACPS was established in 1931 by the Empire of Japan for its occupied Asian populations to promote cultural and economic unity. Its declared intention was to create a self-sufficient bloc of Asian nations, led by Japan, and thus promoting Japanese superiority over other Asians.

47. Commanded by Claire Lee Chennault, the First American Volunteer Group of the Chinese Air Force (1941–1942), nicknamed the Flying Tigers, comprised pilots from the US Navy, Marines and Army. They were originally recruited to defend China against Japanese forces, before the U.S. and Japan declared war.

48. In recognition of his role in the campaign, after the war Slim would be appointed Chief of the Imperial General Staff and Governor-General of Australia (1953–60).

49. Information on the India and Burma campaigns of the Second World War was drawn from various sources, including William Slim's *Defeat into Victory: Battling Japan in Burma and India, 1942–1945* (2000), Michael Lowry's *Fighting Through to Kohima: A Memoir of War in India & Burma*, (2003), Trevor N. Dupuy's *Asiatic Land Battles: Expansion of Japan in Asia* (1963), and Louis Allen's *Burma: The Longest War 1941–45* (1984).

50. Oakes's personal records.

51. The Chinese 38th and 22nd Divisions driven into India in the retreat from Burma would become the backbone units of Stilwell's newly established Chinese Army in India, reinforced by soldiers arriving from Kunming via the 'Hump'.

52. The Lend-Lease policy was a programme under which the United States supplied the Republic of China along with the British Commonwealth and Free France with oil, food and weapons between 1941 and 1945.

53. Beginning with 27 aircraft in May 1942, by its end in July 1945 there were 640 aircraft in service and a total of 156,977 trips made. 594 aircraft were lost in the operation, with 1,659 personnel killed or missing.

54. An estimated 2.1 to 3 million people died of starvation, malaria and other diseases aggravated by malnutrition, population displacement and unsanitary conditions in Bengal province alone between 1943 and 1944.

55. The 14th Army was formed from IV Corps (Imphal), XV Corps (Arakan) and XXXIII Corps (reserve) – later joined by XXXIV Corps.

56. Festing would decorate Oakes with his MBE at an investiture ceremony in the town of Mongmit, Burma, on 31 Mar 1945, soon after its capture from the Japanese.

57. Army records. Personal collection of Oakes family.

58. Ledo Road was the alternative overland connection built during the war between India and China to deliver supplies, after the Japanese cut off the Burma Road. The Chindits, otherwise known as the Long Range Penetration Groups, the creation of British Army Brigadier Orde C. Wingate, were special operations units of the British and Indian armies during the Burma Campaign.

59. Japanese casualties would amount to approximately 200,000 overall, of which between 144,000 to 164,500 were believed to have died. Estimates for Burmese civilians killed throughout those four years of fighting range from 250,000 to 1,000,000. Japanese casualties for Kohima and Imphal were 60,643, with many of these deaths attributed to starvation, malnutrition and disease.

60. The CWGC website records that Kohima War Cemetery and Cremation Memorial contain 1,422 and 917 casualties, respectively. Imphal War Cemetery contains 1,603 casualties, its Cremation Memorial 868 remains of Hindu and Sikh soldiers, and the Indian Army War Cemetery with 868 Commonwealth burials, consisting mostly of Muslim servicemen.

61. CWGC Archives: CWGC/1/2/H/T 571 Colin St Clair Oakes; Letter from IWGC to Oakes dated 2 Nov. 1945.

62. CWGC Archives: Minutes of 289th Meeting on 20 Feb. 1947. Adopted the recommendation to appoint a Principal Architect for the Commission's India and South East Asia District, and offer that appointment to Oakes effective 1 Mar. 1947.

Chapter 6: Singapore

1. After the Japanese surrender, Takuma Nishimura would be tried by the British for his involvement in the Sook Ching massacre and given life imprisonment. En route to Tokyo, he was forcibly removed from his ship by the Australians, brought to Manus Island and tried and executed for the Parit Sulong massacre in Malaya.

2. The Japanese 25th Army, from bases in Indochina, launched an amphibious assault into Thailand and northern Malaya on 8 December 1941.

3. Tomoyuki Yamashita earned the sobriquet 'Tiger of Malaya' for his conquering of Malaya and Singapore. After the surrender, he would be tried for war crimes committed by forces under his command in the Philippines and executed.

4. Part of the Australian 22nd Brigade and 1st Malaya Infantry Brigade, Dalforce volunteers proved themselves formidable in the fighting, earning the British sobriquet 'Dalley's Desperadoes'. Suffering high casualties, they were disbanded on 13 February1942, two days before the surrender of Singapore. Refer to Kevin Blackburn and Daniel Chew Ju Ern, 'Dalforce at the Fall of Singapore in 1942: An Overseas Chinese Heroic Legend', *Journal of Chinese Overseas* 1, no. 2 (2005): 233–259.

5. After the Allied surrender, Maxwell served as a prisoner of war in Taiwan, where he confided to Brigadier Arthur Blackburn that he deliberately directed his men to retreat to avoid unnecessary death under the hopeless circumstances. After the war, he gave evidence

at the military trial of Bennett on charges of abandoning his command after the fall of Singapore. Peter Brune, *Descent into Hell: The Fall of Singapore – Pudu and Changi – The Thai-Burma Railway* (2014), 442.

6. Accompanying Percival and their Japanese escort Lieutenant-Colonel Ichiji Sugita were Captain Cyril H.D. Wild carrying the white flag, a staff officer and Japanese-speaking interpreter, Brigadier T.K. Newbigging, the Chief Administrative Officer, Malaya Command, carrying the Union Flag, and Brigadier K.S. Torrance, General Staff Malaya Command.

7. CWGC Add 1/6/17 Box 2003. Oakes Report on his Tour Nov. 1945 to Dec. 1945. Oakes mentions that prior to leaving Delhi on their way to the battlefield sites, he and Obbard visited the Historical Section at GHQ to obtain direction on likely sites, taking into account key battles and engagements.

8. A.J. Hill, 'Hobbs, Sir Joseph John Talbot (1864–1938)', *Australian Dictionary of Biography*, National Centre of Biography, Australian National University, http://adb.anu.edu.au/biography/hobbs-sir-joseph-john-talbot-6690/text11539, published first in hardcopy 1983, accessed online 23 Jan. 2020. Four of the five memorials Hobbs proposed in Europe were of his design. The memorial at Polygon Wood was dedicated to the 5th Division, his former command.

9. Ibid. Hobbs's proposal for a memorial in Villers-Bretonneux gained traction in Australia, with its wartime Prime Minister Billy Hughes announcing a national design competition for its conception in 1925. Open only to Australian veterans and their parents, the winning design by Melbourne architect William Lucas was approved by the French Government in 1929, but the Great Depression soon after placed it on hold. The IWGC would eventually step in with the current design by Sir Edwin Lutyens.

10. http://www.delvillewood.com/wood.htm

11. Directorate of Graves Registration and Enquiries, *Technical Instructions*, Directorate of Graves Registration And Enquiries (Revised to 1 Feb., 1918).

12. Ibid., 3–4.

13. CWGC Archives, CWGC/1/1/5/12 and SDC 15. *Exhumation and Repatriation of Remains*.

14. Maria Tumarkin, *Traumascapes: The Power and Fate of Places Transformed by Tragedy* (2013), 12.

15. Ibid.

16. Ibid. In his tour report on Kohima, Oakes presents evidence of his awareness of the significance of sites, as he informs that 'the site has considerable historical significance as it was on the actual ground of the present cemetery that, in 1944 the Kohima Garrison made their final stand against the surrounding Japanese'.

17. Fought in three stages, the Battle of Kohima began on 4 April 1944 and ended with the Allies finally pushing the Japanese out of Imphal and lifting the city's siege on 22 June. British and Indian forces' casualties of dead, missing and wounded would amount to 4,064 men. The Japanese battle casualties of 5,764 were for the Kohima area alone. The figure would reach almost 7,000 by the time they were pushed back into Burma, with many of them later subsequently dying of disease, starvation or taking their own lives.

18. Field-Marshal Viscount William Slim, *Defeat into Victory: Battling Japan in Burma and India, 1942–1945*, 322–323, and Michael Lowry, *Fighting Through to Kohima: A Memoir of War in India & Burma*, 205–255. Referred to as the 'Battle of the Tennis Court', a small contingent of Commonwealth soldiers encircled by the Japanese held out against repeated assaults over 35 days from 8 April to 13 May 1944.

19. *The WWII Battle Fought Across a Tennis Court 10.07.14* [online video], Forces TV, 11 Jul. 2014, https://youtu.be/cS7KeDxkEbM, accessed 26 Jan. 2020.

20. CWGC Add 1/6/17 Box 2003. Interest in the existing military cemetery siting, layout and development had in fact commenced with the Deputy Commissioner Charles Pawsey, who had remained in the city during the siege, and the late garrison engineer Major R.E. Oakes Wells identified the tennis court's significance (an area about 150 feet by 130 feet) and requested it be left clear as a possible memorial site and reserved against further concentration of graves.

21. *Romusha* is a Japanese term for labourer that now specifically denotes the forced labourers during WWII.

22. Colonel E. Foster Hall, 'The Graves Service in the Burma Campaigns', *Royal United Services Institution. Journal,* 92:566, 240–244. Foster Hall would chronicle in detail the difficulties and challenges faced by the Graves Registration Units in the recovery and concentration of remains in Burma, in particular the time between registration and consolidation of remains. He would go on to make one of the earliest proposals to the Imperial War Graves Commission to consider cremation.

23. Australian Government, Department of Veteran Affairs, ANZAC Portal, https://anzacportal.dva.gov.au/history/conflicts/australia-and-second-world-war/events/victory-8-may-194515-august-1945/coming-home, accessed 31 Jan. 2020.

24. Ibid.

25. McLean became Military Secretary in 1949 and Chief Staff Officer, Ministry of Defence in 1951. Denning was promoted to General Officer Commanding Northern Ireland District in 1949.

26. CWGC Add 1/6/17 Box 2003. Oakes Report on his Tour Nov. 1945 to Dec. 1945.

27. Ibid.

28. Romen Bose, *Singapore at War: Secrets from the Fall, Liberation & Aftermath of WWII*, 356–357, 432–433.

29. Melaik stems from the Malay *mel-lak-ka,* referring to a rubber tree farm.

30. CWGC Add 1/6/17 Box 2003. Oakes Report on his Tour Nov. 1945 to Dec. 1945.

31. Ng Beng Yeong, *Till the Break of Day: A History of Mental Health in Singapore 1841–1993*; and Joshua Chia Yeong Jia, 'Woodbridge Hospital', Infopedia (2010), National Library Board, Singapore, https://web.archive.org/web/20110914180735/http://infopedia.nl.sg/articles/SIP_1094_2010-05-27.html, accessed 29 Nov. 2018.

32. Dusun is a Malay term for orchard. It also refers to an indigenous minority tribal group found throughout Sabah, Sarawak and Brunei.

33. Wan Meng Hao, 'More Than Meets The Eye: Remembering the War Dead in Singapore', 236–237, from Kevin Tan (ed.), *Spaces of the Dead: A Case from the Living* (2011).

34. CWGC Add 1/6/17 Box 2003. Oakes Report on his Tour Nov. 1945 to Dec. 1945.

35. International Criminal Court: ICC Legal Tools Database, https://www.legal-tools.org/doc/412496/ and http://www.singaporewarcrimestrials.com/case-summaries/detail/128, accessed 30 Jan. 2020. Known as the Fukudome Case (3rd Seletar Beheading Case), Fukudome, Asakura and Ino were found guilty of committing a war crime and sentenced to 3, 2 and 3 years' imprisonment respectively. In May 1945, eight further prisoners of war were beheaded and their bodies buried at Nee Soon. The perpetrator, Lieutenant Miyawaki Fumio, was tried and sentenced to death by hanging, later commuted to 20 years' imprisonment.

36. Obbard would make a point of insisting that a restriction be placed on the erection of any memorial within the Joraneu Cemetery so as to avoid it diminishing the stature of the future Muslim War Cemetery.

37. Ibid.

38. CWGC SDC 97 Box 2004. Obbard's Tour Reports 1945–46. Annexure 6. In his notes on the selection of sites for permanent military cemeteries on Singapore, Obbard highlights that Foster Hall's original proposal was for three Christian cemeteries – at Buona Vista, Kranji and Changi – and one Muslim cemetery at Nee Soon. Agreeing on Nee Soon for the Muslim site, Foster Hall indicated it contained the ashes of Hindu cremations and there was the need to scatter them.

39. Lex Arthurson, *The Story of the 13th Australian General Hospital: 8th Division A.I.F. Malaya*, 25. Prior to their relocation at Changi, the 13th Australian General Hospital (AGH) was moved according to the shifting front lines. Up to 12 February 1942, their dead were buried at the Ulu Pandan British Military Cemetery on Reformatory Road (Clementi Road). The shift in front lines saw the AGH then re-form at St Patrick's School, where a new cemetery was created in Martia Road. Hospital records indicate 21 men buried there in the last days of the Japanese push.

40. Ibid., 35.

41. Ibid., 37. Hunt, one of the senior medical officers of the AGH, would follow up the service with the prophetic statement, 'You will be POWs for years so get yourselves in the right frame of mind to endure whatever is heaped upon you.'

42. CWGC SDC 97 Box 2004. Obbard's Tour Reports 1945–46. Annexure 6.

43. CWGC Add 1/6/17 Box 2003. Oakes Report on his Tour Nov. 1945 to Dec. 1945.

44. CWGC SDC 97 Box 2004. Obbard's Tour Reports 1945–46.

45. CWGC Add 1/6/17 Box 2003. Oakes Report on his Tour Nov. to Dec. 1945.

46. Blackburn, Kevin and Edmund Lim, 'Singapore's "Little Japan": and its Japanese Cemetery', 190–193, from Tan (ed.), *Spaces of the Dead*.

47. Bose, *Singapore at War*, 47–50. This was also referred to as the Bukit Batok Memorial, and along with the Allies' memorial cross, it was constructed under the engineering commander-in-charge Yasugi Tamura, using 500 Australian POWs from the Sime Road and Adam Park camps.

48. Nippon News No. 122 broadcast on 6 October 1942, information from NHK Video Bank. From November 1941, NHK (*Nippon Hoso Kyokai* aka Japan Broadcasting Corporation), along with all public news agencies in Japan, was nationalised. Their productions became official announcements of the Imperial Army General HQ, with hundreds of similar propaganda films produced and screened throughout the duration of the war.

49. CWGC Add 1/6/17 Box 2003. Oakes Report on his Tour Nov. 1945 to Dec. 1945, 51–53.

50. Ibid.

51. Ibid.

52. Ibid.

53. CWGC SDC 97 Box 2004. Obbard's Tour Reports 1945–46. In a special note to Annexure 6.

54. Ibid.

55. Brown had also concurred with Obbard's initial recommendations of Changi and Nee Soon for Christian and Muslim war graves, respectively.

56. CWGS ADD/7/14/1 War Office – Far East Land Forces Grave Registration Reports (TNA), 10 Jan. 1947.

Chapter 7: Kranji

1. Kranji was preceded by Taiping War Cemetery in Perak, which had its preliminary design layout completed in 1947, and its IWGC redevelopment design approved in 1949.

2. CWGC Archives: RA/41595 Pt 1 Kranji War Cemetery Singapore. Telegram sent from Melbourne to IWGC on 10 Jul. 1947. Brigadier John K McNair of the IWGC would request assistance from Major-General Valentine Blomfield DSO, War Office.

3. Ibid.

4. No. 61 GCU was dispatched from Melbourne, and was responsible for the whole of Malaya and Singapore.

5. Japanese Surrendered Personnel (JSP) was a designation for captured Japanese servicemen at the end of the war, used particularly by British forces. It was proposed by the Japanese to circumvent their military's service code and cultural norms prohibiting military personnel being taken prisoner.

6. Reuters-Australian Associated Press.

7. Reuters-AAP, 'Japs Allowed to Picnic Among War Graves at Singapore', *Canberra Times*, Monday 7 Jul. 1947, 1.

8. Ibid.

9. Ibid.

10. The Japanese aerial attack of Darwin occurred on 19 February 1942, followed by submarine attacks on Allied warships in Sydney Harbour on the night of 31 May–1 June 1942.

11. Australian War Memorial, *General information about Australian prisoners of the Japanese*, https://www.awm.gov.au/articles/encyclopedia/pow/general_info, accessed 6 Jan. 2019.

12. KTM, otherwise known as Malayan Railways Limited, is the main rail operator throughout Peninsular Malaysia.

13. Museum of Military Medicine, RAMC/PE/1/341/COLL, *Report on Karanji Prisoner of War Camp May 1944 to August 1945*, from Lt. Col. JC Collins' papers (SMO Malaya), 1. The colloquial term 'Karanji' was occasionally used during and immediately after the war to refer to Kranji.

14. Ibid.

15. Yoshikawa Taira would be tried at the Singapore War Crimes Trials. With almost 1,900 POWs formerly under his supervision, Yoshikawa was accused of providing poor living conditions, inadequate medical and food supplies, disruption of Red Cross deliveries and the physical punishment meted out by himself personally and his subordinates. He was found guilty and sentenced to four years' imprisonment. ICC Legal Tools Database, https://legal-tools.org/doc/a958a9/ accessed 17 Feb. 2020.

16. Collins, *Report on Karanji Prisoner of War Camp,* 1.

17. Lex Arthurson, *The Story of the 13th Australian General Hospital: 8th Division A.I.F., Malaya,* (2009), 76. Arthurson also provided an account of the first casualty at Kranji: 'The first person to die at this newly established hospital had cardiac *beri-beri*. He had been riddled with this deficiency disease – swelling in the legs followed by a huge bloated stomach and his sudden collapse on the 5th June [1944].'

18. Geoffrey Bingham, *Love is the Spur* (2004), 46–47.

19. Personal communication by Glenda Godfrey, 25 Nov. 2019.

20. Ray Watson, 'Kranji', *Far Eastern Heroes,* https://www.far-eastern-heroes.org.uk/Mister_Sam/html/kranji.htm accessed 30 Jan. 2020.

21. Philip Longworth, *The Unending Vigil: A History of the Commonwealth War Graves Commission 1917–1984* (1985), 42–44, 83. This was compounded by the Commission's

Charter, under which a discharged soldier who died as a result of his wartime service was not entitled to a war grave. The deaths of severely malnourished prisoners of war after liberation would test this entitlement. It would take years for the Commission to properly address and refine the policy of war graves entitlement.

22. CWGC Archives: CWGC_1_2_H_T 571 Colin St. Clair Oakes. The agreement with the Commission would run through to 31 March 1953.

23. 'An Ex-PoW on War Cemeteries', *The Straits Times*, 27 Dec. 1947, 9.

24. Ibid.

25. Ibid.

26. Royston Oliver, 'A Singapore War Cemetery', *The Straits Times*, 6 Jan. 1948, 6. The same article would appear in the *Cambridge Daily News*, UK, a month later on 6 Feb. 1948.

27. Ibid.

28. BBC Online Archive: 'Capt Cecil D Pickersgill, architect and designer of the Changi Lychgates, Part 1: A Prisoner of the Japanese', *WWII People's War*. https://www.bbc.co.uk/history/ww2peopleswar/stories/15/a6871115.shtml accessed 3 Oct. 2019.

29. 'Dale man designed gate to honour men who died at infamous Japanese prison', *The Teesdale Mercury*, 3 March 1999, 10. Also 'Capt Cecil D Pickersgill, architect and designer of the Changi Lychgates, Part 1: A Prisoner of the Japanese', and 'Part 2: From Tanglin to Alrewas'. Pickersgill put Warrant Officer Turkentine, of the Royal Anglian Regiment, in charge of timber gathering, and volunteers were called to assist on the project. Two draughtsmen, Sappers D. Lawrence and J. Munton of the 560 Field Coy, Royal Engineers, assisted with the drawings. https://www.bbc.co.uk/history/ww2peopleswar/stories/49/a6871449.shtml accessed 3 October 2019.

30. Pickersgill departed Changi with the first batch of officers to be sent to the Siam-Burma Railway. He died of cerebral malaria on 24 October 1943. His name is located on Column 37 of the Singapore Memorial. The Changi Prison lychgate now resides within the National Memorial Arboretum, Staffordshire, UK.

31. CWGC Archives: RA/41595 Pt 1 Kranji War Cemetery Singapore. Memorandum dated 17 February 1948, from Frank Roy Sinclair, Secretary of the Department of the Army to Secretary, Prime Ministers Department.

32. Ibid., Items 1(4) and 1(5).

33. Ibid. Yokohama War Cemetery, located in Hodogaya-ku, Yokohama, comprises four distinct burial grounds interconnected by landscaped pathways: a British section, a Canadian and New Zealand section, an Australian section, and an Indian section.

34. CWGC Archives: CWGC RA/41595 Pt 1 Kranji War Cemetery Singapore. Personal letter dated 17 Apr. 1948 to McNair IWGC HQ from Obbard.

35. Ibid. Letter dated 21 May 1948 from Secretary, IWGC to Secretary-General, IWGC Anzac Agency

36. Ibid.

37. CWGC Archives: CWGC RA/41595 Pt 1 Kranji War Cemetery Singapore. Cable dated 20 Jul. 1947 from SEALF (South East Asia Land Force) to the War Office.

38. The numbers of victims would eventually be revised to 69 members.

39. Sook Ching (肅清), meaning 'purge through cleansing', was the systematic purge and massacre of thousands of Chinese perceived as hostile by the Japanese military, between 18 February and 4 March 1942, soon after their occupation of Singapore and Malaya. Overseen by the Imperial Japanese Army's Kempeitai secret police, the exact casualty figures have never been confirmed, though it is estimated that somewhere between 25,000 and 50,000 Chinese were killed. See Kevin Blackburn, 'The Collective

Memory of the Sook Ching Massacre and the Creation of the Civilian War Memorial',
JMBRAS, Vol. 73, Part 2, 71–89.

40. CWGC Archives: RA 41595 Pt 1 Kranji War Cemetery Singapore, letter dated 11 September 1947, from Brigadier Obbard, CAO I&SEA District to IWGC Headquarters.

41. Ibid., Obbard recounting Gimson.

42. Ibid.

43. Ibid. Letter from Obbard to IWGC Headquarters on 12 Sept. 1947. Aside from the local interest generated, the Chinese burial area would also resolve the caretaker problems encountered by a foreign, isolated site, some 14 miles from Singapore town and 3 miles from the nearest village.

44. Serving most of his career in the Colonial Office, Acheson would in 1948 switch to the Cabinet Office, heading the Historical Section as Assistant Secretary. McNair, who had taken over from Sir Fabian Ware as the Director-General of the Directorate of Graves Registration and Enquiries (DGR&E) in London, and had joined the IWGC after the war ended, would in 1948 be promoted to Foreign Relations Officer.

45. Ibid. Note of File A/41495, by Brig. John K McNair, dated 14 Oct. 1947.

46. Otherwise commonly known as British Protected Persons (BPP), this class of British nationality is associated with former protectorates, protected states, and territorial mandates and trusts under British control, which Malaya and Singapore fell under at the time. BPPs are deemed to be British nationals, but are neither British nor Commonwealth citizens.

47. CWGC Archives: RA/41595 Pt 1 Kranji War Cemetery Singapore. Tour Notes, Singapore 10th to 13th Nov. 1947.

48. Ibid. Handwritten letter from Obbard to Brig. John K McNair, 31 January 1948, confirming his provisional approval of the Chinese mass grave location and conditions, followed up by the Commission's formal acceptance via NLT 18 November 1947.

49. The Government was established in April 1946 to administer the running of Singapore after the interim post-war British Military Administration.

50. Ibid. Notes of Conference dated 4 March 1947, held in London between representatives of the IWGC and the Army's GR&E. Brigadier Higginson decided that the commemoration of British Service bodies along with others from the mass grave be on a screen wall or other memorial at Kranji, leaving the Colonial Office free to treat the mass grave as they wished.

51. Upon the occupation of Singapore, the Civil General Hospital was relocated to the Mental Hospital in Yio Chu Kang, but a second relocation took place nine months later to Tan Tock Seng Hospital. Some of the medical staff were also sent to Kandang Kerbau Hospital on Bukit Timah Road.

52. 'Memorial Service to Dr. Bowyer', *The Straits Times*, 11 Apr. 1947, 3.

53. Not interned immediately, Wilson tended to the hospitalised and prisoners of war before being arrested on 17 October 1943 as part of the 'Double Tenth' episode. He was then sent to Outram Road Jail, headquarters of the Kempeitai, where he was interrogated, before being sent to the Sime Road Camp.

54. 'Fence only memorial to 500 war dead', *The Singapore Free Press*, 3 Nov. 1947, 5, and 'The Big Pit: Memories of the siege of Singapore', *The Straits Times*, 5 Dec. 1947, 6. Strang would replace Bowyer as Chief Medical Officer, Singapore General Hospital, after the war ended.

55. The final total of victims within the mass grave came to 407, of which 108 would eventually be listed as Commonwealth servicemen.

56. CWGC Archives: CWGC_1_2_A_A.202.3.4 Pt 1 The Singapore Civil Hospital Grave Memorial – Kranji War Cemetery, and RA/41595 Pt 1 Kranji War Cemetery Singapore. Note of conference held 4 Mar. 1948. Aside from Higginson, Vale and McNair, also present were Major W.K.K. Kinnear and E.J King.

57.. Ibid.

58. CWGC Archives: CWGC_1_2_A_A.202.3.4 Pt 1 The Singapore Civil Hospital Grave Memorial – Kranji War Cemetery. Letter from IWGC to Trafford Smith, Colonial Office, 4 May 1951, including drawings and proposed inscription.

59. Bidadari Christian Cemetery was used for military burials between 1907 and 1941. Those Christian soldiers buried there were re-interred in 1957 at Ulu Pandan War Cemetery, then moved to Kranji Military Cemetery adjacent to the war cemetery. Bidadari was closed in 1972, with its remaining graves exhumed between 2001 and 2006.

60. CWGC Archives: RA 41595 Pt 1 Kranji War Cemetery Singapore. Letter from Brig. H.F Barker CAO I&SEA District IWGC to IWGC Headquarters, 21 Sept. 1948, and letter from Barker to the Dutch War Graves Authorities Kantoor Gravendienst, 1 Oct. 1948. Along with the numbers of Dutch graves throughout Southeast Asia, Barker confirmed that there were 174 Dutch graves within Kranji and 6 in Bidadari.

61. Ibid. Letter from Major H.M. Lang, ADGR&E (Records) to the Under Secretary of State, War Office, 27 Apr. 1948. Army regulations governing the layout of war cemeteries required plots to be numbered connectively from left to right, lower to upper, in a single direction. Kranji's layout followed an alternating pattern across a central path.

62. CWGC Archives: RA 41595 Pt 2 Kranji War Cemetery Singapore. Letter from Director of Works, CWGC to Legal Advisor, 1 Aug. 1958, confirming Oakes's position on the accessway.

63. Ibid., Letter from Obbard to Higginson, IWGC HQ, 28 July 1951.

64. Commemorating the British soldiers born or living in Singapore and who died during the First World War, it was designed by Denis Santry of Swan & Maclaren Architects and completed in 1922.

65. Stephen Sim, 'Looking After War Graves', *The Singapore Free Press*, 5 Aug. 1950, 1, and R.A. Phillips, 'Chinese Keeps Vigil on Aussie War Dead', *Brisbane Telegraph*, 29 Nov. 1950, 18, and 'General Commends Caretaker', *Singapore Standard*, 12 Aug. 1950.

66. 'And a Visit to Chinatown', *Malaya Tribune*, 6 Nov. 1949, 4. The *Sunday Tribune* carried the same advertorial on the same day. Similarly, 'What to See in Singapore', *Qantas Empire Airways,* Jun. 1948, No. 6, Vol. 14, 2.

67. CWGC Archives: RA 41595 Pt 2 Kranji War Cemetery Singapore. Letter from IWGC SEA District to IWGC HQ, 5 Dec. 1950.

68. Ibid. Letter from Obbard to Area Superintendent, IWGC Far East, 18 Aug. 1952.

69. Ibid. Letter from Oakes to Director of Works, IWGC HQ, 12 Sept. 1952.

70. Longworth, *The Unending Vigil*, 93–95. The Scottish architect Sir Robert Lorimer was tasked with the design of the Naval Memorials.

71. IWGC MoP 303, 22 Apr. 1948, 4–5. It was the seventh meeting of the Air Council Committee on War Memorials. For the UK, the Air Council had favoured the Commission's suggestion of Runnymede as the main RAF Memorial.

72. Ibid.

73. IWGC MoP 311, 20 Jan. 1949, 6.

74. Ibid.

75. Later renamed the Civil Hospital Grave Memorial, it refers to the Singapore General Hospital in Bukit Merah.

76. CWGC Archives: CWGC/7/3/2/1/20 Form A: Kranji War Cemetery. Remarks by Oakes on the design for approval by the Commission.

77. IWGC MoP 321, 15 Dec. 1949, 8.

78. In the case of Kranji, the Senior Architect signing off on the Form A was George Vey.

79. Prior to joining the Commission, Steedman was Chief Engineer Southern Command, Indian Army.

80. IWGC MoP 361, 16 Jul. 1953.

81. Ibid.

82. Ibid.

83. The Australian-born Longmore would rise to become Commander-in-Chief of the RAF Middle East Command in 1940.

84. IWGC MoP 361, 16 Jul. 1953, 12.

85. Ibid.

86. Mason, in the year prior to his appointment to the High Commission, had completed his *Official History: Prisoners of War, 1939–1945*, an account of New Zealand's POWs during the war.

87. CWGC: Minutes of 393rd Meeting of IWGC, 21 Jun. 1956, 5. Richard H. Perry, the IWGC Chief Administrative Officer for India, Pakistan and South East Asia District, was authorised to sign the Memorandum of Transfer on behalf of the Commission. A rood is a historic English and international inch-pound measure of area. Similarly, a pole is a measure of length often between 3 and 8 metres.

Chapter 8: Building a War Cemetery

1. *Nanyang Siang Pau*, 3 Mar. 1957, 5.

2. *Nanyang Siang Pau*, 2 Mar. 1957, 6.

3. The Taiping Military Cemetery was established, landscaped and constructed by Major J.H. Ingram, War Graves Registration Unit, in 1946. The IWGC approved Oakes's war cemetery design on 21 July 1949. *'From Malaya to Mill Control'*, unknown newspaper.

4. CWGC Archives: RA 41595 Pt 3 Kranji War Cemetery Singapore, letter from IWGC Legal Advisor H.L. Simmons to CAO, IWGC India Pakistan & South East Asia District, 28 Oct. 1955.

5. The Cross of Sacrifice specified for Kranji was a Type B, the second-largest of the four sizes designed by Blomfield for cemeteries of varying burial numbers. With an octagonal stone podium spanning 15 feet across, the Cross stands at an overall height of 24 feet 9⅛ inches (7.55 metres).

6. 'Graves of 1,300 Discovered: Victims of Jap firing parties', *The Straits Times*, 13 Sept. 1951. The graves were discovered by Chang Cheng Yean and Lai Hsin Jen, who both survived the massacres and led officers from the War Graves Inquiry Services and the Joint Appeal Committee of Jap-Massacred Chinese to the location.

7. CWGC Archives: RA 41595 Pt 2 Kranji War Cemetery Singapore. Letter from Graves Registration & Enquiries, FARELF, to War Office, 11 Oct. 1950. The ten soldiers were identified as members of the Manchester Regiment who were in holding positions against the Japanese. The Perseverance Estate, stretching from Geylang Serai to Jalan Eunos in Singapore's east, was owned by the wealthy Arab Alsagoff family, and cultivated *serai* (lemongrass) from the latter half of the 19th century.

8. CWGC Archives: RA 41595 Pt 3 Kranji War Cemetery Singapore. 'Removal of Netherlands War Graves from Saigon to Singapore (Secretary-General's Report: Item vii)',

Minutes of the Second Meeting of the Commonwealth-Netherlands Joint Committee held at the Hague on 8th & 9th Apr., 1954; and IWGC MoP 369, 15 Apr. 1954, 5. There were a total of 162 graves removed from Saigon, of which 18 were of Netherlands soldiers. The reburial at Kranji was completed on 31 March 1954.

9. 'Budget, National Development Division – General', Parliamentary *Hansard Records* 28, Sitting No. 8, 20 Dec. 1968.

10. Personal communication of architectural drawings and documents provided by CWGC. Interestingly, the design drawings do not identify the authority commissioning them nor the designer.

11. 'Special cemetery for nation's great', *The Straits Times*, 19 Nov. 1970, 3.

12. 'Yusof: How a few months turned into 2½ years', *The Straits Times*, 31 Dec. 1970, 3.

13. The Controller of Land Revenue signed on behalf of the Singapore President, and William John Chalmers on behalf of the CWGC.

14. A 10-month-long water-rationing exercise was enacted between April 1963 and February 1964.

15. CWGC Archives: Note to CWGC by T.W. Chatterton, 19 Jun. 1971

16. Though not native to Singapore or Malaya, the fern tree grows in humid climates, particularly in the tropical zones of Africa, India and Sri Lanka. Evergreen with thick and roundish crown, it grows to between 5 and 10 metres tall.

17. The *bagua* are eight symbols used in Taoist cosmology to represent the fundamental principles of reality, seen as a range of eight interrelated concepts. This is commonly manifested in architectural forms throughout Southeast Asia and the Far East.

18. CWGC online resource, www.cwgc.org/find-a-cemetery/cemetery/2004200/kranji-war-cemetery/ accessed 1 Mar. 2020.

19. Better known for his illustrated maps, in particular the 1914 'Wonderground Map' of London's Underground, Gill also designed the numbers and regimental badges for all the Commission's military headstone inscriptions.

20. 'Memorial to Flyers Planned', *The Straits Times*, 7 Oct. 1953, 1.

21. CWGC website, www.cwgc.org/find/find-cemeteries-and-memorials/109600/runnymede-memorial Last accessed 25 Feb. 2019.

22. CWGC Archives: Form_A_CWGC_7_3_2_1_58, Malta Air Forces Memorial. Notes by Edward Maufe on 25 Oct. 1951, in his capacity as Artistic Advisor to the Commission.

23. Stamp (2006), 162–165. Stamp chronicles in detail the extent of the problems faced by Lutyens's brick face selection and the many remedial measures undertaken over the years by the Commission.

24. IWGC MoP 309, 18 Nov. 1948, 8–9. The bronze plaque had in fact first been used in the cemeteries of the Gallipoli peninsula, where seismic activity and sandy conditions made it patently impractical to use the upright Portland stone headstone. The Anzac Agency would revert to this low marker throughout its work in Southeast Asia and within selected Australian sites.

25. IWGC MoP 307, 16 Sept. 1948, 8. Bateman (1902–1951) was the Director of Works from 1945 to 1951.

26. Ine Wouters, et al. (eds.), *Building Knowledge, Constructing Histories, Vol. 1: Proceedings of the 6th International Congress on Construction History (6ICCH 2018), July 9–13, 2018, Brussels, Belgium*. Conference paper by Charles Lai, 'Cement and 'Shanghai plaster' in British Hong Kong and Penang (1920s–1950s)'.

27. CWGC Archives: RA/41595 Pt 1 Kranji War Cemetery Singapore. Letter from Obbard, IWGC I&SEA Agency to Vice-Chairman, IWGC HQ copied to Colonial

Secretary, Government of Singapore, 11 Sept. 1947. Obbard was strongly in support of allocating a Chinese burial area within the greater Kranji Military Cemetery.

28. Joiner, Sarah, 'The Evolution of the Planting Influences of the Imperial War Graves Commission from its Inception to the Modern Day', *Garden History*, Vol. 42, Supplement 1: Memorial Gardens and Landscapes: Design, Planting and Conservation (Autumn 2014), 92.

29. Notwithstanding Lutyens's involvement in all these cemeteries as either Principal Architect or through his Stone of Remembrance, Trouville Hospital Cemetery was designed by Reginald Blomfield, and Warlincourt Halte British Cemetery by Charles Holden.

30. Miller (2013), 77. Miller cites Mandy Morris's 'Gardens "For Ever England"' in this interpretation.

31. From Yves-Marie Allain and Janine Christiany, *L'Art des Jardins en Europe*, Citadelles (2006); Elizabeth Boults and Chip Sullivan, *Illustrated History of Landscape Design*, (2010) https://en.wikipedia.org/wiki/English_landscape_garden, accessed 27 Feb. 2019.

32. Mandy S. Morris, 'Gardens "For Ever England": Landscape, Identity and the First World War British Cemeteries on the Western Front', *Ecumene*, Vol. 4, No. 4 (Oct. 1997), 411.

33. Ibid., 425.

34. Longworth, Philip, *The Unending Vigil: The History of the Commonwealth War Graves Commission* (1985), 74. Arthur William Hill, Assistant Director, Royal Botanic Gardens, Kew, and Botanical Advisor to the Imperial War Graves Commission, contributed the essay to the *Journal of the Royal Horticultural Society*.

35. Taiping's annual rainfall of about 4000 mm is far above the average for Peninsular Malaya at 2000–2500 mm.

36. CWGC Archives: CWGC/7/3/2/1/22 Form A - Taiping War Cemetery.

37. Sarah Joiner, *Garden History*, 96–98.

38. Director of the Singapore Botanical Gardens from 1925, Richard Eric Holttum (1895–1990) was allowed to continue working there throughout the duration of the Japanese Occupation.

39. CWGC Archives: RA/41595 Pt 2 Kranji War Cemetery Singapore. Handover certificate for Stage II.

40. 'Those trees won't grow here, says professor', *The Straits Times*, 13 Nov. 1953, 2.

Chapter 9: Post-War

1. Nan Hall, 'Thoughts of the past move 81-year-old war heroine to tears', *The Straits Times*, 3 Mar. 1957, 1; and Karl Hack and Kevin Blackburn, *War Memory and the Making of Modern Malaysia and Singapore* (2012), 110–111.

2. Ibid.

3. Ibid., 108–111.

4. Ibid., 110 and Nan Hall (1957), 1.

5. Ibid. Private Sim Chin Foo, Dalforce, Service No. DAL/46, died 1 September 1942. His name is inscribed within Column 399 of the Singapore Memorial.

6. IWGC MoP 400, 21 Febr. 1957, 3; and 'British War Widows at Unveiling', *The Birmingham Post & Gazette*, 26 Feb. 1957, 6.

7. *The Australian Women's Weekly*, a weekly news and current affairs journal, would extensively cover the Kranji Memorial unveiling ceremony and report back to the general public, including the first-known colour coverage of the event.

8. Gavin Long, *The Final Campaigns: Australia in the War of 1939–1945, Series 1 – Army, Vol. VII*, 1965, 634. https://www.awm.gov.au/collection/RCDIG1070206/ accessed 10 Mar. 2020.

9. CWGC online figures for Kranji War Cemetery and Memorial.

10. Dorothy Drain, 'Singapore Memorial', *The Australian Women's Weekly*, 27 Feb. 1957, 21.

11. Ibid.

12. Lex Arthurson, *The Story of the 13th Australian General Hospital: 8th Division A.I.F., Malaya*, (2009), 80–81. Changi University, a vocational guidance education scheme, was established to both instruct and maintain morale during the years of internment. Classes began in the week of 28 August 1944, and included such varied subjects as bookkeeping, agriculture, music theory, horticulture and market gardening, poultry farming, building and mathematics.

13. Albert Coates and Newman Rosenthal, *The Albert Coates Story: The Will That Found the Way*, (1977).

14. Ian W. Shaw, *On Radji Beach*, (2010). Formerly the Sarawak royal yacht, the SS *Vyner Brooke* was carrying 65 nurses of the Australian Army Nurses Service when it was sunk. Twenty-two of the original nurses would reunite amongst the survivors on nearby Radji Beach at Bangka Island. The civilian women and children would leave for Muntok whilst the nurses remained to care for the wounded, where they were intercepted by the Japanese forces.

15. Dorothy Drain, 'Singapore Memorial: Fifteen Australians will fly to unveiling', *The Australian Women's Weekly*, 27 Feb. 1957, 21.

16. The Australian involvement on the Gallipoli peninsula in Anatolia (Turkey) commenced on 25 April 1915 with their landings at what became known as Anzac Cove. Over the following eight months before their final withdrawal on 20 December 1915, the Australian suffered 26,111 casualties, including 8,141 deaths. Source: AWM.

17. Joan Beaumont, 'Contested Trans-national Heritage: The Demolition of Changi Prison, Singapore', *International Journal of Heritage Studies* 15, no. 4 (2009).

18. As sites of 'dark tourism', these locations have become destinations for visitors seeking a connection with Australia's military heritage. Along with Gallipoli, they have also become somewhat 'rites of passage' for younger members seeking to identify with a nationalistic construct of what it is to be an Australian.

19. Gurmukhi is the official script of the Punjabi language. The Hindi script also accommodated those Gurkhas/Nepalese who died, in lieu of a separate Nepali text. The Malay inscription is rendered in Jawi script.

20. 'Singapore memorial Unveiled', *Northern Daily Mail*, 2 March 1957, 5.

21. *MacGregor Herald*, 24 Jan. 1957, 2. The CWGC corrected figures indicate that Canada records 184 missing persons on the Singapore Memorial from the total of 24,320, and 3 identified graves within the war cemetery.

22. Junko Tomaru, *The Postwar Rapprochement of Malaya and Japan, 1945–61: The Roles of Britain and Japan in South-East Asia* (2000), 81–126.

23. Dorothy Drain, 'Poignant Links with Australia', *Australian Women's Weekly*, 21 Jan. 1959, 44.

24. The Cenotaph within Singapore's Esplanade Park is a good example of war commemoration through foreign representation. Designed by the architect Denis Santry of Swan & Maclaren, and unveiled in 1922 to commemorate the memory of 124 British soldiers who died in the First World War, the memorial was modelled on Lutyens's Whitehall Cenotaph in London. To acknowledge those who died in the Second World War, many of

whom were from the local Chinese, Malay and Indian communities, a dedication without names was added.

25. Hamzah Muzaini and Brenda Yeoh, 'Memory-making "From Below": Rescaling Remembrance at the Kranji War Memorial and Cemetery, Singapore', *Environment and Planning* 39 (2007): 1303–1304. DOI 10.1068/a3862. Muzaini and Yeoh do highlight, though, that whilst Singaporeans have no connection with the people interred at the cemetery, Kranji today is perceived as a national and global landscape, bringing with it a sense of affiliation with the site.

26. 'An Occupation Relief Fund', *The Straits Times*, 3 Apr. 1951, 8. By way of comparison and allowing for inflation, the initial allocation of £17,000 (S$145,000) in 1951 equates to almost £174,742 (S$1.451m) in 2020.

27. 'Welfare Fund Now $599,000', *The Singapore Free Press*, 4 Oct. 1947, 5.

28. 'Farm Will Aid Families', *The Straits Times*, 1 Apr. 1951, 11.

29. 'War widows start new farm life: Help waits for others', *The Straits Times*, 24 Oct. 1951, 4.

30. Ibid.

31. 'New Homes for War Victim Families', *The Singapore Free Press*, 12 Jul. 1951, 5.

32. Similar self-farming resettlement schemes had been attempted in the past to various degrees of success, notably the refugee villages in northern Greece after the Balkan Wars and population exchanges with Turkey in the early 1920s, and the Soldier Settlement Scheme in Australia providing land to returning discharged servicemen after both the world wars.

33. Named after the military campaign medal awarded to British and Commonwealth forces who served in Burma between 1941 and 1945, the Burma Star Association was formed in 1951 for those ex-servicemen who had taken part in that campaign.

34. Vera Lynn, who visited the Burma front during the war, had in fact entertained the troops in March 1944 at Shamshernagar airfield in Bengal before the Battle of Kohima. For her courage and contribution to the morale of the troops, in 1985 she received the Burma Star.

35. http://www.victorianweb.org/art/architecture/astonwebb/bio.html last accessed 16 Mar. 2020.

36. 'The Dedication of the War Memorial', *The Britannia Magazine*, Vol. LXII, No. 97, Christmas 1949, 4–5. The memorial was unveiled on 29 October 1949, by Admiral of the Fleet Lord Cunningham. The buildings of the current campus of the Britannia Royal Naval College, Dartmouth, were originally designed by Sir Aston Webb and completed in 1905.

37. Edward Bottoms, 'AA School of Architecture – History', from an abridged version of an introductory lecture to Archives for London & the Twentieth Century Society, Feb. 2010.

38. For a comprehensive account of the Centenary celebrations, refer to the dedicated edition of *The Architectural Association Journal* LXIII, no. 718 (Jan. 1948).

39. MARS was an architectural think tank founded in 1933 and involved in the British modernist movement. Established by several prominent architects and architectural critics of the time, it disbanded in 1957. Aside from Oakes, the Exhibition Committee consisted of Gordon Brown, Robert Furneaux-Jordan, Joan Burnett, Grave Lovat-Fraser, Major A. Longden, G.E. Marfell, John Summerson, G.R. Wiltshire and Frank R. Yerbury.

40. 'The Centenary Exhibition: 17th December – 8th January', *The Architectural Association Journal*, Jan. 1948, 106.

41. Chris Bateman, 'The Life and Death of Peter Dickinson and The Inn on the Park', *Spacing Toronto*, 23 Aug. 2016, http://spacing.ca/toronto/2016/08/23/life-death-peter-dickinson-inn-park/ accessed 26 Apr. 2019.

42. *Architecture Illustrated*, Dec. 1948, 129. First presented at the Royal Academy Exhibition of 1947, Oakes's initial proposal for Kohima comprised a Memorial to the Missing, designed as a pantheon structure upon the hill. The memorial would not be realised and was replaced by the present-day layout.

43. *Beacon*, Oct. 1949. In-house publication of Boots Pure Drug Company. Oakes's joining Boots in 1949 saw him enter into an arrangement with the Imperial War Graves Commission to hand over those outstanding war cemeteries whilst committing to completing the remainder. This arrangement ended 31 March 1953.

44. CWGC Archives: CWGC/1/2/H/T 571 Colin St. Clair Oakes. Letter from Director of Works, IWGC to Oakes on 18 Dec.1952, setting out the formal relinquishment of service, and letter from IWGC's Establishment Officer to Chief Accountant 19 Jan. 1953. The outstanding concentration cemeteries in India, Pakistan and Burma, namely Kirkee, Delhi, Madras, Karachi and Taukkyan, would be passed to another architect.

45. Paula Hamilton, 'Contested memories of the Pacific War in Australia', in Christina Twomey and Ernest Koh (eds.), *The Pacific War: Aftermaths, Remembrance and Culture* (2015), 50–52.

46. Janet Watson, 'A sideshow to the war in Europe: Nation empire, and British commemoration of the Pacific War', in Christina Twomey and Ernest Koh (eds.), *The Pacific War: Aftermaths, Remembrance and Culture* (2015), 33.

Bibliography

Allen, Louis. *Burma: The Longest War 1941–45*. London: J.M. Dent & Sons, 1984.

Andrews, Maggie (Ed.). *Lest We Forget: Remembrance & Commemoration*. Brimscombe Port: The History Press, 2011.

Arthurson, Lex. *The Story of the 13th Australian General Hospital, 8th Division A.I.F., Malaya*. Melbourne: Lex Arthurson, 2000.

Barker, Michael. *Sir Edwin Lutyens: An Illustrated Life (1869–1944)*. Botley, UK: Shire Publications Ltd, 2010.

Bingham, Geoffrey C. *Love is the Spur*. North Parramatta, NSW: Eyrie Books, 2004.

Blackburn, Kevin and Karl Hack. *War Memory and the Making of Modern Malaysia and Singapore*. Singapore: NUS Press, 2012.

Bose, Romen. *Kranji: The Commonwealth War Cemetery and the Politics of the Dead*. Singapore: Marshall Cavendish Editions, 2006.

Bose, Romen. *Singapore at War: Secrets from the Fall, Liberation & Aftermath of WWII*. Singapore: Marshall Cavendish Editions, 2012.

Brodie, Antonia, et al. *Directory of British Architects 1834–1914 Vol. 2 (L–Z)*. London: Continuum, 2001.

Brune, Peter. *Descent Into Hell: The Fall of Singapore – Pudu and Changi – The Thai-Burma Railway*. Sydney: Allen & Unwin, 2014.

Bryan, J.N. Lewis. *The Churches of the Captivity in Malaya*. London: Society for Promoting Christian Knowledge, 1946.

Bullard, Steven. *Blankets on the Wire: The Cowra Breakout and its Aftermath*. Canberra: Australian War Memorial, 2006.

Campbell, Louise. 'A Call to Order: The Rome Prize and Early Twentieth-Century British Architecture.' *Architectural History*, Vol. 32, pp. 131–151. London: SAHGB Publications, 1989.

Chomsky, Noam and Edward S. Herman. *After The Cataclysm: Postwar Indochina and the Reconstruction of Imperial Ideology*. Rev. ed.; first published 1979. Chicago: Haymarket Books, 2014.

Coates, Albert and Newman Rosenthal. *The Albert Coates Story: The Will that Found the Way*. Melbourne: Hyland House, 1977.

Cohen, Jean-Louis. *Architecture in Uniform: Designing and Building for the Second World War*. Paris: Canadian Centre for Architecture and Editions Hazan, 2011.

Commonwealth War Graves Commission. *A Guide to the Commonwealth War Graves Commission.* London: Third Millennium Publishing, 2018.

Connah, Roger. *Finland: Modern Architectures in History.* London: Reaktion Books, 2005.

Crane, David. *Empires of the Dead: How One Man's Vision Led to the Creation of WWI's War Graves.* London: William Collins, 2014.

Dakers, Caroline. *Forever England: The Countryside at War 1914–1918.* Rev. ed.; first published 1987. London: I.B. Tauris, 2013.

Davies, Philip. *Splendours of the Raj: British Architecture in India, 1660 to 1947.* London: John Murray, 1985.

Dhoraisingam, S. Samuel. *Singapore's Heritage: Through Places of Historical Interest.* Singapore: Elixir Consultancy Service, 1991.

Dupuy, Trevor Nevitt. *Asiatic Land Battles: Allied Victories in China and Burma.* New York: Franklin Watts, 1963.

Dupuy, Trevor Nevitt. *Asiatic Land Battles: Expansion of Japan in Asia.* New York: Franklin Watts, 1963.

Ellis, John and Michael Cox. *The World War I Databook: The Essential Facts and Figures for all the Combatants.* London: Aurum Press, 2001.

Faulk, Henry. *Group Captives: The Re-education of German Prisoners of War in Britain, 1945–1948.* London: Chatto & Windus, 1977.

Frei, Henry. *Guns of February: Ordinary Japanese Soldiers' Views of the Malayan Campaign and the Fall of Singapore 1941–42.* Singapore: Singapore University Press, 2004.

Foster Hall, E. 'The Graves Service in the Burma Campaigns.' *Royal United Services Institution Journal,* 92:566, 240–44, DOI: 10.1080/03071844709433994 (1947).

Geurst, Jeroen. *Cemeteries of the Great War by Sir Edwin Lutyens.* Rotterdam: 010 Publishers, 2010.

Gibson, Edwin and G. Kingsley Ward. *Courage Remembered: The Story Behind the Construction and Maintenance of the Commonwealth's Military Cemeteries and Memorials of the Wars of 1914–1918 and 1939–1945.* London: Her Majesty's Stationery Office, 1989.

Hack, Karl and Kevin Blackburn. *Did Singapore Have to Fall?: Churchill and the Impregnable Fortress.* New York City: RoutledgeCurzon, 2004.

Hurst, Sidney C. *The Silent Cities: An Illustrated Guide to the War Cemeteries and Memorials to the 'Missing' in France and Flanders: 1914–1918.* London: Methuen & Co. Ltd, 1929.

Hynes, Samuel. *The Edwardian Turn of Mind.* Princeton: Princeton University Press, 1968.

Institute of Mental Health. *Loving Hearts, Beautiful Minds: Woodbridge Hospital Celebrating 75 Years.* Singapore: Armour Publishing, 2003.

Irving, Robert Grant. *Indian Summer: Lutyens, Baker, and Imperial Delhi.* New Haven: Yale University Press, 1981.

Jones, David and Anna Teo. *Saint George's Church: Celebrates One Hundred Years.* Singapore: Straits Times Press, 2012.

Kenyon, Frederic. *War Graves. How the Cemeteries Abroad will be Designed.* Report to the Imperial War Graves Commission. London: His Majesty's Stationery Office, 1918.

Khan, Hasan-Uddin. *International Style: Modernist Architecture from 1925 to 1965.* Cologne: Taschen, 2009.

Kwok, Jung Yun, *Voices of the Fallen: Singaporean and Australian Memories of the Fall of Singapore.* PhD thesis, School of History and Politics, University of Wollongong, 2010.

Lane, Arthur. *Kranji War Cemetery.* Stockport, UK: Lane Publishers, 1995.

Lang, Jon. *A Concise History of Modern Architecture in India.* Delhi: Permanent Black, 2002.

Lee, Amaris. 'A Case of Renewed Identity: The Fading Role of WWII in Singapore's National Narrative.' *Singapore Policy Journal*. Singapore: Harvard Kennedy School, 9 November 2005.

Lee, Geok Boi. *The Syonan Years: Singapore Under Japanese Rule 1942–1945*. Singapore: National Archives of Singapore, 2005.

Leemon, Jack. *War Graves Digger: Service with an Australian Graves Registration Unit*. Sydney: Australian Military History Publications, 2010.

Lim, P. Pui Huen and Diana Wong (Eds.). *War and Memory in Malaysia and Singapore*. Singapore: Institute of Southeast Asian Studies, 2000.

Loh Kah Seng. *Making and Unmaking the Asylum: Leprosy and Modernity in Singapore and Malaysia*. Petaling Jaya: Strategic Information and Research Development Centre, 2009.

Long, Gavin. *The Final Campaigns: Australia in the War of 1939–1945, Series 1 – Army*. Vol. VII. Canberra: Australian War Memorial, 1965.

Longworth, Philip. *The Unending Vigil: A History of the Commonwealth War Graves Commission 1917–1984*. Rev. ed.; first published 1967. London: Leo Cooper, 1985.

Lowry, Michael. *Fighting Through to Kohima: A Memoir of War in India and Burma*. Barnsley: Leo Cooper, 2003.

Miller, Kristine F. *Almost Home: The Public Landscapes of Gertrude Jekyll*. Amsterdam: Architectura & Natura Press, 2013.

Morris, Jan. *Stones of Empire: The Buildings of the Raj*. Oxford; New York: Oxford University Press, 1983.

Morris, Mandy S. 'Gardens "For Ever England": Landscape, Identity and the First World War British Cemeteries on the Western Front.' *Ecumene*, 4, no. 4 (1997), 410–434.

Murray, Jacqui. *Watching the Sun Rise: Australian Reporting of Japan, 1931 to the Fall of Singapore*. Lanham: Lexington Books, 2004.

Muzaini, Hamzah and Brenda S.A. Yeoh. *Contested Memoryscapes: The Politics of Second World War Commemoration in Singapore*. Abingdon, UK: Routledge, 2016.

Nelson, David. *The Story of Changi, Singapore*. Perth: Changi Publication Company, 1974.

Ng, Beng Yeong. *Till the Break of Day: A History of Mental Health Services in Singapore 1841–1993*. Rev. ed.; first published 2001. Singapore: NUS Press, 2016.

Scates, Bruce. *ANZAC Journeys: Returning to the Battlefields of World War II*. Cambridge: Cambridge University Press, 2013.

Shaw, Ian W. *On Radji Beach*. Sydney: Pan Macmillan Australia, 2010.

Slim, William. *Defeat into Victory: Battling Japan in Burma and India, 1942–1945*. Rev. ed.; first published 1956. New York: Cooper Square Press, 2000.

Smith, Neil C. *Understanding Australian Military Speak*. Adelaide: Unlock the Past, 2016.

Soh, Fiona and Vera Soo (Eds.). *Heartening Minds: IMH 80th Anniversary 1928–2008*. Singapore: Institute of Mental Health/Woodbridge Hospital, 2008.

Spark, Seumas. *The Treatment of the British Military War Dead of the Second World War*. PhD Thesis, University of Edinburgh, 2009.

Stamp, Gavin. *Silent Cities: An Exhibition of the Memorial and Cemetery Architecture of the Great War*. London: RIBA Publications, 1977.

Stamp, Gavin. *The Memorial to the Missing of the Somme*. London: Profile Books, 2006.

Stamp, Gavin. 'The Imperial War Graves Commission.' *Journal of the Society for the Study of Architecture in Canada*, Vol. 33, No. 1, 2008.

Summers, Julie. *Remembered: The History of the Commonwealth War Graves Commission*. London: Merrell Publishers, 2007.

Summers, Julie. *British and Commonwealth War Cemeteries*. Oxford: Shire Publications, 2010.

Swinson, Arthur. *Kohima*. London: Cassell, 1966.

Tan, Kelvin Y.L. (Ed.). *Spaces of the Dead: A Case from the Living*. Singapore: Ethos Books, 2011.

Thomas, Sally, *Family Histories 1850–2000, Book 2: Dorothy*. Southborough, UK: The Ink Pot, 2007.

Thomas, Sally. *Family Histories 1850–2000, Book 4: May*. Fletching, UK: Red Letter Books, 2013.

Thompson, Julian. *Forgotten Voices of Burma*. London: Ebury Press, 2009.

Tomaru, Junko. *The Postwar Rapprochement of Malaya and Japan, 1945–61: The Roles of Britain and Japan in South-East Asia*. London: Palgrave Macmillan, 2000.

Tumarkin, Maria. *Traumascapes: The Power and Fate of Places Transformed by Tragedy*. Melbourne: Melbourne University Press, 2005.

Twomey, Christina and Ernest Koh (Eds.). *The Pacific War: Aftermaths, Remembrance and Culture*. Milton Park, Abingdon, Oxon: Routledge, 2015.

Wallace-Hadrill, Andrew. *The British School at Rome: One Hundred Years*. Rome: Studio Lodoli Sud, 2001.

Ware, Fabian. *The Immortal Heritage: An Account of the Work and Policy of the Imperial War Graves Commission during Twenty Years 1917–1937*. Cambridge: Cambridge University Press, 1937.

Winter, Jay. *Sites of Memory, Sites of Mourning: The Great War in European Cultural History*. Cambridge: Cambridge University Press, 1995.

Wyatt, Stephen. *Memorials to the Missing: A Play for Radio*. 2008.

Yang, Daqing and Mike Mochizuki (Eds.). *Memory, Identity, And Commemorations of World War II: Anniversary Politics in Asia Pacific*. Lanham: Lexington Books, 2018.

Yap, Siang Yong, et al. *Fortress Singapore: The Battlefield Guide*. Rev. ed.; first published 1992. Singapore: Marshall Cavendish Editions, 2011.

Ziino, Bart. *A Distant Grief: Australians, War Graves and the Great War*. Crawley: University of Western Australia Press, 2007.

Image Sources

Courtesy of the Commonwealth War Graves Commission
Page 14, 17, 20, 29, 81, 83, 131, 132, 133, 143, 147, 157, 159, 166, 168, 169, 173, 176, 177, 195, 196–197, 198–199, 202, 207, 208, 209, 210, 215, 218–219, 251

Courtesy of the Oakes family
Page 97, 101, 103, 107, 110, 111, 112, 115, 119, 240, 248

Page 24: Courtesy © Imperial War Museum [E(AUS) 4945]
Page 48: Courtesy © National Portrait Gallery, London [NPG x154756]
Page 53: Courtesy © National Portrait Gallery, London [NPG x123028]
Page 63: Courtesy of Janet Sebald
Page 67: Courtesy of Alisdair Ferrie
Page 69: Courtesy of the Australian War Memorial [AWM 117206]
Page 105: Courtesy © National Portrait Gallery, London [NPG x86518]
Page 106: Courtesy of the Borough of Croydon
Page 130: Courtesy of Guy Obbard
Page 134: Courtesy of Vicky Nash
Page 141: Courtesy © Imperial War Museum [Art.IWM ART LD 7487 10]

Page 152: Courtesy of Brian Spittle
Page 153: Courtesy of the Australian War Memorial
Page 182: Nanyang Siang Pau © Singapore Press Holdings Limited. Reprinted
    with permission
Page 184: Nanyang Siang Pau © Singapore Press Holdings Limited. Reprinted
    with permission
Page 185: Courtesy of Ho Yap Hoi (何益辉)
Page 186: Courtesy of the Ho Family
Page 223: Courtesy of Bauer Media Pty Ltd / The Australian Women's Weekly
Page 230: Nanyang Siang Pau © Singapore Press Holdings Limited. Reprinted
    with permission
Page 238: Courtesy of the author
Page 243: Courtesy of The Boots Archive

Maps by Yoke Lin Wong

Cover: Photograph by Weixiang Lim

Back cover: Photograph of Colin St Clair Oakes courtesy of the Oakes family;
    other images courtesy of Commonwealth War Graves Commission

Index

Acheson, Andrew B. 163
Aitken, C. 45, 74, 75, 82
Akyab 87, 116, 117–18
Alexander, H.R.L. 113
Alexandra Hospital 137, 166
Allen, Maxwell 106, 108
Allied Land Forces South East
    Asia (ALFSEA) 34, 155
Alphonso, Arthur G. 191
Ambon 135, 175, 227
Ambon War Cemetery 88
American Volunteer Motor
    Ambulance Corps 48
Arakan 116–18, 120
Architectural Association (AA)
    11, 54, 84, 96, 104, 106,
    108, 121, 237–41
*Architectural Association Jour-
    nal, The* 240
Arthurson, Lex 152
Artists Rifles 84
Aslett, Alfred R. 119
Atkinson, Fello 239
Australian Broadcasting Cor-
    poration (ABC) 222
Australian General Hospital
    (13th) 142, 152, 225
Australian Women's Weekly, The
    222, *223*, 229

Bailey, Rev. P.F. 20
Baker, Herbert 30, 45, 53, 66,
    74–5, 79, 82, 94, 98, 100,
    121, 211
Barrett, Leslie D. 84
Barrie, Sir James 74
Bartlett, Percy J. 242, 244
Bateman, Lt.-Col. R.W. 205

Bedok 118
Bennett, Maj.-Gen. H. Gordon
    100, 126, 224
Bennett, T.P. (& Son) 100
Bhanipur (Bhowanipore) 34
Bidadari Christian Cemetery
    88, 137, 168–9, 188
Bingham, Geoffrey 153–4
Binnie, William B. 84
Black, Sir Robert. 15–20, *17*,
    181, *184*, 220, 227
Blomfield, Reginald. 30, 53–4,
    66, 79, 82, 88, 98, 100, 121
Blunden, Edmund 47, 73
Boots Pure Drug Company 11,
    30, 235–6, 242–6, *243*,
    248
Bourail 175
Bowyer, Dr. John H. 165
Bradshaw, Harold C. 84, 100
Bridgeford, Maj.-Gen. William
    171
Brindley, John 26, 68–9, *69*
Britannia Royal Naval College
    11, 237
British Broadcasting Corpora-
    tion (BBC), 19, 45–6
British Legion 18
British Overseas Airways Cor-
    poration (BOAC) 32, 172
British Red Cross Society 45,
    47–9, 151
British School at Rome (BSR)
    27, 56, 70, 100, 101, *101*,
    102, 103, 121
Brooke, Rupert 211
Brookwood Military Cemetery
    54, 87

Brown, Brig. Athol E. 60–4,
    63, 135, 146, 148, 161, 224
Brown, Henry J. 86, 87, 88
Brown, Raymond G. 96, *105*,
    239, 245
Bruce, Stanley 61
Bukit Batok Hill (Point 348)
    127, 136, 143–6, 172, 247
Bukit Mandai *147*
Bukit Panjang 126
Bukit Timah 143, 221
Bukit Timah Race Course 189
Bullwinkel, Sister Vivian 225
Bunji, RAdm. Asakura 140
Bunning, W.H. 181
Buona Vista 136–7, 142–3, 145
Burma Star Association 235
Burnet, John J. 79, 204
Buthidaung 118

Calcutta 34, 108, 109, *109*,
    111, 114
Capon, Kenneth 239
Casson, Hugh 36
Centenary Exhibition, Archi-
    tectural Association 239,
    240, 241
Cenotaph, London 236
Cenotaph, Singapore 171, 231
Chambers, John 111
Changi 9–10, 31, 38, 66, 136
Changi Aerodrome 142, 155
Changi Beach 140
Changi Cemetery 68–9, 140–2,
    145–6, 157–61
Changi Hospital 151–4, 165
Changi Prison 8, 69, 138, 140,
    150–1, 165, 172, 226

Changi Prisoner-of-War Camp 16, 26, 28, 38, 60, 68–9, 141–2, 151, 159, 160, 224, 227
Changi University 69, 224
Cheng Seang Ho 221–2, 230
Chettle, H.C. 70
Chindwin River 113, 116, 118
Chinese High School 16
Chinese Memorial 164, 209
Chittagong 34, 111, 115, 117
Chittagong War Cemetery 21
Chungkai 34
Chungkai War Cemetery 40, 43, 130, 132, 134, 214
Churchill, Winston 81, 127
Citizen Military Force 63, 68
Coates, Sir Albert E. 224–5
Collins, Lt.-Col. Joseph C. 151, 154
Colonial Office 16, 57, 62, 122, 156, 163, 167, 232
Colquhoun, Alan 239
Cowlishaw, William H. 84
Cowra 63
Cowra Japanese War Cemetery 64
Cox, Maj.-Gen. Lionel 164
Cox, Oliver 239
Cox's Bazar 115–16
Cremation Memorial 178, 201
Cross of Sacrifice 19, 20, 54, 80, 82, 83, 90, 91, 131, 132, 175, 187, 190, 208
Croydon, Borough of 11, 106–7
Croydon Civic Centre 106
Curtin, John 58

Dacca (Dhaka) 34, 111
Dalforce 25, 123, 126, 162, 221
Dalley, Lt.-Col. John 123, 221
Davis, Group Capt. R.H. 224
de Soissons, Louis 30, 55, 56, 73, 94, 100, 121, 236
Dedicatory Inscription Panel 201, 220, 227
Delhi 21, 34, 86–7, 130
Denning, Maj.-Gen. Reginald 136, 142
Dickinson, Peter 241–2
Digboi 89, 156
Digboi War Cemetery 88
Dimapur 115, 118
Directorate of Graves Registration & Enquiries (DGR&E) 34, 49, 50, 52, 74, 129, 134–5, 167
Drain, Dorothy 222, 224, 229
Duckham, Richard 86, 88

École des Beaux-Arts 56
Edmonds, John M. 67
Edmondson, Thomas 109–10
Edwards, Barry 91
Eiichi, Cdr. Ino 140
Eklund, Jarl 100
El Alamein 174, 203, 228
Englezos, Lambis 91
Enthoven, Roderick E. 239

Far East Air Force 19–20
Far East Land Forces 20, 87, 136, 164
Far Eastern Relief Fund 233
Faubourg d'Amiens British Cemetery 46
Federated Malay States Volunteer Force (FMSVF) 162
Feilden, Bernard 239
Ferrie, James 26, 65–8, 67
Festing, Maj.-Gen. Sir Francis 87, 114, 119, 119
Foster Hall, Col. Eric 134–5, 134, 140, 146
Furneaux-Jordan, Robert 106, 108, 239

Garrison Hill 66–7, 130
Gauhati 156
George, David L. 50
Giffard, Gen. George 117
Gill, MacDonald 200
Gimson, Sir Franklin 162–4, 167
Glasgow School of Architecture 66
Gloucester, Duke of 16
Goddard, David 239
Goldsmith, George H. 84
Gordon-Finlayson, Sir Robert 52
Greater East Asian Co-Prosperity Sphere 37
Green, William C. 100
Guillemont Farm 24

Hall, Nan 220, 221
Hanaya, Lt.-Gen. Tadashi 117
Hardisty, William C. 97
Harrow County School 98
Helbert, Col. G. 128
Hepworth, Philip 55–6, 73, 121, 236
Higginson, Brig. Frank 52, 70, 167, 171
Hill, Capt. Arthur W. 78
Hill, Vernon 203
Ho Bock Kee 21, 29, 184, 184–5, 186–7, 186, 229

Hobbs, Lt.-Gen. Sir Talbot 128
Hobday, Ralph 86–8
Hock Lee Amalgamated Bus Company 16
Holden, Charles 53, 79
Holford, William 36, 89–90, 96, 101, 105, 245
Holttum, Prof. Eric 214, 216
Hong Kong 17, 21, 23, 33, 39, 62, 73, 86, 112, 130, 131, 135, 163, 170, 175, 188, 195, 208, 214
Hong Kong render 186, 208
Hong Kong Singapore Royal Artillery (HKSRA) 162
Horsburgh, Patrick 239
Hospital Grave Memorial 178
Howard, Ebenezer 56
Hubbard, Robert 101
Hunt, Maj. Bruce 142
Hutton, Arthur J.S. 26, 65–6, 68
Hutton, John 203
Hutton, Lt.-Gen. Thomas 113

Iida, Lt.-Gen. Shojiro 113
Imperial War Graves Endowment Fund 52, 61–2
Imphal 34, 114, 115, 118, 120, 121, 130, 156
Imphal-Kohima Road 130
Imphal War Cemetery 130–1
Indian National Army (INA) 150, 153
Irrawaddy River 113
Irwin, Lt.-Gen. Noel M.S. 116
Ishak, Yusof 190–2

Jauhati 34
Jekyll, Gertrude 37, 103, 210–12
Jenkins, Martin 46
Jones, Arthur C. 167
Jorhat 34, 115
Jurong 126
Jurong River 126

Kalewa 114
Kanchanaburi 34, 43, 130, 214
Kanchanaburi War Cemetery 132, 133, 134, 205, 242
Kates, Norman 88
Kavanagh, John F. 101, 101
Kawabe, Gen. Masakazu 118
Kempeitai 165, 221
Kenyon, Lt.-Col. Sir Frederic 27, 53–5, 53, 65, 70, 75–83, 86, 88–9, 94, 102, 169, 180

Kimura, Lt.-Gen. Hyotaro 120
Kipling, Rudyard 80, 200
Kohima 34, 115, 118, 121,
  130–1, 156, 214, 247
Kohima, Battle of 66, 67, 118,
  120
Kohima War Cemetery 40, 67,
  68, 132, 242, 249
Kokoda (Track) 31, 150, 227
Kranji Farm 233
Kranji Military Cemetery 138,
  147, 148, 161, 163, 169,
  194
Kranji Prisoner-of-War Camp
  150–6
Kranji Prisoner-of-War and
  Hospital Cemetery 143,
  153
Kranji Racecourse 189
Kranji Reservoir 189
Kranji River 122, 123, 126,
  150, 189
Kuala Lumpur (Cheras Road)
  Civil Cemetery 88
Kunming 116

Labuan 175
Lae 175
Lawrence, Anthony 19
Lea, Nancy 95, 112, 112, 121,
  235, 244
Ledo 115
Ledo Road 120
Lee Kuan Yew 193
Leemon, Jack 58–9
Leith, Gordon 73
Lim Yew Hock 16
Lin, Maya 246
Lincoln, Abraham (Gettysburg
  Address), 18–19
Liverpool Municipal School of
  Art 240
Longmore, Air Chief Marshal
  Sir Arthur 15, 174, 180
Lorimer, Robert 53, 79, 94,
  121, 210
Lutyens, Edwin 30, 37–8, 43,
  45–6, 53–6, 66, 74–82, 81,
  84, 87–8, 94, 98, 100, 102,
  121, 180, 187, 194, 204,
  210–11, 236–37, 246

MacArthur, Gen. Douglas
  58, 228
MacFarlane, Maj. Andrew
  32–4
Maclauchlan, Rev. Francis 67
MacLeod, E. 52
Macready, Sir Nevil 49

MacRitchie Reservoir 126–7
Magwe 34
Malayan Emergency 156, 222,
  228
Mandai Columbarium 192–3
Mandai River 122, 150
Mandalay 34, 87, 113, 120
Mason, Walter W. 181
Maufe, Edward 44, 54–6, 73,
  87, 89, 179–80, 203, 246
Maungdaw 118
Maxwell, Brig. Duncan 123,
  126
Maynamati 34
Maynamati War Cemetery 88
Mayu Ranges 116
Mayu Tunnels 118
Mazargues Indian Cemetery 66
McCormick, James 154
McLean, Maj.-Gen. Kenneth
  136
McNair, Brig. J.K. 64, 65, 163
Meiktila 87, 120
Melaik 136, 138
Memmo, Guido N. 55
Memorial to the Civilian
  Victims of the Japanese
  Occupation 25, 231
Merdeka Talks 17
Merepas Island 43
Middlesex County Council 97,
  104, 106
Modern Architectural Research
  Group (MARS) 105, 239
Mogaung 120
Morris, Mandy 29, 42, 211–12
Moulmein 113
Mountbatten, Adm. Lord Louis
  34, 117, 136, 155, 171
Myitkyina 120

Nadzir Ugana Haji Ibrahim bin
  Yusoff 19
Nair, Devan 192
Nanyang Siang Pau 21, 182,
  183, 186, 229–30, 230
Nee Soon 126, 136, 139, 140
Nee Soon Military Cemetery
  139, 140, 145
Nee Soon Rifle Range 140
Netherlands War Graves
  Foundation (Oorlogsgra-
  venstichting) 169, 187
New Delhi 156, 33, 94
Newell, Rev. I.E. 19
Ngakyedauk 118
Ngakyedauk Pass 118
Nishimura, Maj.-Gen. Takuma
  122, 126

Northern Polytechnic 99, 121
Norton, Richard 48

Oakes, Leonard R. 97, 97
Obbard, Brig. Harry N. 26,
  29, 32–3, 36, 129, 130,
  134, 137–46, 156, 158–9,
  161–4, 169–72, 173, 189,
  209, 213–4, 216, 233
Oliver, Col. Royston 158
Order of St John of Jerusalem
  47
Outram Road Jail 43

Parit Sulong 68, 69
Pasir Panjang 43, 137–8
Pasir Panjang Military Ceme-
  tery (Buona Vista) 137, 194
Pawsey, Charles 130
Pegu 34, 113
Peirce Reservoir 126–7
Penang 33, 172, 206, 214,
  216, 235
Percival, Lt.-Gen. Arthur
  126–7
Perseverance Estate 188
Pickersgill, Capt. Cecil D.
  139, 160
Pike, Rev. Victor J. 17, 19
Pite, William 54
Pooley, Sir Ernest 241
Port Moresby 175
Port Moresby (Bomana) War
  Cemetery 179
Portsmouth Naval Memorial
  56, 79, 174
Public Works Department
  (PWD) Singapore 66, 186,
  190, 231
Public Works Department,
  Bengal 109–10
Purvis, Samuel 154

Qantas 172

Rabaul 175
Ranchi 116
Rangoon 34, 113, 120
Rangoon Memorial, 21, 87,
  244
Rawalpindi War Cemetery 88
Recovery of Allied Prisoners
  of War and Internees
  (RAPWI) 134–5, 155
Rees, Verner O. 84
Rew, Noel A. 84
RIBA Journal 71, 85, 230
Richmond, Sir Ian 102
Rimau 43

Robertson, Howard 239
Royal Academy of Arts 56, 100
Royal Academy Exhibition 102, 107, *107*
Royal Academy School 56
Royal Australian Engineers Chapel 69
Royal Botanic Gardens, Kew 78, 213
Royal College of Art 54
Royal Engineers 33, 56, 66, 84, 86, 111, 139, 160
Royal Institute of British Architects (RIBA) 70, 84–5, 99, 242
Rumah 231
Runnymede Memorial 203, 228, 246

Saarinen, Eero 100
Saarinen, Eliel 100
Sahmaw 87
Sai Wan Bay 130, 170, 214
Sai Wan Memorial 21, 175, 242
Sai Wan War Cemetery 21, 39, 40, 73, *131*, 195, 208, 249
Saigon Military Cemetery 168, 188
Salisbury, Sir Edward 216
Scott, Sir Giles G. 100
Sek Hong Choon, Ven. 20
Seletar Airfield 138
Seletar Naval Base 140
Seletar Reservoir 126
Seletar River 139
Sharma, Pundit Bhoj Raj. 19
Sheares, Benjamin H. 192
Sheldon, William & Noel 103, *103*
Shigeru, VAdm. Fukudome 140
Shinozaki, Yuzuru 43
Siam-Burma Railway 31, 34, 36, 58, 61, 69, 132, 134–5, 150, 154, 160, 224, 227
Siglap 188
Sigvaldason, J.P. 174
Silchar 34
Sim Chin Foo 221
Singapore Botanic Gardens 29, 213, 216
Singapore General Hospital 138, 147, 164–8, *166*, *168*, 209
Singapore General Hospital Memorial 209
Singapore Hui Ann Association 29, 185

Singapore Memorial (Kranji), 15–23, 30, 39–40, 44, 68, 96, 160, 175, *182*, 184, 186, *186*, 190, 195, *196–7*, *198–9*, 203, 206, 209, *209*, 220–31, *223*, 233, 242, 246–50
Singapore Social Welfare Department 233–5
Singapore State Cemetery 29, 40, 189–93
Sir Aston Webb & Son 237–8
Sittang River 113
Skeaping, John 101
Slim, Lt.-Gen. William 67, 113, 116–18, 120, 236
Sook Ching massacre 162, 188, 234
South East Asia Command (SEAC) 34, 57, 65
Spragg, Cyril D. 70
St George's Church (Tanglin Barracks) 139, 159–60
St John's Island 138
Stamp, Gavin 80, 87
Stanley War Cemetery 39, 195
Steedman, Maj.-Gen. John F.D. 179, 181, 220
Stephenson, Cecil 99
Stevenson, William 240
Stewart, Alan 86
Stilwell, Lt.-Gen. Joseph W. 115, 117
Straits of Johore 18, *83*, 122–3, 148, 170, 175, 189
Straits Settlements Volunteer Force (SSFV) 25, 162, 221
Straits Times, The 157, 158, 203, 220, 230
Strang, Dr. T.F. 166
Summerson, John 239
Sun Yat-sen 184
Sylhet 34

Taiping 213
Taiping War Cemetery 156, 179, 187, 208, 213
Taira, Sgt.-Maj. Yoshikawa 152
Tan Beng Kiat 190–1
Tan Tong Toh 171
Tange, Kenzo 37
Tatura German Military Cemetery 64
Taukkyan War Cemetery 21, 87
Taylor, Brig. Harold B. 123, 224
Territorial Army 111, 160

Thanbyuzayat 34, 130, 132, 214
Thanbyuzayat War Cemetery 43, 132–4, *133*, 205, 242
Thiepval Memorial 33, 38, 45–6, 87, 204, 246
Tobin, Rev. P. 20
Toungoo 34
Truelove, John R. 84

Ulu Pandan 137, 194
Ulu Pandan Military Cemetery 138, *169*, 194
United States Army Forces in Australia (USAFIA) 60
University of Hong Kong 106
Unmaintainable Graves Memorial 168, 178, 206

Vale, Brig. Croxton S. 167
Valletta, Malta Memorial 174, 203, 228
Ventris, Michael 239
Vey, George 86, 88–9, 167, *168*
Vietnam Veteran's Memorial 246
von Berg, Wilfred C. 84

War Graves Service (Australian Army) 57–61, 68, 146, 157–8, 216
War Graves Service (British Army) 58, 157–8, 169
War Office 49, 51, 64, 86, 111, 148, 156, 161, 166–7, 169
Ware, Sir Fabian A.G. 27, 45, 47–50, *48*, 61, 74–5, 80, 129, 169
Warren, Edward 79
Webb, Sir Aston 237
Webb, G.W. 234
Wee Kim Wee 192
Williams, Sir Owen 242, 244
Wilson, Bishop John L. 165
Wing Loong Cemetery 136, 138, 139, 159
Wing Loong Estate 138
Woodlands 126, 127, 151, 157, 170–1
Worthington, Hubert 53–4, 56, 203, 204, 236
Wyatt, Stephen 45–6

Yamashita, Lt.-Gen. Tomoyuki 122–3, 126–7
Yokohama 64
Yokohama War Cemetery 90, 160–1